The Digital Journey of Banking and Insurance, Volume II

"*Digitalization and Machine Learning*, the second volume of *The Digital Journey of Banking and Insurance, Volume II*, offers the necessary but often missing link between business and technical view."

—Dr. Carsten Stolz, *CFO Baloise Group*

"This three-volume book series spans from a business view in the first volume up to a technical view in the last volume. This second volume is the bridge between the business view and the technical view, the frequently required but often missing link. This link makes the book series a comprehensive work."

—Bernhard Hodler, *Former CEO Julius Baer Group*

"My experience shows me that one of the most important topics is to build the link between business and technical view or in other words to have real business (use)cases; it is great to see that in *Digitalization and Machine Learning*, the second volume of *The Digital Journey of Banking and Insurance, Volume II* as one of the hottest topics in our time."

—Gerhard Lahner, *COO of Vienna Insurance Group*

"Virtually all financial institutions have embarked on ambitious digital journeys, both to provide better products and customer experience more efficiently and in response to the threat of industry disruption by FinTech competitors. There is no doubt that there will be winners, and there will be losers. I am convinced that *The Digital Journey of Banking and Insurance, Volume II* series is indispensable reading for the future winners."

—Thomas C. Wilson, *CEO, President and Country Manager at Allianz Ayudhya*

"We do remember when we started our digital journey, but we do not know when it will be over. Therefore, we are definitely in the middle. The book series *The Digital Journey of Banking and Insurance, Volume II* is a must-read for of all of us."

—Christian Peter Kromann, *CEO, SimCorp*

Volker Liermann · Claus Stegmann
Editors

The Digital Journey of Banking and Insurance, Volume II

Digitalization and Machine Learning

Editors
Volker Liermann ⓘ
ifb SE
Grünwald, Germany

Claus Stegmann
ifb Americas, Inc.
Charlotte, NC, USA

ISBN 978-3-030-78828-5   ISBN 978-3-030-78829-2 (eBook)
https://doi.org/10.1007/978-3-030-78829-2

© The Editor(s) (if applicable) and The Author(s), under exclusive license to Springer Nature Switzerland AG 2021
This work is subject to copyright. All rights are solely and exclusively licensed by the Publisher, whether the whole or part of the material is concerned, specifically the rights of translation, reprinting, reuse of illustrations, recitation, broadcasting, reproduction on microfilms or in any other physical way, and transmission or information storage and retrieval, electronic adaptation, computer software, or by similar or dissimilar methodology now known or hereafter developed.
The use of general descriptive names, registered names, trademarks, service marks, etc. in this publication does not imply, even in the absence of a specific statement, that such names are exempt from the relevant protective laws and regulations and therefore free for general use.
The publisher, the authors and the editors are safe to assume that the advice and information in this book are believed to be true and accurate at the date of publication. Neither the publisher nor the authors or the editors give a warranty, expressed or implied, with respect to the material contained herein or for any errors or omissions that may have been made. The publisher remains neutral with regard to jurisdictional claims in published maps and institutional affiliations.

Cover credit: Stutterstock/Paul

This Palgrave Macmillan imprint is published by the registered company Springer Nature Switzerland AG
The registered company address is: Gewerbestrasse 11, 6330 Cham, Switzerland

Acknowledgments

The three-book series was the natural next step from the book *The Impact of Digital Transformation and FinTech on the Finance Professional* and an exciting project for us. We look back with gratitude at the many discussions with clients, partners and colleagues at ifb. Without this vital community, such an undertaking would not be possible.

We would first like to thank all contributors (clients, partners and colleagues), whose expertise was invaluable in exploring and formulating such a comprehensive work with a wide overview and deep insights. Their insightful feedback helped us to sharpen this work to this amazing level.

In addition, we would like to thank Tula Weis and her team from Palgrave Macmillan for advice and support in this project.

We like to thank Satzanstalt for supporting us in the development and realization of the book covers idea.

We would also like to thank our colleagues Julia Horstmann, Davin Radermacher and Jenny Klein for their support in all the small, but important things that make such an undertaking a success.

Volker Liermann
Claus Stegmann

Introduction to Volume II—Digitalization and Machine Learning

Looking at the whole book series *The Digital Journey of Banking and Insurance, Volume II*, this second volume might be the most important one in the context of digital transformation. Practical experience in digital transformation shows that the combination of in-depth knowledge of the business processes and the ability to leverage the new technology are the keys to a successful digital transformation.

The starting point of digital transformation is a key decision to be made. Some institutions start with the technology and build up teams for machine learning, cloud computing and data lakes. Once the infrastructure is ready, they look for cases to leverage the technology. Other organizations start with a focus on the more pressing business challenges and look for tools in the lucky bag of digital transformation. The second approach tends to deliver a more efficient digital strategy. One of the reasons for this is the dilemma of vision and value (see Stegmann and Ludwig 2021): after a few years with mixed success in digital transformation, the stakeholders demand a long-term value (and profit) strategy, which is challenging due to narrowed margins, new competitors and technology and infrastructure investments to be made.

The challenge posed by the second approach (driven by the business unit needs, internal/external business units) is to anchor the technology knowledge and enable the business units to leverage the technology. Studying and discussing successful use cases will enable the business units to discover certain promising patterns. The business units will then be able to project these patterns onto their own business needs.

The deep dive into practical use cases offers an understanding of the ingredients of digital transformations. When looking at the many use cases, certain structures come to light: e.g. pattern identification to group and cluster transactions and use these clusters for processing similar transactions in a standardized way (for fraud detection see [Enzinger and Li 2021], or for optimization of regression tests see [Liermann, Li and Wünnemann], Use Case—Optimization of Regression Tests—Reduction of the Test Portfolio Through Representative Identification 2021) and for projection of terminations see (Schmüser et al. 2021). Another important design is to continuously learn from humans and improve automation through automated decision-making using machine learning (see [Liermann et al. "Hyperautomation (Automated Decision-Making as Part of RPA)" 2021] and [Gabriel 2021]).

In-depth business knowledge is inevitable. Only the business units can identify the application of the new technologies with the best leverage. The implementation of most of the technologies is to some extent complex or needs at least some good IT fundamentals. The tasks can only be solved by a team working closely together. The close collaboration of business units and IT is not a new approach. However, not only do the boundaries need to be overcome, but the two parties need to merge their knowledge to understand the other side in a deeper fashion than before.

Lloyd Blankfein (Goldman Sachs CEO) stated "We are a technology firm," emphasizing that IT is the major tool to transform data into information and knowledge. Dave McKay took the different viewpoint "If a bank thinks it is a tech company, then it is wrong. We are still business-to-consumer and business-to-business companies, trying to meet customer needs. Banks are using technology to anticipate those needs and meet them in a creative way, but we don't derive our income from technology." It is correct that no income is generated by technology and the customer needs are at the center of attention. Dave McKay's view is supported by the creative use of technology to analyze and anticipate customer behavior (outside digitalization). Inside digitalization helps the institute to optimize the tasks and reduce costs or provide more insights with the same costs.

Figure 1 illustrates inside and outside digitalization and their impact on cost reduction and revenue increase.

Most of the use cases presented in this book are in the lower areas of analytics and predictive analytics as well as process and process automation and contribute to the cost reduction of internal tasks.

Another important aspect of digital transformation originates from the processes or, to be more precise, the functions documented in the functional architecture linked by processes to get the required tasks done. To improve

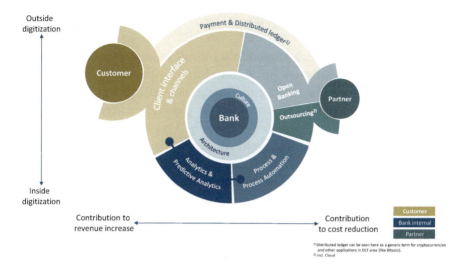

Fig. 1 Overview digital transformation © ifb SE

the processes, two roads could be taken: (A) improve the processes with the functions already existing and (B) improve the functions and the ways the tasks are handled.

Process improvement—up to a certain level—could be achieved by RPA and other techniques to adjust automation within the processes. Process mining can help to identify the slow and weak parts of a process. RPA can provide the organization with incremental process improvements, which could subsequently lead to significant cost reductions.

More potential lies in the deeper, functionally oriented analysis of the underlying tasks and a recomposition of the functions in the existing processes. This is still far from a disruptive process improvement (or at least a rare outcome). On the one hand, these functionally driven process improvements generally have a greater potential for optimization. On the other, the potential for failure is higher in the implementation, as with all significant changes. The focus on incremental process improvements or functional process improvements is accompanied by a risk/return assessment, calculation and evaluation.

Cyber risk is omnipresent for all institutions and is continuously rising due to the growing portion of data available electronically. While the IoT[1] and the risk of attacks on remotely managed physical machines are significant in the industry, the principal[2] cyber risk arises from the threat of disclosure of client

---

[1] Internet of Things.
[2] In terms of the impact on reputational risk.

or position data. Cyber risk will not go away, but the management could be improved continuously.

Quantum computing is a groundbreaking technology. Practical implementation is not at hand for every institution, but it is within sight and expected to become a standard practice in the coming decade. The way algorithms are structured is significantly different from the classical (binary) programming paradigm. The differing programming paradigm is a challenge for all nontheoretical physicists and some aspects might demand different thinking even for mathematicians. The hurdle is even higher for all others, but a basic knowledge about the idea behind quantum computers is again the key to identifying the relevant use cases, helping to improve the business. Quantum computing will contribute to scenario generation and analysis, making it a powerful tool for all risk managers and controllers.

Overview of Book Series

This book is the second volume of the three-volume book series *The Digital Journey of Banking and Insurance, Volume II*. The first volume *Disruption and DNA* focuses on change and the things staying stable in the banking and insurance market (outside view) as well as the effect on accounting, risk management and regulatory departments (inside view). The inside view is completed by an analysis of cultural alterations. This volume "Digitalization and Machine Learning Applications" mainly emphasizes use cases as well as the methods and technologies applied (such as processes, leveraging computational power and machine learning models). In the last volume of the series, "Data Storage, Processing and Analysis," the view of the way we deal with data shifts. The angle shifts over the volumes from a business-driven approach in the *Disruption and DNA* volume to a strong technical focus in the *Data Storage, Processing and Analysis* volume, leaving the *Digitalization and Machine Learning Applications* volume with the business and technical aspects in-between.

Overview of the Parts of This Book

This volume indicates the technological requirements and builds a bridge between the business-inspired first volume and the technology-driven third volume.

The first part offers insights into use cases in the context of inside digitalization. All use cases show the importance of models to identify patterns and demonstrate how to work with the results. The use cases discussed are applied in accounting and risk management.

The second part illustrates how the improved availability of computational power and innovation can encourage new applications in the context of risk management and planning. One example is the visualization of scenario results via a dynamic dashboard.

Quantum computing is the topic of the third part of the volume. Reports from practical applications in a lab setting and beyond are combined with a compact and focused deep dive into the setup of programming: quantum computing and quantum annealing.

Processes and process optimization (including process automation) are major areas in a digital transformation. The fourth part is dedicated to processes and process optimization and presents the tools to improve the processes tactically and sustainably.

The last part visits the space of open source and explores the origins of this omnipresent paradigm. It investigates the success of open source and defines the areas in which open source is most successful. A summary of all parts closes this volume.

Literature

Enzinger, Philipp, and Sangmeng Li. 2021. "Fraud Detection Using Machine Learning Techniques." In *The Digital Journey of Banking and Insurance, Volume II—Digitalization and Machine Learning*, edited by Volker Liermann and Claus Stegmann. New York: Palgrave Macmillan.

Gabriel, Jens. 2021. "RPA Use Case—'IFRS 9/SPPI'." In *The Digital Journey of Banking and Insurance, Volume II—Digitalization and Machine Learning*, edited by Volker Liermann and Claus Stegmann. New York: Palgrave Macmillan.

Liermann, Volker, Sangmeng Li, and Christoph Wünnemann. 2021. "Use Case—Optimization of Regression Tests—Reduction of the Test Portfolio Through Representative Identification." In *The Digital Journey of Banking and Insurance, Volume II—Digitalization and Machine Learning*, edited by Volker Liermann and Claus Stegmann. New York: Palgrave Macmillan.

Liermann, Volker, Sangmeng Li, and Johannes Waizner. 2021. "Hyperautomation (Automated Decision-Making as Part of RPA)." In *The Digital Journey of Banking and Insurance, Volume II—Digitalization and Machine Learning*, edited by Volker Liermann and Claus Stegmann. New York: Palgrave Macmillan.

Schmüser, Arne, Farah Skaf, and Harro Dittmar. 2021. "Use Case—NFR—HR Risk." In *The Digital Journey of Banking and Insurance, Volume II—Digitalization *and Machine Learning*, edited by Volker Liermann and Claus Stegmann. New York: Palgrave Macmillan.

Stegmann, Claus, and Sven Ludwig. 2021. "Digitalization Strategy." In *The Digital Journey of Banking and Insurance, Volume I—Disruption and DNA*, by Volker Liermann and Claus Stegmann. New York: Palgrave Macmillan.

Contents

Use Cases

Use Case: Optimization of Regression Tests—Reduction of the Test Portfolio Through Representative Identification   5
Volker Liermann, Sangmeng Li, and Christoph Wünnemann

Use Case—Nostro Accounts Match   21
Volker Liermann, Sangmeng Li, and Johannes Waizner

Use Case—Fraud Detection Using Machine Learning Techniques   33
Philipp Enzinger and Sangmeng Li

Use Case: NFR—HR Risk   51
Harro Dittmar, Arne Schmüser, and Farah Skaf

Sentiment Analysis for Reputational Risk Management   73
Daniel Schröder and Marian Tieben

Use Case: NFR—Using GraphDB for Impact Graphs   99
Volker Liermann and Marian Tieben

High-Performance Applications

Distributed Calculation Credit Portfolio Models 119
Volker Liermann, Sangmeng Li, and Johannes Waizner

BSDS: Balance Sheet Dynamics Simulator 135
Volker Liermann and Harro Dittmar

Dynamic Dashboards 155
Volker Liermann and Sangmeng Li

High-Performance Applications 181
Xenia Bogomolec

Quantum Computing

Post-quantum Secure Cryptographic Algorithms 189
Xenia Bogomolec and Jochen Gerhard

Quantum Technologies 201
Peter Nonnenmann and Xenia Bogomolec

Categorical Quantum Theory 221
Peter Nonnenmann

Process and Process Optimization

Processes in a Digital Environment 233
Marie Kristin Czwalina, Chiara Jakobs, Christopher Schmidt, Matthias Jacoby, and Sebastian Geisel

Process Mining 259
Lars Rautenburger and Alexander Liebl

Hyperautomation (Automated Decision-Making as Part of RPA) 277
Volker Liermann, Sangmeng Li, and Johannes Waizner

RPA Use Case—"IFRS 9/SPPI" 295
Jens Gabriel

Open Source

Open-Source Software 313
Volker Liermann

Summary 325
Volker Liermann and Claus Stegmann

Index 329

Notes on Contributors

Xenia Bogomolec is a Mathematician and Information Security Specialist with a background in Computer algebra, system engineering, network programming and lawful telecommunication interception. She has worked as an analyst and functional-technical coordinator with a strong regulatory focus in various IT and information security projects in the financial and biotech industry. Since 2017, she has also worked with various collaborators on post-quantum security analyses. This includes identification of post-quantum secure cryptographic algorithms with regard to known quantum attacks. Since autumn 2020, a small team from her recently founded company Quant-X Security & Coding has also been working on quantum algorithm tests on quantum annealing processors.

Marie Kristin Czwalina Senior Consultant, has been working at ifb group in the Core Banking Team since 2020. She deals with further development in the area of innovation management and digitalization topics around the areas of sales and processing in banks and specializes in process automation, customer-oriented advice and the implementation of GDPR requirements in IT applications. She studied business informatics with a focus on IT management in her master's degree at the FOM University of Applied Sciences.

Dr. Harro Dittmar Senior Consultant at ifb SE, is a Passionate Programmer with a confident and structured approach to the modeling of complex systems. His aspiration is the thorough understanding, implementation and troubleshooting of scenario calculations, predictions and optimization problems from a holistic perspective. After his academic career in statistical modeling and pattern recognition of molecular systems, he started a career in the banking sector. His consulting focus includes quantitative risk modeling, strategic approaches to the optimization of data architectures and data management.

Philipp Enzinger is Managing Consultant at ifb and responsible for insurance analytics and risk topics. At ifb, Mr. Enzinger leads the digitalization workgroup for insurance data science. As project manager and subject matter expert, he has been advising financial institutions on credit risk and financial transformation topics for more than five years. In recent years, Mr. Enzinger has focused on insurance companies' IFRS 17/9 implementation—in particular new risk calculations as well as impacts on planning, reporting and financial steering. Mr. Enzinger holds an M.Sc. degree in economics from the University of Cologne.

Notes on Contributors

Jens Gabriel Director at ifb SE, has been working as a consultant in the banking industry in Europe for more than fifteen years. He has in-depth experience both in advising business departments and in implementing standard software. In addition to this, he possesses in-depth knowledge of accounting and reporting standards (IFRS and local GAAP), especially of financial instruments. He is also an expert in IT as well as functional architecture and has focused on SAP Bank Analyzer and SAP S/4HANA FPSL implementation regarding IFRS 9 and project management. He has also co-authored books and professional articles on IFRS and Basel III. He graduated in economics from Technical University of Cologne.

Sebastian Geisel works at ifb as a Senior Consultant in the Finance Process Excellence Team. Before joining ifb, he gained significant experience in optimization and digitalization of financial and operational processes with a special focus on real estate. Now, he also works on the development and implementation of target operating models for insurance companies and engages in the development of digitalization and process automation topics. He did his master's degree in business administration at the LSE (London School of Economics and Political Science) and the University of Trier.

Dr. Jochen Gerhard is a Risk Specialist in Group Risk Management at Commerzbank AG. In his former role as Manager at BearingPoint, he advised financial institutions and supervisors in various projects about risks, data collection and analytics systems. He has always combined the business aspects with the technology challenges in the area of security, analytics and artificial intelligence. He studied mathematics and computer science and has worked as a theoretical physicist.

Matthias Jacoby Director at ifb, is head of the Finance Process Excellence Team. During his studies in business administration with a major in finance and accounting, he gained international work experience in Germany, Switzerland and Spain. Before joining ifb International AG (Zurich, Switzerland), he spent five years working for Ernst & Young in Assurance & Advisory Services and successfully completed his Swiss CPA qualification in 2011. During the last nine years working for ifb, he has mainly been involved in large finance transformation projects at financial service providers. Based on his expertise in financial processes and benchmark know-how, he has led several process optimization projects, including Fast Close or Outsourcing within Europe.

Chiara Jakobs Senior Consultant, has been working at ifb group in the area of Regulation and Reporting since 2018. She is mainly involved in regulatory projects from a functional perspective, focusing on business analysis for clients within the financial services sector in Germany and Luxembourg. Additionally, she strongly focuses on innovation and digitalization topics in terms of process optimization and automation. She studied international business at Maastricht University—School of Business and Economics (Maastricht, The Netherlands) and successfully completed her master's degree with a major in strategy and innovation.

Dr. Sangmeng Li Senior Consultant at ifb SE, has primarily worked as a Data Scientist for quantitative risk management in the financial industry with a focus on data analysis, risk modeling and technical implementation. She received her doctorate in mathematics from the University of Münster, having conducted research on stochastic differential equation and Monte Carlo simulation as part of her Ph.D.

Alexander Liebl joined ifb group as a Senior Consultant in April 2019 after gathering several years of experience in consulting projects in the financial services industry. He is part of the Insurance unit at ifb group and the leading process mining expert. The business information scientist advises and supports insurance companies in their digitalization programs. His focus lies on agile project management, business process management and operational excellence. He also has a profound academic background in technology and innovation management and holds a master's degree (Master of Science).

Volker Liermann Partner at ifb group, worked in the banking industry for over two decades, primarily focusing on financial risk management. Throughout his career, he has focused on developing integrated and comprehensive frameworks to help organizations correctly project risk at a strategic and tactical line of business and departmental level. He has also focused on developing frameworks to integrate stress testing and regulatory stress tests. In recent years, his focus has shifted to digitalization, machine learning and digital processes including improvements to classical financial and nonfinancial risk management. He has a background in economics and a degree in mathematics from the University of Bonn.

Dr. Peter Nonnenmann Senior Scientist at Quant-X Security & Coding GmbH, is a highly experienced Computer Scientist and Quantum Theory Expert who prefers to work on solutions for problems with a clear industrial focus. The most recent projects at Quant-X Security & Coding involved work on quantum algorithm solutions for chosen industrial problems and quantum security analyses of globally used symmetric crypto algorithms. Before that, he co-authored a contribution in DIGITALE WELT magazine on a novel approach to AI and 3D computer vision by defining a preliminary but mathematically rigorous concept for "holistic, global information," incorporating category and sheaf theory into neural networks. He holds a degree in informatics with a strong focus on mathematics from the University of Frankfurt.

Lars Rautenburger Director and Head of Operational Excellence. He is responsible for the digital transformation of insurance companies, including topics like process mining, robotic process automation, data science, change management and agile project management. Before joining ifb, he acquired extensive know-how in the insurance industry for more than 20 years. At Sopra Steria SE, he led the insurance consulting workforce in ASG. At MSG Systems AG, he was responsible for business consulting insurance. He started his career in consulting with Accenture, where he worked for nearly ten years. He has an economics background with a degree in business administration from the University of Siegen.

Notes on Contributors   xxiii

Christopher Schmidt joined the ifb group in April of 2019. The Senior Consultant has a strong record of managing complex projects in international environments as well as a proven skillset in developing automated processes with RPA technology. The certified RPA Advanced Developer focuses on the development of software robots as well as the design of target operating models and overall RPA strategy. Before joining ifb, he already gathered experience as a consultant in projects within the financial sector, at both insurance companies and banks.

Arne Schmüser Senior Consultant at ifb SE since 2015, has been working in the banking industry with a focus on data governance, data architecture and data quality management. His work as a Business Analyst is often related to elements of risk management. Since 2020, he has been co-lead of the Non-Financial Risk (NFR) working group at ifb, where he has conceived methods of managing NFR as well as various use cases of ifb's best practice approach.

Daniel Schröder Managing Consultant at ifb group, has been working in the financial industry for over seven years, focusing on data engineering and data integration. At ifb, he leads an internal working group on Natural Language Processing and Applications. He holds a degree in business mathematics from the Technical University of Dortmund with a focus on quantitative data analysis and econometrics.

Farah Skaf works as a Consultant at ifb group. She focuses on strategy and architecture topics. She has a master's degree in administration and business management from HEC, Morocco, as well as a Business Manager certification from ATV seminars in Würzbug, Germany. Her interests include agile transformation and agile methodologies. Furthermore, she is both a certified Scrum Master and Business Owner.

Claus Stegmann has as Co-CEO of ifb group—an international consulting firm—acquired extensive know-how over the last three decades in the financial industry regarding finance transformation, risk management and regulatory compliance. He is intensively engaged with the current challenges of the financial industry, which result from strong changes to customer behavior, a changing competitive environment and new technologies due to digitalization. He has also co-authored books on *Stress Tests in Banks, Basel III* as well as *Digitalization in the Finance Industry*, and graduated from Business School at the University of Passau, Germany.

Marian Tieben holds an M.Sc. degree in economics from the University of Cologne with a focus on finance and started his career at ifb group in 2019. He has mainly worked on technical implementations of several data science tasks with R or Python. Marian is an active member of the internal Research & Development working groups in the context of digitalization and has already gained practical project experience in this field.

Dr. Johannes Waizner began his career at ifb in 2018 in a group dedicated to credit risk and is now a Senior Consultant. His focus lies on the technical side, where his work ranges from implementations using Access databases, to novel use cases in the field of robotic process automation, to, most recently, work in Hadoop systems. He also specializes in Python integration due to the great potential of machine learning in the realm of credit risk models. Before ifb, he obtained his Ph.D. in theoretical physics at the University of Cologne modeling resonances in helical magnetic solid-state systems.

Christoph Wünnemann has worked at ifb group since 2006. He has supported numerous customers in the field of regulatory reporting, in particular with the widely used reporting software ABACUS360. As a team leader and topic manager in the competence center Regulatory Reporting, he promotes innovative ideas in this context. Christoph holds an M.Sc. degree in information systems from the University of Muenster.

List of Figures

Use Case: Optimization of Regression Tests—Reduction of the Test Portfolio Through Representative Identification

Fig. 1	Exemplary situation in the context of ABACUS360 (© ifb SE)	7
Fig. 2	Idea and goals of the test portfolio reduction through representative identification (© ifb SE)	7
Fig. 3	Phases and steps of the approach (© ifb SE)	9
Fig. 4	Implementation of the approach in an ABACUS360 environment (© ifb SE)	9
Fig. 5	Clustering—center (© ifb SE)	12
Fig. 6	Clustering—center and edge elements (© ifb SE)	12
Fig. 7	Hard clustering and soft clustering (© ifb SE)	13
Fig. 8	Identifying the edge elements (© ifb SE)	14
Fig. 9	Assignment probabilities (© ifb SE)	15
Fig. 10	Clustering result: hard vs soft (© ifb SE)	15
Fig. 11	Introduction with adaptive method (© ifb SE)	17
Fig. 12	Cost effects/benefit analysis (© ifb SE)	18

Use Case—Nostro Accounts Match

Fig. 1	Involved parties (© ifb SE)	24
Fig. 2	Different matching situations (© ifb SE)	24
Fig. 3	Brute force search (© ifb SE)	26
Fig. 4	Levenshtein distance (© ifb SE)	26
Fig. 5	Longest common substring distance (© ifb SE)	27

| Fig. 6 | Levenshtein distance (© ifb SE) | 28 |
| Fig. 7 | Prefiltering of invoices and payments: select the top N invoices/payments with the highest match probability (© ifb SE) | 29 |

Use Case—Fraud Detection Using Machine Learning Techniques

Fig. 1	Imbalanced dataset (© ifb SE)	37
Fig. 2	Variable importance (© ifb SE)	40
Fig. 3	Insured_hobbies vs. label (© ifb SE)	40
Fig. 4	Insured_education_level vs. label (© ifb SE)	41
Fig. 5	Reconstruction error vs. label (© ifb SE)	42
Fig. 6	Ensemble model (© ifb SE)	43
Fig. 7	Variable importance (© ifb SE)	43
Fig. 8	Calibration statistics (© ifb SE)	44
Fig. 9	Target operating model fraud (© ifb SE)	46
Fig. 10	Example setup of fraud detection dashboard (© ifb SE)	48

Use Case: NFR—HR Risk

Fig. 1	Connection between HR sub-risks and resignation risk (© ifb SE)	54
Fig. 2	Example of impact graph with one resignation trigger (© ifb SE)	56
Fig. 3	Comparison of the tree of indicators and impact graph (© ifb SE)	56
Fig. 4	Indicator tree for resignation risk (© ifb SE)	60
Fig. 5	Example calculation for resignation score of an employee, along an impact graph (© ifb SE)	61
Fig. 6	ROC curves for 10 trials with independent splits of the data into training set and test set. The curves correspond to a 90:10 split ratio on the left and to a 50:50 split ratio on the right. The blue curves were obtained for a generalized linear model and the golden curves for a gradient boosting tree (© ifb SE)	67
Fig. 7	Relative importance of the 10 most important variables for the predictions of the GLM (left) and the GBM (right) (© ifb SE)	70
Fig. 8	Attrition by Overtime (yes/no) for the GLM predictions in percent (© ifb SE)	70

Sentiment Analysis for Reputational Risk Management

| Fig. 1 | Approach overview (© ifb SE) | 75 |
| Fig. 2 | Graphical representation of reputation over time (© ifb SE) | 77 |

| Fig. 3 | Latent Dirichlet allocation example and overview (© ifb SE) | 86 |

Use Case: NFR—Using GraphDB for Impact Graphs

Fig. 1	Impact graph ESG (© ifb SE)	102
Fig. 2	Symbols in an impact graph (© ifb SE)	103
Fig. 3	Impact graph ESG (tool view) (© ifb SE)	104
Fig. 4	Predecessor and successor analysis of ESG graph (tool view) (© ifb SE)	105
Fig. 5	Management aggregation of ESG graph (tool view) (© ifb SE)	107
Fig. 6	Expected values of the probabilities of occurrence—numerical example (© ifb SE)	108
Fig. 7	Distribution of losses—numerical example (© ifb SE)	109
Fig. 8	Distribution of losses—numerical example—normally distributed damage amounts (© ifb SE)	110
Fig. 9	Score integration (© ifb SE)	111
Fig. 10	Change activity status of vulnerabilities (© ifb SE)	112
Fig. 11	Example reporting (© ifb SE)	113

Distributed Calculation Credit Portfolio Models

Fig. 1	Overview CreditMetrics (© ifb SE)	121
Fig. 2	Parameter CreditMetrics (© ifb SE)	123
Fig. 3	Overview of the parts to be parallelized (© ifb SE)	123
Fig. 4	Natural calculation block building—Variant A (lhs) and Variant B (rhs) (© ifb SE)	125
Fig. 5	Overview of queuing for the calculation blocks (© ifb SE)	126
Fig. 6	Hybrid approach to designing the calculation blocks (split by runs)—Variant C (© ifb SE)	127
Fig. 7	Overview of queuing for the calculation blocks—Variant C (© ifb SE)	128
Fig. 8	Hybrid approach to designing the calculation blocks (main split by clients)—Variant D (© ifb SE)	129
Fig. 9	sparklyr configuration (© ifb SE)	130
Fig. 10	Executors in Spark UI: Spark.executor.cores = 2; Spark.executor.instances = 4; Spark.executor.memory = "1500 M" (© ifb SE)	131
Fig. 11	Executors in Spark UI: Spark.executor.cores = 2; Spark.executor.instances = 5; Spark.executor.memory = "1500 M" (© ifb SE)	131
Fig. 12	Calculation performance comparison (© ifb SE)	133

BSDS: Balance Sheet Dynamics Simulator

| Fig. 1 | ABM—essential elements (© ifb SE) | 137 |

Fig. 2	BSDS—hierarchy of agents in a class diagram (© ifb SE)	138
Fig. 3	BSDS—topology of directional communication links between groups of agents (© ifb SE)	139
Fig. 4	BSDS—sequence of actions and messages of the actor model. The diagram shows blocks of actions that are executed by all individual members of the corresponding color-coded agent group (© ifb SE)	141
Fig. 5	BSDS—outline of the steps performed by the matching algorithm of the markets (© ifb SE)	142
Fig. 6	BSDS—details of the technical implementation and code dependencies (© ifb SE)	145
Fig. 7	BSDS—Input for system initialization and output of simulation runs (© ifb SE)	147
Fig. 8	BSDS—evolution of the total exposure in the system in a pre-run over 500 iterations. On the left side, the number of loans per client is limited to a maximum of 5, on the right side to a maximum of 20 (© ifb SE)	149

Dynamic Dashboards

Fig. 1	Definition dynamic dashboarding (© ifb SE)	156
Fig. 2	Example of actual portfolio composition (© ifb SE)	161
Fig. 3	Limit usage in t_0 (© ifb SE)	162
Fig. 4	Shiny dashboard: portfolio manager dashboard (© ifb SE)	163
Fig. 5	Shiny dashboard: portfolio manager dashboard: drop-down menus (© ifb SE)	164
Fig. 6	MicroStrategy dashboard: portfolio manager dashboard (© ifb SE)	165
Fig. 7	Impairment projection dashboard: business year (© ifb SE)	166
Fig. 8	Impairment projection dashboard: PD modeling (© ifb SE)	167
Fig. 9	Impairment projection dashboard: PD modeling under the GDP impact (© ifb SE)	167
Fig. 10	Impairment projection dashboard: predicted expected loss (© ifb SE)	168
Fig. 11	Impairment projection dashboard: predicted expected loss under increased LGD (© ifb SE)	168
Fig. 12	Impairment projection dashboard: predicted expected loss under modified portfolio components (© ifb SE)	168
Fig. 13	Overview of integrated stress test—bank (© ifb SE)	169
Fig. 14	Integrated stress tests—architecture layers (© ifb SE)	170
Fig. 15	Overview of visuals in Power BI (© ifb SE)	172
Fig. 16	Example of dynamic dashboard—Power BI (© ifb SE)	173
Fig. 17	Power BI including R Script Editor (© ifb SE)	174
Fig. 18	Example of SAC dashboard (© ifb SE)	175

Fig. 19	MicroStrategy developing desktop (© ifb SE)	175
Fig. 20	Word cloud and interactive map (© ifb SE)	176
Fig. 21	R Shiny script example (© ifb SE)	177

High-Performance Applications

Fig. 1	Math functions (© Quant-X Security & Coding GmbH)	182
Fig. 2	Minimum iterations and required number of years (original screenshot) (© Quant-X Security & Coding GmbH)	184
Fig. 3	Maximum iterations and required number of years for mask attack (original screenshot) (© Quant-X Security & Coding GmbH)	184

Quantum Technologies

Fig. 1	Entangle circuit (original image) (© Quant-X Security & Coding GmbH)	210
Fig. 2	Entangle probability (original image) (© Quant-X Security & Coding GmbH)	211
Fig. 3	Entangle sphere (original image) (© Quant-X Security & Coding GmbH)	212
Fig. 4	Quantum gate U_f (© ifb SE)	214
Fig. 5	Deutsch algorithm—quantum circuit (© ifb SE)	214
Fig. 6	Deutsch algorithm—applying the Hadamard gate (© ifb SE)	215

Categorical Quantum Theory

| Fig. 1 | Natural transformation (© ifb SE) | 225 |

Processes in a Digital Environment

Fig. 1	Main components of a digital environment (© ifb SE)	234
Fig. 2	The value chain (© ifb SE)	236
Fig. 3	The different types of processes (© ifb SE)	236
Fig. 4	Four phases of process optimization (© ifb SE)	238
Fig. 5	The magic triangle (© ifb SE)	239
Fig. 6	Standalone vs. embedded BPE (© ifb SE)	241
Fig. 7	Overview of process automation solutions (© ifb SE)	243
Fig. 8	Overview—advantages and challenges of BPEs (© ifb SE)	246
Fig. 9	Overview—advantages and challenges of process mining (© ifb SE)	248
Fig. 10	Overview—advantages and challenges of RPA (© ifb SE)	250

Process Mining

Fig. 1	Minimal event log analyzed by process mining (simplified illustration) (© ifb SE)	262
Fig. 2	Steps during a process mining project (© ifb SE)	263
Fig. 3	Structure of event logs (example), own representation acc. to (van der Aalst 2016)	265
Fig. 4	Processes in theory and practice (© ifb SE)	266
Fig. 5	Example of the effect of a general process adjustment (© ifb SE)	268
Fig. 6	Typical tasks performed by RPA bots (© ifb SE)	269
Fig. 7	Main tasks of a process mining expert (© ifb SE)	271
Fig. 8	Technologies used to reach hyperautomation (© ifb SE)	273

Hyperautomation (Automated Decision-Making as Part of RPA)

Fig. 1	Modern RPA (© ifb SE)	278
Fig. 2	Five-step decision automation model (© ifb SE)	279
Fig. 3	Blocks for a step-by-step implementation (© ifb SE)	279
Fig. 4	Overview of label "Value" (© ifb SE)	285
Fig. 5	Correlation matrix (© ifb SE)	285
Fig. 6	Object.Type vs. Value (© ifb SE)	286
Fig. 7	(Object.Type, Object) vs. Value (© ifb SE)	287
Fig. 8	Random forest: cross-validation result (© ifb SE)	287
Fig. 9	UiPath.Python.Activities module in the UiPath Packages manager (© ifb SE)	288
Fig. 10	Python scope and properties in UiPath (© ifb SE)	288
Fig. 11	Architecture of the integration of Python into UiPath (© ifb SE)	289
Fig. 12	Email regarding an invoice announcement (© ifb SE)	290
Fig. 13	Coarsest grained flow graph of the automation procedure in UiPath (© ifb SE)	291

RPA Use Case—"IFRS 9/SPPI"

Fig. 1	Focus of IFRS 9 (© ifb SE)	297
Fig. 2	Business requirements regarding classification of financial assets (IFRS 9) (© ifb SE)	299
Fig. 3	Challenges in practice (© ifb SE)	302
Fig. 4	General classification of use case "IFRS 9/SPPI" (© ifb SE)	304
Fig. 5	Suitability test for implementation of use case "IFRS 9/SPPI" with RPA (© ifb SE)	305
Fig. 6	Proposed process for use case "IFRS 9/SPPI" using RPA (© ifb SE)	306

Fig. 7	Using digitalization as a driver for increased efficiency in Accounting and Controlling (© ifb SE)	308

Open-Source Software

Fig. 1	Standard software—open source—individual development (© ifb SE)	320

List of Tables

Use Case: Optimization of Regression Tests—Reduction of the Test Portfolio Through Representative Identification

Table 1	Selected attributes of dataset "German Credit" (© ifb SE)	14

Use Case—Nostro Accounts Match

Table 1	Data example of match = 1 (© ifb SE)	27
Table 2	Data example of match = 0 (© ifb SE)	27
Table 3	Ten cross-validation results (© ifb SE)	28
Table 4	Prediction (© ifb SE)	29
Table 5	Example of result with no matched pairs (No.Match = 0) (© ifb SE)	30

Use Case—Fraud Detection Using Machine Learning Techniques

Table 1	Numeric attributes (©ifb SE)	38
Table 2	Categorical attributes (© ifb SE)	38
Table 3	Random forests: performance (© ifb SE)	39
Table 4	Autoencoder: performance (© ifb SE)	41
Table 5	Pros and cons of supervised and unsupervised learning (© ifb SE)	42
Table 6	Combined model: performance (© ifb SE)	43

Use Case: NFR—HR Risk

Table 1	Overview of the 28 employee features of the example dataset that can be utilized as possible predictors for the binary classification of the attrition tendency (© ifb SE)	66
Table 2	Summary of different model families (and their ensembles) that were compared with the AutoML function of the h2o R package. The AUC measure is highlighted as the performance metric that was used to rank the models (© ifb SE)	68

Sentiment Analysis for Reputational Risk Management

Table 1	Example calculation of expected mean sentiment for three documents (© ifb SE)	76
Table 2	Token level results of spaCy's NLP pipeline showing lemmatization and POS tagging (© ifb SE)	80
Table 3	Span level results of spaCy's NLP pipeline showing results of named-entity recognition (© ifb SE)	81
Table 4	Ten most similar word vectors by **cosine similarity** with respect to search phrase "**european_central_bank|ORG**" (© ifb SE)	81
Table 5	Ten most similar word vectors by **cosine similarity** with respect to search phrase "**ecb|ORG**" (© ifb SE)	82
Table 6	Ten most similar word vectors by **Levenshtein similarity** with respect to search phrase "**european_central_bank**" (© ifb SE)	82
Table 7	Ten most similar word vectors by **Levenshtein similarity** with respect to search phrase "**ecb**" (© ifb SE)	82
Table 8	Special mapping rules to be applied in preprocessing (© ifb SE)	83
Table 9	Special mapping rules for large amounts of money (© ifb SE)	83
Table 10	Examples of sentence classifications (© ifb SE)	93

Use Case: NFR—Using GraphDB for Impact Graphs

Table 1	Comparison between SQL and Cypher from (Neo4J, n.d.) (© ifb SE)	104

Distributed Calculation Credit Portfolio Models

Table 1	CPU usage (© ifb SE)	132
Table 2	Comparison of splitting variants (© ifb SE)	133

BSDS: Balance Sheet Dynamics Simulator

Table 1	BSDS model parameters (© ifb SE)	144

| Table 2 | BSDS results for the efficiency of the matching algorithm (gold columns) at different combinations of parameters (blue columns). The indicators were averaged in the steady states that were reached after 250 iterations (© ifb SE) | 149 |

Dynamic Dashboards

Table 1	Example limit structure (© ifb SE)	161
Table 2	Limit usage in t_0 (© ifb SE)	162
Table 3	Pros and cons of tools (© ifb SE)	171

Processes in a Digital Environment

| Table 1 | Characteristics of heavyweight and lightweight IT (© ifb SE) | 252 |
| Table 2 | Categorization of process automation technologies (© ifb SE) | 252 |

Hyperautomation (Automated Decision-Making as Part of RPA)

| Table 1 | Head of the dataset (© ifb SE) | 284 |

List of Equations

Sentiment Analysis for Reputational Risk Management

Equation 1:	Expected topic-word vector representation	87
Equation 2:	Expected document-word vector representation	87
Equation 3:	Most suitable vector	87
Equation 4:	Probabilistic measure of relevance	88

Use Case: NFR—Using GraphDB for Impact Graphs

Equation 1:	Path probability—risk event 1 to financial situation	108
Equation 2:	Path probability—risk event 1 to cash flows	108

Distributed Calculation Credit Portfolio Models

Equation 1:	Factor-loadings (©ifb SE)	122
Equation 2:	One-factor variant (©ifb SE)	122

BSDS: Balance Sheet Dynamics Simulator

Equation 1:	Average number of actual loan agreements	143
Equation 2:	Ratio matched loan amounts	143
Equation 3:	Averaged incongruity of target and actual rating structures	143

Post-quantum Secure Cryptographic Algorithms

Equation 1:	Generator matrix	193

Equation 2:	Affine transformation 1	196
Equation 3:	Affine transformation 2	196
Equation 4:	Quadratic map	196

Quantum Technologies

Equation 1:	Vector of complex numbers	206
Equation 2:	Canonical basis	206
Equation 3:	Representation of a qubit	207
Equation 4:	Definition tensor product	207
Equation 5:	Two-qubit system	207
Equation 6:	n-qubit state space	208
Equation 7:	Quantum gate	208
Equation 8:	Examples of quantum gates (Pauli matrices)	208
Equation 9:	Unitary group	209
Equation 10:	Pauli group	209
Equation 11:	Clifford group	209
Equation 12:	Generic state as a vector	210
Equation 13:	Hadamard (H) gate	210
Equation 14:	Controlled NOT gate	210
Equation 15:	Application Hadamard gate and CNOT to $q3$	211
Equation 16:	Actual distribution	211
Equation 17:	Deutsch's algorithm functions	213
Equation 18:	Equivalence 1	213
Equation 19:	Equivalence 2	213
Equation 20:	Tensor product of qubits	214
Equation 21:	Definition of U_f	214
Equation 22:	Deutsch algorithm—applying U_f	215
Equation 23:	Top qubit	215
Equation 24:	Applying a Hadamard gate to the top qubit	215
Equation 25:	Final state measure—f is constant	215
Equation 26:	Final state measure—f is balanced	215

Categorical Quantum Theory

Equation 1:	Category identity	222
Equation 2:	Category source	222
Equation 3:	Category target	222
Equation 4:	Category composition	222
Equation 5:	Source and target of the identity	223
Equation 6:	Left / Right identity	223
Equation 7:	Associativity	223
Equation 8:	Source and target	223
Equation 9:	Functor identity	224

Equation 10:	Functor—Source/target commutativity	224
Equation 11:	Functor is a category morphism	224
Equation 12:	Natural transformation	224
Equation 13:	Commutativity	225
Equation 14:	Tensor product	225
Equation 15:	Source /Target of tensor product	226
Equation 16:	Middle four exchange	226
Equation 17:	Identity of tensor product	226
Equation 18:	n - gubit gates	226
Equation 19:	Scalars	227
Equation 20:	Post - selection	227
Equation 21:	Preparation	227
Equation 22:	Circuit evaluation	227
Equation 23:	eval	227
Equation 24:	NN - Sum	228
Equation 25:	NN—Activation	228

Use Cases

Successful digitalization happens when urgent customer demands and business needs are met by leveraging data and technology. As soon as this is agreed, the next crucial point to overcome is to convince the organization, i.e., employees, that this would work. One might convince the C-level decision-makers, and sometimes they do understand the potential. To make a difference, it is equally important to convince the people on the ground because they must perform the transformation.

One can start top-down and invest in technology, infrastructure and building up the workforce with data scientists. The real driver for fundamental changes in culture and in the way things are done is an inspiration through successful examples. This inspiration is far more positive when it serves satisfied customers and optimized and better internal departments.

Long-term investment in these skills and infrastructure is important and must be executed at a certain point in the journey, but it is even more important to have the support of the whole organization (including the people on the ground). Understanding the technology in depth and implementing the infrastructure is more of an IT task. Infrastructure only comes to life and the technology is only leveraged with the right business challenge—even more if the business challenge can be divided into different and smaller use cases. A convincing case is proven in shorter time and the investment and involvement are achieved much easier because quick gains are possible.

In some cases, the driver has an IT background, but, due to mixed experiences in the past, IT does not always have positive connotations in the business department. Anyone who wants to bring about digital transformation must convince the organization that IT and projects are different this time. Agile projects (or even agile organizations) have the potential to speed up the process of getting what is really needed (see Part V in the first volume of this book series).

The first chapter in this part (Liermann et al. "Use Case—Optimization of Regression Tests—Reduction of the Test Portfolio Through Representative Identification" 2021) presents a common use case in changing the bank/insurance company[1] as well as running the bank/insurance company. Regression tests are usually carried out when a new release of a standard software or a minor change in the data mapping is deployed. The classical regression test aims to ensure the stability of the system and environment, so it is primarily used in RtB/RtI.[2] In the CtB/CtI[3] context (while implementing new software and functionalities), when a certain quality is established, the regression test can ensure that this quality remains stable, while still making major changes at different ends of the whole context. The use case presents an approach to reduce the number of transactions tested on a smaller set (representatives) aiming to cover all functions, so that a comprehensive test can be carried out with a significantly smaller dataset.

The next chapter (Liermann et al. "Use Case—Nostro Accounts Match" 2021) illustrates an improvement of the process of nostro account matching that is partially still carried out manually. The approach goes beyond an exact string match and works with similarity measures like Levenshtein distance (LSD) and longest common substring distance (LCS distance).

The third chapter (Enzinger and Li 2021) provides a machine-learning-driven solution to fraud identification in the insurance claims process. The chapter delivers a model calibrated to car insurance data in which the model selection and calibration process are documented. All components (including a dashboard) are developed by using open-source tools.

The fourth chapter of the part is (Schmüser et al. 2021). The chapter explores a subtopic of the nonfinancial risk universe: the HR risk. The chapter introduces HR risk as a part of the nonfinancial risk and focuses on resignation risk as a specific HR risk. As a practical example, a model using machine learning for estimating the probability of a resignation is presented.

The next chapter is (Schröder and Tieben 2021). Another risk category in nonfinancial risk is reputation risk. The chapter uses the methods of sentiment analysis to estimate the reputation risk of an institute. Different types of methods are presented spanning from dictionary-based approaches up to natural language processing (NLP). The subjects discussed include NLP

---

[1] Thinking of projects and establishing new things or renewing existing ones (CTB/CTI).
[2] Run the Bank/Run the Insurance.
[3] Change the Bank/Change the Insurance.

preprocessing like word embedding and named entity recognition (NER) as well as topic modeling.

The last chapter (Liermann and Tieben "Use Case—NFR—Using GraphDB for Impact Graphs" 2021) covers another important subject of nonfinancial risk: the connectedness of nonfinancial risk categories across the nonfinancial risks. The impact graph is introduced as a tool to document and analyze the connectedness of risk events. The underlying technology implementing the impact graphs is GraphDB. The toolset developed enables the organization to implement a holistic approach to communicating and reporting the connected risks in nonfinancial risk.

Literature

Enzinger, Philipp, and Sangmeng Li. 2021. "Fraud Detection Using Machine Learning Techniques." In *The Digital Journey of Banking and Insurance, Volume II—Digitalization and Machine Learning*, edited by Volker Liermann and Claus Stegmann. New York: Palgrave Macmillan.
Liermann, Volker, and Marian Tieben. 2021. "Use Case—NFR—Using GraphDB for Impact Graphs." In *The Digital Journey of Banking and Insurance, Volume II—Digitalization and Machine Learning*, edited by Volker Liermann and Claus Stegmann. New York: Palgrave Macmillan.
Liermann, Volker, Sangmeng Li, and Christoph Wünnemann. 2021. "Use Case—Optimization of Regression Tests—Reduction of the Test Portfolio Through Representative Identification." In *The Digital Journey of Banking and Insurance, Volume II—Digitalization and Machine Learning*, edited by Volker Liermann and Claus Stegmann. New York: Palgrave Macmillan.
Liermann, Volker, Sangmeng Li, and Johannes Waizner. 2021. "Use Case—Nostro Accounts Match." In *The Digital Journey of Banking and Insurance, Volume II—Digitalization and Machine Learning*, edited by Volker Liermann and Claus Stegmann. New York: Palgrave Macmillan.
Schmüser, Arne, Farah Skaf, and Harro Dittmar. 2021. "Use Case—NFR—HR Risk." In *The Digital Journey of Banking and Insurance, Volume II—Digitalization and Machine Learning*, edited by Volker Liermann and Claus Stegmann. New York: Palgrave Macmillan.
Schröder, Daniel, and Marian Tieben. 2021. "Sentiment Analysis for Reputational Risk Management." In *The Digital Journey of Banking and Insurance, Volume II—Digitalization and Machine Learning*, edited by Volker Liermann and Claus Stegmann. New York: Palgrave Macmillan.

Use Case: Optimization of Regression Tests—Reduction of the Test Portfolio Through Representative Identification

Volker Liermann, Sangmeng Li, and Christoph Wünnemann

1 Introduction

The situation for traditional banks is critical. On the revenue side, fintech companies and, more and more, Big Tech (GAFAM[1] and BATX[2]) are putting pressure on traditional banks. Therefore, all initiatives helping to cut costs are welcome.

The complexity of processes and systems has risen continuously. A core task of bank management is now to transform data from the core banking system into valuable and interpretable key figures to enable decision-makers (especially in senior management) to make the right call.

---

[1] Google, Amazon, Facebook, Apple, and Microsoft, also named the Big Five or the Tech Giants. Before Microsoft joined the club the GAFA were often referred to as Big Four, The Four Horsemen.
[2] Baidu, Alibaba, Tencent, and Xiaomi are the biggest tech firms in China mirroring the GAFAM.

V. Liermann (✉) · S. Li · C. Wünnemann
ifb SE, Grünwald, Germany
e-mail: Volker.Liermann@ifb-group.com

S. Li
e-mail: Sangmeng.Li@ifb-group.com

C. Wünnemann
e-mail: Christoph.Wuennemann@ifb-group.com

Bank management continuously needs to adjust and reinforce the usability of these figures. The driver of these changes could be internal (as continuous improvement) and external (new regulatory requirements). The continuous change process needs to be implemented in the systems.

Due to this continuous change situation, the importance of testing is obvious. It is important to distinguish between two aspects of testing: (A) testing new functionalities and (B) testing existing functionalities (often referred to as regression tests). Even though the nature of the two aspects is similar, there are some significant differences. In case (A), the expected results and functionalities must be defined by the test management. In (B), the expected results and mechanics already exist. They only need to be tested if they are still operating and if no ricochet is introduced by changes in other parts of the system or infrastructure.

In the test context, the revaluation of a full portfolio is—given a certain complexity of the calculation/transformation—a process that consumes a great deal of time, disk space, and calculation resources. Often the portfolios consist of structurally similar transactions that follow structurally comparable patterns. This phenomenon offers the opportunity to significantly reduce the number of considered transactions while simultaneously keeping the test data quality at a high and appropriate level.

1.1 Initial Situation—By Example

To illustrate the potential for cost cutting, we analyze a fictional but specific case. The numbers can easily be mapped to a real-world example. The figures presented in the chapter are taken from the context of the regulatory reporting software ABACUS360[3] but can be applied to any other analytical software in any other business context. In the following, the term analytical software system is used generally; ABACUS is only mentioned explicitly when it comes to ABACUS specifics.

Figure 1 sums up the requirements for the use case and the potential cost reduction in terms of hard disk memory and computational power.

1.2 General Idea

In the upper part of Fig. 2, we see the idea and the goals of the approach. Regression tests can be optimized if representative transactions of the entire

---

[3] Vendor: BearingPoint Software Solutions GmbH.

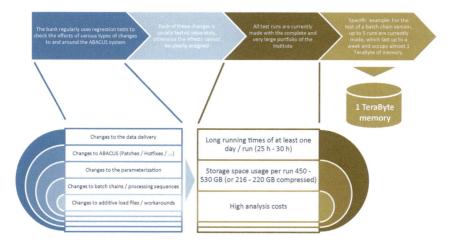

Fig. 1 Exemplary situation in the context of ABACUS360 (© ifb SE)

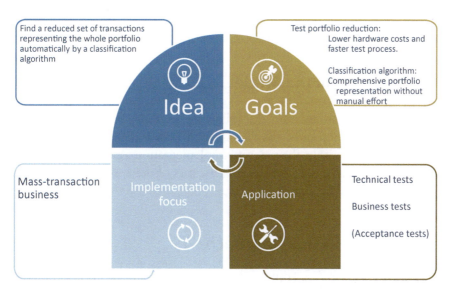

Fig. 2 Idea and goals of the test portfolio reduction through representative identification (© ifb SE)

portfolio (representatives) are compiled in a reduced test portfolio, which then enables a statement to be delivered about the effects on the entire portfolio (analogous to the extrapolations for elections). Since maintaining a representative test portfolio manually is very extensive and will not necessarily lead to a comprehensive representation of the full portfolio, it should be done automatically by classification algorithms in the context of machine learning (ML).

The test portfolio reduction has a variety of benefits. Firstly, the running times can be significantly reduced and, therefore, the test procedure as a whole is completed earlier. Secondly, significantly less storage space is used, also in the archive. Thirdly, the reduced computational power can reduce server requirements. In a cloud- and usage-based IT environment the costs are affected directly. In a non-usage-based IT environment, at least the machine availability and flexibility improve.

The application of classification algorithms for portfolio reduction potentially leads to a better portfolio representation without manual efforts.

The targeted bank or financial institution should have a mass transaction business. A large retail portfolio (e.g., credit cards) of a bank could be significantly reduced. All other types of business are further tested with all data. The reduced portfolio represents a supplement that can be used if suitable.

The reduced portfolio can be definitely used for technical tests, e.g., batch chains, as well as for business tests, e.g., when trying out parameters, additive load files, processing sequences, etc. If acknowledged by business representatives, it can also be taken as the basis for acceptance tests.[4]

1.3 Structure of the Article

The chapter is organized into the following sections: Firstly, the approach used is explained. Secondly, the model performance is discussed on a freely available dataset. Thirdly, the practical implementation aspects and challenges are examined. Finally, the essential cornerstones of the approach are summed up.

2 Phases in the Approach

The approach reducing the full portfolio to a meaningful set of representatives consists of five main steps which can be assigned to three phases. These steps and phases are shown in Fig. 3.

In the model phase the model is developed and trained with a certain set of training data. In the apply phase the trained model is applied to the "real" business. The final validation phase is a kind of feedback loop, where the classification made is challenged by an automated error analysis.

In the following sections, the corresponding steps of the phases are explained in detail and are illustrated in Fig. 4 in the context of ABACUS360.

---

[4] For further discussions on this see Chapter 4.

Use Case: Optimization of Regression Tests ...

Fig. 3 Phases and steps of the approach (© ifb SE)

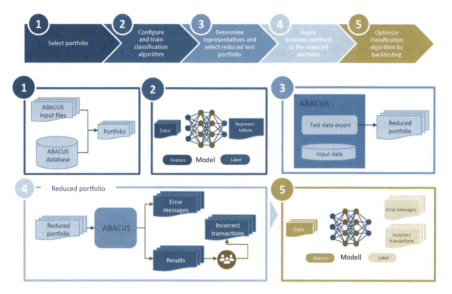

Fig. 4 Implementation of the approach in an ABACUS360 environment (© ifb SE)

2.1 Step I: Select Portfolio

The first phase identifies and selects the portfolio that should be used for the training of the model. Retail portfolios with a significant number of transactions give good leverage when applying and reducing the computational time and the storage consumption. In addition, large numbers of transactions in a retail portfolio offer a good and valid starting point for the classification models.

To improve the stability and the explanatory power of the classification, the portfolio should not only be a one-day snapshot. The model training with multiple portfolio stages over time avoids overfitting to the specific one-day situation in the portfolio.

As illustrated in Fig. 4, in an ABACUS360 environment portfolio selection can be set up on the basis of the ABACUS360 input data files or alternatively directly on the ABACUS360 database.

2.2 Step II: Configure and Train Classification Algorithm

In the training phase, all transactions of the portfolio (maybe on different dates) will be passed on to the classification model. One of the most important parameters is the number of classes and the corresponding size of the classes (the number of transactions associated with the class). If the number of classes is too small, the representative will not reflect the variety of structures, which can lead to errors. On the other hand, if the number of classes is too big and the number of transactions associated with the class is small, the leverage for resource reduction will be small.

2.3 Step III: Determine Representatives and Select Reduced Test Portfolio

Once the model is trained, it is used to associate all transactions of the "real" business with one class and one or more representatives are chosen for each class. The list of representatives is then used to select the related datasets. Therefore, not only the transactions themselves have to be selected but every related entity, such as business partners, ratings, cash flows, etc., as well. This total quantity of data forms the reduced test portfolio.

The selection might be put either on the input data layer of the analytical software system or alternatively already on the database which is used as the data basis for the population of input data into the system (e.g., an underlying data warehouse).

As illustrated in Fig. 4, in ABACUS360 there is already a test data export functionality available which can be used for this. The functionality is able to extract all related data to certain transaction or partner IDs.

2.4 Step IV: Apply Business Methods to the Reduced Test Portfolio

The data of the reduced test portfolio is now passed on to the (regulatory) methods and is monitored in terms of errors generated by the system and unexpected deviations from a reference value (e.g., a result of a former run, before any changes in customizing or coding).

2.5 Optimize Classification Algorithm

To perform an optimization of the classification model, the explanatory power of the representatives must be evaluated. The full portfolio (set A) and the representatives (set B) are calculated. The comparison of the system-generated errors and unexpected deviations from a reference value for these two sets is then analyzed. If all transactions associated with a class generate the same errors or unexpected deviations from a reference value, the classification is optimal.

This feedback loop is the only alternative to validate the chosen classification, as classification in our case is unsupervised learning[5] it cannot be backtested. The efficiency of the chosen representatives can only be challenged by the application of the business methods to the reduced set and the full portfolio calculation. By doing so, the faulty transactions not identified can be identified and the classification algorithm can be optimized (e.g., by varying the number of classification clusters).

3 Model Development and Application

3.1 Model

3.1.1 Cluster Algorithms

Clustering is an unsupervised machine learning method aimed at dividing data objects into several groups in such a way that the objects from the same group have similar structure to each other. Simply speaking, the aim is to segregate data objects with similar traits and assign terms into groups (clusters). For more details, we refer to (Liermann et al. 2019).

In this article, each business object is treated as a single data object. The business features, assigned to each business object, contain the information and can be used for extracting clustering. This means that business objects with similar feature structure can be assigned to the same cluster. As illustrated in Fig. 5, the cluster center represents all cluster members.

---

[5] A classification of machine learning algorithms can be found in Liermann et al. (2019).

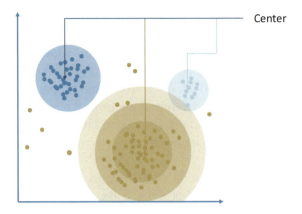

Fig. 5 Clustering—center (© ifb SE)

3.1.2 Hard and Soft Clustering

Besides the cluster center, it is also necessary to consider the edge objects (Fig. 6) for which the cluster assignment is not certain, therefore the cluster center might not be able to represent these outliers appropriately. In this article, we suggest collecting these edge objects in the representation pool and testing them especially carefully.

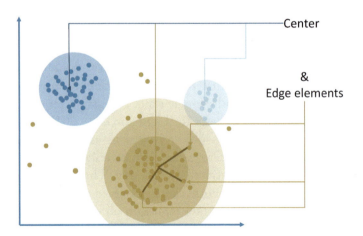

Fig. 6 Clustering—center and edge elements (© ifb SE)

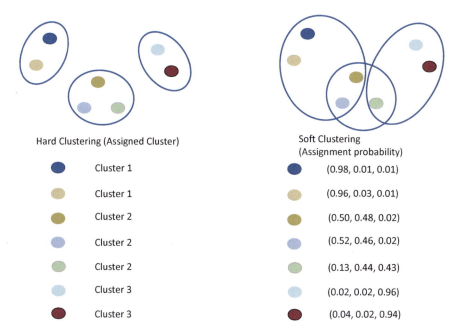

Fig. 7 Hard clustering and soft clustering (© ifb SE)

This fact suggests that we should apply soft clustering (fuzzy clustering), in which each data object can potentially belong to more than one cluster. Instead of one single assigned cluster label, a vector of assignment probabilities is computed, where the length of vector should be equal to the number of clusters and the sum of vector elements should be equal to one. We compare hard and soft clustering in Fig. 7, where the assignment labels and assignment probabilities are listed below the figure, separately.

In the case of soft clustering, we can identify the edge objects according to the assignment probabilities. For instance, we compute the difference between the first two maximum assignment probabilities and identify the edge elements if the difference is smaller than 0.1 (Fig. 8).

3.2 Experiment Results—German Credit

In this section, we want to conduct a numerical experiment where we use the dataset "German Credit" from the machine learning dataset repository (UCI Open Datasets, n.d.). The following clustering analysis is implemented in R by using *dtwclust* package (cran.r-project.org 2019). We use the first five attributes of the dataset, which contain both categorial and numerical variables (Table 1).

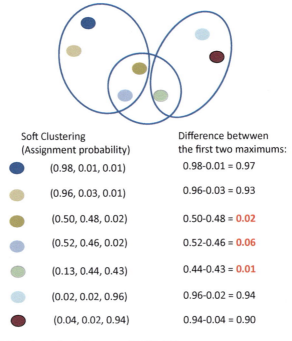

Fig. 8 Identifying the edge elements (© ifb SE)

Table 1 Selected attributes of dataset "German Credit" (© ifb SE)

Attribute 1	Categorial; five categories
Attribute 2	Numerical; integers between 4 and 72
Attribute 3	Categorial; five categories
Attribute 4	Categorial; 11 categories
Attribute 5	Numerical; integers between 250 and 18,424

The similarity between data samples is computed by summing up the similarity for pairs of each attribute, where the Hamming metric is used for categorical attributes and the Euclidean metric for numerical attributes. In addition, it is necessary to normalize the numerical attributes first, so that the value can be changed to a common comparable scale. We illustrate the clustering result by using the t-SNE (T-Distributed Stochastic Neighbor Embedding) algorithm (Maaten and Hinton 2011), where the clustering result is visualized in a two-dimensional space.

- Assignment cluster 3:

Cluster_1	Cluster_2	Cluster_3	Cluster_4	Cluster_5
0.056654	0.037566	0.851446	0.037839	0.016494

- Edge element:

Cluster_1	Cluster_2	Cluster_3	Cluster_4	Cluster_5
0.220152	0.303061	0.327815	0.064431	0.084541

Fig. 9 Assignment probabilities (© ifb SE)

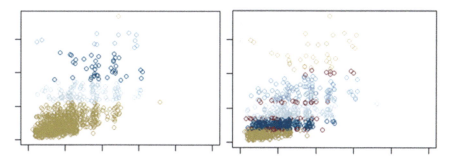

Fig. 10 Clustering result: hard vs soft (© ifb SE)

For both results, five clusters are constructed. In the hard clustering result, the cluster members are not equally distributed, with the yellow cluster and the light blue cluster strongly dominating the dark blue cluster. In contrast, soft clustering provides five clusters of nearly equal sizes due to the high assignment tolerance. In addition, we can identify the edge elements based on the assignment probabilities. In the following figure (Fig. 9), we provide examples of two points, where the first one is assigned to cluster 3 due to the dominated probability and the second one is an edge element. In Fig. 10, the edge elements are marked as red points.

3.3 Backtesting and Continuous Improvement

Once a reasonable model is trained it is important to keep up the good model performance. There are multiple reasons why the trained model does not keep up with the initial good performance. The portfolio and the transactions in the portfolio are dynamic over time. The requirements and methods used for transforming the portfolio data into regulatory key figures can be altered: (A) by design (new regulatory requirement), (B) by implementation (changes by the vendor), (C) changes in the parametrization of the software (customizing), and (D) changes in the data transfer from the source systems. These are only a few sources of possible changes in the model accuracy.

4   Challenges in the Practical Application

In the practical application, maintaining a representative test portfolio manually often fails due to high efforts in identifying the representatives and the unnecessary low priority. It is therefore indisputable that generating a test portfolio automatically by an algorithm is very beneficial.

However, the main challenge is not reducing the test data but the acceptance of reduced test data by the business representatives due to the following reasons:

- For the user acceptance test (UAT) and final approval business representatives often rely more on full datasets because they are afraid that special cases are not covered.
- Defective datasets from the production environment may not be available 1:1 in the test environment so the error analysis cannot be carried out adequately.
- Key figures or evaluations referring to the full portfolio may not deliver reasonable results.

Therefore, for the acceptance of reduced test data it is very important (a) to prove that the reduced test portfolio represents the full portfolio almost comprehensively and (b) to still enable test runs with the full portfolio.

Both expectations can be met by a hybrid approach containing a certain set of test runs with the full portfolio as well as a certain set of test runs with the reduced test portfolio. Regular test runs on the full portfolio on the one hand cover the requirements of UAT approval and full portfolio evaluation. On the other hand, they should be used to establish a regular backtesting/validation process to ensure the representativeness of the reduced test portfolio. All other test runs in between the approval phases are performed on the reduced test portfolio.

As illustrated in Fig. 11, the transition from a full portfolio to a reduced test portfolio should occur successively in a smooth transition process. At the beginning, the cluster algorithm needs a couple of full portfolio runs as the basis for training. Once the algorithm is trained as much as desired, the full portfolio runs can be reduced in favor of more and more runs with

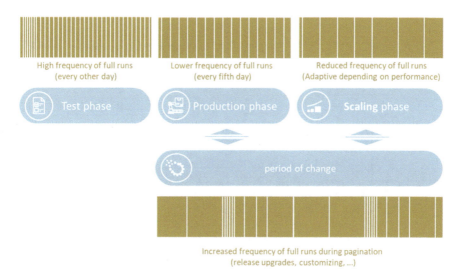

Fig. 11 Introduction with adaptive method (© ifb SE)

the reduced test portfolio. In the target scenario, full portfolio runs are only scheduled for UAT approval phases and, in exceptional cases, for full portfolio evaluations.

Although it is not recommended to perform tests only on the reduced test portfolio, the execution part of the test runs already promises to save a lot of calculation time and storage. It can be used either to undertake a larger test program or to dismantle hardware capacities. The latter is even promising with a consumer-oriented cloud IT infrastructure like Azure,[6] Google Cloud, or AWS,[7] because fewer storage and machine utilization requirements will reduce the cost directly. In a traditional IT infrastructure, reducing IT infrastructure is more difficult to realize, because the performance of the remaining full portfolio runs might be compromised.

5 Summary

Today, there is a great deal of pressure on the business model of traditional banks. In an overcrowded market and with low interest rates it is hard to realize improvements on the revenue side. On the cost side, there are two options: (A) cost cutting by reducing or removing functionality or (B) cost

---

[6] Azure—cloud services of Microsoft.
[7] Amazon Web Services—cloud services of Amazon.

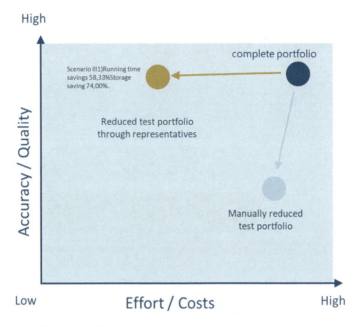

Fig. 12 Cost effects/benefit analysis (© ifb SE)

cutting by optimizing the existing functionality. The approach presented addresses the latter option. This effect is shown in Fig. 12.

In the upper part, we see the full portfolio evaluation (dark blue dot, which can be seen as the truth). The reduced portfolio (representatives) is illustrated by the golden dot, which has a similar level of accuracy (if the model is well trained) but shows a significant reduction in the computational and storage costs. The light blue dot in the lower part expresses our expectation of the performance of a manually reduced test portfolio.[8] The accuracy will be significantly lower and cost cutting will not be at the same level as the optimized test portfolio model.

The approach presented can significantly reduce the computational and storage cost. The cost cutting is immense even if all three to five calculations are applied to the full portfolio (giving the opportunity of a close-meshed valuation and backtesting, finding all errors or significant reference value deviations).

The approach can be applied to all testing, independent of the bank management calculation used (accounting, controlling, regulatory reporting, or risk management). Therefore, infrastructure costs in data lake-like storage,

---

[8] The relevance of this approach in productive environments is not to be underestimated.

machine learning environments, and employee know-how (data scientist) can be easily leveraged via the bank management departments.

Literature

cran.r-project.org. 2019. *Package 'dtwclust'*. December 11. Accessed January 8, 2021. https://cran.r-project.org/web/packages/dtwclust/dtwclust.pdf.

Liermann, Volker, Sangmeng Li, and Norbert Schaudinnus. 2019. "Mathematical Background of Machine Learning." In *The Impact of Digital Transformation and Fintech on the Finance Professional*, edited by Volker Liermann and Claus Stegmann. New York: Palgrave Macmillan.

Maaten, Laurens van der, and Geoffrey Hinton. 2011. "Visualizing Data Using t-SNE." *Journal of Machine Learning Research*, August.

UCI Open Datasets. n.d. *Statlog (German Credit Data) Data Set*. Accessed January 5, 2021. https://archive.ics.uci.edu/ml/datasets/statlog+(german+credit+data).

Use Case—Nostro Accounts Match

Volker Liermann, Sangmeng Li, and Johannes Waizner

1   Introduction

Cost pressure in the banking industry is, as of today (2021), ever-present. Some issues originated a long time ago, like the low interest rates and their impact on profitability. Other aspects are caused by singular events (such as the COVID-19 pandemic) and their impact on higher impairments in the loan portfolios. New players have entered the marketplace: Fintech companies, but also the Big Tech companies (GAFAM[1]). They cut certain parts of the banking value chain and therefore reduce the margins.

It is expected that these trends will continue in the years to come. Cost pressure is going to rise even more. Thus, there is a strong imperative to seek efficiency improvements and cut costs.

---

[1] Google, Apple, Facebook, Amazon, and Microsoft (and in Asia Tencent and Alibaba).

V. Liermann (✉) · S. Li · J. Waizner
ifb SE, Grünwald, Germany
e-mail: Volker.Liermann@ifb-group.com

S. Li
e-mail: Sangmeng.Li@ifb-group.com

J. Waizner
e-mail: Johannes.Waizner@ifb-group.com

RPA (see Czwalina et al. 2021; Soybir 2021) is a pragmatic way to automate simple and recurring processes. Process mining can reveal the parts of a process worth a deeper analysis.

The process of matching nostro accounts has long been known and—due to its repetitive nature combined with a high frequency (daily)—was a target for optimization long before the digitalization hype began. Matching the two lists (incoming payments and expected payments) is a challenge that has only been solved by IT to a certain extend. Except for trivial cases, the matching itself remained an intellectual challenge for a real person.

1.1 General Idea

Matching by nostro account is tricky, because a brute force approach[2] is—due to computational complexity—only feasible for a small number of payments. A brute force approach would in addition not use the text for identifying the payments.

This chapter shows a matching approach using machine learning. The two-step approach is a combination of a clustering algorithm and a brute-force-style match. The clustering algorithm is used to identify and narrow the possible candidates down to a reasonable number (step one). Within the second step, the remaining (reduced number of) candidates are matched.

1.2 Structure of the Chapter

The second section introduces the business requirements and the origin of the nostro account match. The next section offers tools and algorithms to solve the challenge of the nostro account match by similarity analysis. The section closes with an example application to a dataset. In Sect. 4, we highlight the potential of NLP in matching business events and billing information (billing text and amount). The fifth section summarizes the findings.

---

[2] Trying out all possible combinations of expected and incoming payments.

2 Business Requirements

2.1 Correspondent Bank System

To better understand the task of matching nostro accounts, this section introduces the purpose and the key elements of the correspondent bank system.

Receiving and paying in a foreign country with a domestic currency is tricky if the bank does not have the required infrastructure and a local bank license. If the bank acts as an affiliate or branch in the foreign country, it works together with a local bank (correspondent bank) to settle with local clients and the foreign currency. Often—due to the affiliate or branch status—the bank does not even have direct access to the foreign central bank settlement system.

Example
A German automotive company (customer of Deutsche Bank) buys steel from a steel manufacturer who is a customer of HSBC for $25 million. Deutsche Bank holds its dollars at The Bank of New York Mellon and HSBC holds its dollars at Bank of America. When the German automotive company instructs its bank to pay the money, HSBC debits the steel manufacturer's account and transfers dollars from its account at BofA to Deutsche Bank's account at BNY. Then, HSBC credits the dollars to the German automotive company's dollar account in Frankfurt.

The accounting terms nostro and vostro (Italian, nostro and vostro; English, "ours" and "yours") are used to differentiate accounts held by a bank for another bank or corporate from an account another bank or corporate holds. A nostro account is held by the other bank. It is an account with our money. Whereas a vostro account holds another bank's money. Therefore, it is an account held by us for another bank or corporate.

In the balance sheet, a debit balance on a nostro account is counted as a cash asset. While a credit balance (i.e., a deposit) on a vostro account is seen as a liability, a debit balance (a loan) on a vostro account is correspondingly taken as an asset.

To keep track of the bank's money being held by the other bank, the nostro account is the right tool. To operationalize, the movements are posted in a shadow account (see Fig. 1). The operational challenge is to keep the shadow account and the nostro account aligned. The alignment is complicated because the booking texts often do not allow a simple one-to-one match of the expected business events and the reported movements on the nostro account. Often—due to manual processing—small alterations occur. Thus, an exact string match is not a promising approach.

Figure 2 shows the different matching situations from simple (top left 1:1) to complex (bottom right—N:M). N is the number of invoice statements and M is the number of incoming payments.

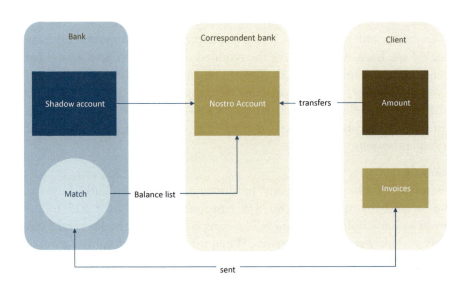

Fig. 1 Involved parties (© ifb SE)

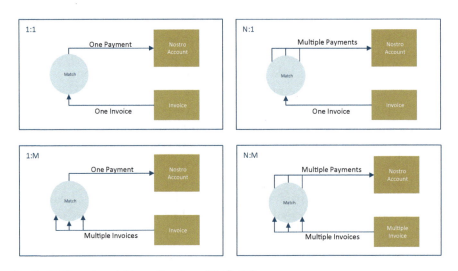

Fig. 2 Different matching situations (© ifb SE)

3 Match Analysis

3.1 Data Collection/Generation

In this chapter we used generated data, which was oriented toward real matching data from project experiences. The data was generated following the different situations in Fig. 2. For each of the situations mentioned (1:1, N:1, 1:M, N:M), we generated several perfectly matching datasets. The task of finding a match was quite easy by using the standard algorithms.

We then contaminated the data by adjusting the text fields, and to make the data like real data we even made small and big changes in invoice and payment numbers. Identification became more challenging, but with some more advanced machine learning models it worked well.

3.2 Brute Force Search

The most common approach in solving match problems such as that mentioned is to use brute force search. This is a very general technique and involves examining all possible combinations and checking whether the amounts match or not. It is simple to implement but usually suffers performance problems, since the computation time grows in linear proportion to the number of data candidates. In this article, we are going to use the power of machine learning algorithms to speed up brute force search. To be more specific, the data candidates are prefiltered according to a match probability, which is predicted by a machine learning model. The number of data candidates can be reduced by deleting the irrelevant candidates or the candidates which are probably not matched.

3.3 Data Analysis/String Similarity

The largest challenge is to figure out how to predict the match probability between each invoice and payment given in Fig. 3. We achieve this by analyzing the text content of column "Text." In this section, we will firstly focus on the direct text analysis, in fact the string similarity. In the next section, we will introduce some advanced extensions in which the content similarity is analyzed based on natural language processing (NLP).

There are a lot of mathematical metrics for measuring string similarity. In the following, we consider the two most common ones: the Levenshtein

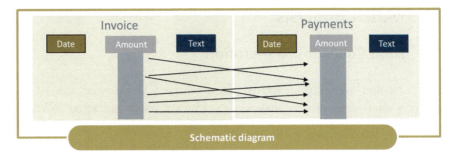

Fig. 3 Brute force search (© ifb SE)

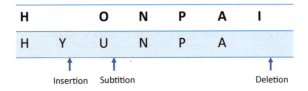

Fig. 4 Levenshtein distance (© ifb SE)

distance (LSD) and the longest common substring distance (LCSD) (Alberto Apostolico 1997).

- Levenshtein distance

The Levenshtein distance measures the difference between two strings by counting the minimum number of single-character edits required to change one into another, where character insertion, deletion, and substitution are considered character edits. As presented in the following example, the Levenshtein distance between HONPAI and HYUNPA is equal to 3, since three-character edits are required (Fig. 4).

- Longest common substring distance

The length of the longest common substring is used as a similarity measure. In comparison to the Levenshtein distance, it is the edit distance only according to insertion and deletion. Again, using the example above, the LCSD between HONPAI and HYUNPA should be equal to 4 (Fig. 5).

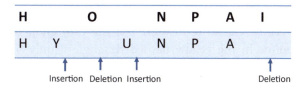

Fig. 5 Longest common substring distance (© ifb SE)

Table 1 Data example of match = 1 (© ifb SE)

	Invoice Text	Payments Text	Match
1	Invoice number: 500537	Ref. 500537	1
2	Invoice number: 500284	Ref: 500284	1
3	Invoice number: 500562	Ref: 500562	1
4	Invoice number: 500800	Ref: 500800	1
5	Invoice number: 500252	Ref: 500252	1
6	Invoice number: 500435	Ref: 500435	1
7	Invoice number: 500438	Ref: 500438	1

Table 2 Data example of match = 0 (© ifb SE)

	Invoice Text	Payments Text	Match
1	Invoice number: 500537	Ref. 500284	0
2	Invoice number: 500537	Ref: 500562	0
3	Invoice number: 500537	Ref: 500800	0
4	Invoice number: 500537	Ref: 500252	0
5	Invoice number: 500537	Ref: 500435	0
6	Invoice number: 500537	Ref: 500438	0
7	Invoice number: 500264	Ref: 500284	0

3.4 Model Training/Features Selection

The following results are implemented in R by using *stringdist* Library (cran.r-project.org 2020) and *h2o* Library (H2O.ai 2019). First, we reconstruct the invoices and payments pairwise as given in the following two tables, where a column "Match" is inserted. This column is binary and shows whether the pair of invoice and payment matches or not (1—match, 0—not match) (Tables 1 and 2).

For each pair of invoice and payment, we compute both Levenshtein distance and longest common substring distance and illustrate them in the following figure, where the blue points stand for matched pairs and the yellow ones for not matched pairs, separately. It is not hard to see that we are not able to achieve a sharp separation by using only one distance. For instance, the points included in the light blue dashed rectangle are hardly separated into blue and yellow classes if we only use the projection on LCSD. The same for the points in the yellow dashed rectangle if only the Levenshtein distance is used (Fig. 6).

This indicates that the classifier constructed based only on a single distance might suffer underfitting and we are able to build a well-performed classifier by combining both distances. The result can be verified by processing cross-validation for different classifiers, where the result is collected in Table 3. We see that the last classifier has a much better performance than each single distance-based classifier. This best classifier will be used in the next section to predict the match probability. The performance indexes used, AUC, Precision, and Recall, are introduced in another article in this book (Liermann and Li 2021).

In Sect. 3.3, we will introduce a natural language processing technology for computing the text similarity in practical application. The features selection introduced above can be carried out to decide which metrics are relevant and to find the best classifier.

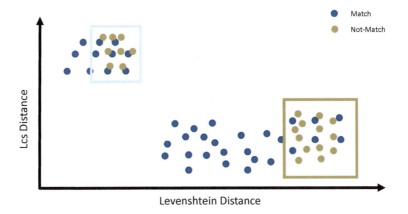

Fig. 6 Levenshtein distance (© ifb SE)

Table 3 Ten cross-validation results (© ifb SE)

Selected features for classifier	AUC (area under the curve)	Precision	Recall
Levenshtein distance	0.9095	0.7345	0.4115
Longest common substring distance	0.8974	0.7545	0.4041
Both distances	0.9972	0.9749	0.9922

3.5 Example of a Match Result

Based on the machine learning model (classifier), we can predict whether a pair of invoice and payment matched or not. In addition, we can also predict the match probability (score). In Table 4, we provide a short example of predictions, where ten pairs of invoice and payment are predicted. The column "Predict" is binary and shows whether the pair matches or not. The remaining two columns indicate the not-match and match probability (p0—not match, p1—match). Not surprisingly, the sum of the last two columns is always equal to 1 by row.

We prefiltered (Fig. 7) the invoices and payments by using the predicted match probability, where the top N candidates with the highest probability can be selected. After that, a brute force search is carried out across the prefiltered candidates. On the one hand, prefiltering/preselection allows us to reduce the number of match candidates and therefore can speed up the brute force search. On the other, it has the risk of losing match accuracy by filtering out matched candidates due to false negative prediction. Therefore, the choice of N plays the key role. In the case of large N, we guarantee a high level of accuracy, but computation time increases. In contrast to that,

Table 4 Prediction (© ifb SE)

Predict	P0	P1
0	0.9414140	0.0585860
0	0.8016686	0.1983314
0	0.8055366	0.1944634
0	0.8016686	0.1983314
1	0.5655805	0.4344195
0	0.8016686	0.1983314
1	0.5655805	0.4344195

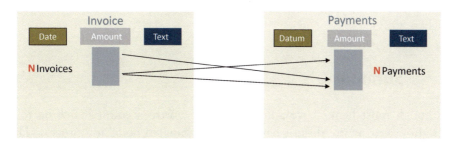

Fig. 7 Prefiltering of invoices and payments: select the top *N* invoices/payments with the highest match probability (© ifb SE)

Table 5 Example of result with no matched pairs (No.Match = 0) (© ifb SE)

No.Match	Type	Date	Identifier	Amount	Text
0	Invoices	01/01/2020	1:1_1	15,700.6	Invoice number: 500537
2	Invoices	01/01/2020	1:1_2	92,649	Invoice number: 500284
2	Payments	01/01/2020	1:1_2	92,649	Ref: 500284
3	Invoices	01/01/2020	1:1_3	39,328	Invoice number: 500562
3	Payments	01/01/2020	1:1_3	39,328	Ref: 500562
0	Payments	01/01/2020	1:1_1	15,690	Ref: 500537

reducing the value of N will speed up the brute force search but increase the risk of losing accuracy.

After processing the brute force, the match result is exported into a CSV file, where a MatchID is assigned to each matched pair. In addition, the invoices and payments for which no matches were found are automatically moved to a pool with MatchID 0 and need to be processed manually (Table 5).

4 Challenges in the Practical Application—NLP

Natural language processing (NPL) is a field of machine learning which aims to give models the ability to read and understand human languages. It can be used in various business areas, for example, sentiment analysis, which analyzes the customer's choices and decisions based on their social media posts. By using NPL, we can extend our use case into a more general case where the text similarity is no longer based on string similarity but keyword similarity or indeed content similarity. Some examples can be found in (Schröder and Tieben 2021).

5 Summary

Although most banks have automated their nostro account matching to a certain extent, many do not have a fully automated matching process. The reasons for partially manual steps are the complexity of different business events. Alterations and situations occur when packaging one or more business events to one booking or by posting one or more bookings to one business event. More complexity is added when a combination of the two preceding situations occur.

String similarity algorithms (near match) and tools like the Levenshtein distance (LSD) and the longest common substring distance (LCSD) are useful in solving most of the challenges and improving the level of automation of tasks that still have to be performed manually to some extent.

Literature

Alberto Apostolico, Zvi Galil. 1997. *Pattern Matching Algorithms.* Oxford: Oxford University Press.
cran.r-project.org. 2020. *stringdist: Approximate String Matching, Fuzzy Text Search, and String Distance Functions.* October 9. Accessed December 17, 2020. https://cran.r-project.org/web/packages/stringdist/index.html.
Czwalina, Marie Kristin, Chiara Jakobs, Christopher Schmidt, Matthias Jacoby, and Sebastian Geisel. 2021. "Processes in a Digital Environment." In *The Digital Journey of Banking and Insurance, Volume II—Digitalization and Machine Learning*, edited by Volker Liermann and Claus Stegmann. New York: Palgrave Macmillan.
H2O.ai. 2019. *h2o.ai Overview.* January 29. Accessed October 29, 2020. http://docs.h2o.ai/h2o/latest-stable/h2o-docs/index.html.
Liermann, Volker, and Sangmeng Li. 2021. "Methods of Machine Learning." In *The Digital Journey of Banking and Insurance, Volume III—Data Storage, Processing, and Analysis*, edited by Liermann Volker and Claus Stegmann. New York: Palgrave Macmillan.
Schröder, Daniel, and Marian Tieben. 2021. "Sentiment Analysis for Reputational Risk Management." In *The Digital Journey of Banking and Insurance, Volume II—Digitalization and Machine Learning*, edited by Volker Liermann and Claus Stegmann. New York: Palgrave Macmillan.
Soybir, Sefa. 2021. "Project Management and RPA." In *The Digital Journey of Banking and Insurance, Volume I—Disruption and DNA*, edited by Volker Liermann and Claus Stegmann. New York: Palgrave Macmillan.

Use Case—Fraud Detection Using Machine Learning Techniques

Philipp Enzinger and Sangmeng Li

1 Introduction

The cost of fraudulent claims for insurers was estimated at around 13 billion euros in 2017 and is second only to tax fraud. Only fraud cases in the amount of 2.5 billion euros have been detected. That is less than one in five fraud cases. Though initiatives to counter insurance fraud exist in many European countries, some were started as early as 1989, detection rates remain low (insurance europe 2019). Fraud leads to competitive disadvantages, moral hazards, adverse selection, reputational damage, and other indirect disadvantages in addition to falsely paid claims. Therefore, insurance companies have tried to detect and prevent fraud manually and automated long before the evolution of machine learning (ML) techniques. They were just not very successful in doing so—right now only one in ten fraudulent claims is correctly detected by insurance companies in Germany. In addition to susceptibility to errors, manual fraud detection processes are complex in maintenance and cost-intensive, not least because forms of fraud

---

P. Enzinger (✉) · S. Li
ifb SE, Grünwald, Germany
e-mail: Philipp.Enzinger@ifb-group.com

S. Li
e-mail: Sangmeng.Li@ifb-group.com

are constantly changing. Added to this is the increasing digitalization of the insurance business and the resulting new data sources.

In times where insurers are constantly looking for new investment opportunities while facing enormous pressure to drive down costs to fulfill the required returns that are needed to stay profitable, the untapped potential of investing in automated fraud detection therefore sounds like a no-brainer. We are going to look into why that is the case, what are the challenges insurers are facing when setting up automated fraud detection systems with ML, and what a process can look like in the new model.

2   A Primer on Insurance Fraud

An insurance contract is a socialization of costs that could endanger the financial welfare of every individual but are bearable when allocated to a large pool of homogeneous individuals. In practice, one of the biggest challenges is the identification of the real costs of the damage the insured individual suffered and whether the circumstances under which the damage was incurred are covered by the insurance contract. These are the two most significant sources of insurance fraud and they basically come down to an information asymmetry problem. This is one of the biggest challenges in avoiding insurance fraud—decreasing the information asymmetry between the insurer and the insured. This is often called "costly state verification" and means that verifying the information the insured individual provides to the insurer comes at a cost. Machine learning is one tool to decrease these costs. Unfortunately, machine learning requires good data quality. But, luckily, insurers have spent the past decade or so **increasing the data availability** (Velauthapillai and Floß 2021), for example, for car insurance contracts. This means that they realized it makes sense to use weather data and geo data when evaluating whether a particular claim is fraudulent or not. But it is not only important to evaluate the data of the claim. You must also take into account the **data at the inception of the contract**. The data might already have been incomplete then, which results in a lack of coverage for the claim. This is a very common phenomenon in health insurance. Fraud can also differ significantly in the degree of criminal energy behind the fraudulent claim. So-called **soft frauds** are opportunistic in nature. The typical case is when your friend claims for the cell phone that you broke yourself using his liability insurance. In contrast, **hard frauds** are planned from the start, often beginning with the deliberate destruction of an insured object. Hard frauds might even become more significant when the insurance company gets a reputation for being lax in fraud detection. It will then fall victim to organized crime syndicates more often. This is known as adverse selection. Knowing this differentiation is important when setting up a fraud detection system because the structure of the data can vary significantly.

Combating fraud is key for insurance companies because high fraud rates pose in themselves a significant competitive disadvantage as the claims paid out are higher than the true insured risk, which results **in higher premiums** and/or lower margins. In addition to this, not being able to "know" the true insured risk also hinders companies in setting up good models as the estimator is always biased. This also poses a significant **model risk** as pricing and customer segmentation models take the cost of fraud falsely into account. Being known as an insurer with lax fraud guidelines can also lead to significant **reputational risks**. Aside from the adverse selection problem mentioned, this can also be alarming for regulators (AML, tax authorities…) and other stakeholders in the company—in particular, shareholders because they end up paying the cost and can opt to invest in a more efficient competitor. Finally, the **financial loss** itself should already be a high enough motivator to try to increase the fraud detection rate as far as possible.

2.1 Current State of Fraud Detection

A study by McKinsey found the following flaws in existing fraud detection systems from an organizational point of view. First of all, fraud is still not a focus topic of top management, although McKinsey estimates potential savings exceeding three percent of claims expenditure. Additionally, the claims department is of limited importance in the organizational and strategic focus of insurance companies. Drilling down into the claims department, fraud detectors historically are the same employees as regular claim handlers—without any additional specializations (McKinsey & Company 2015).

The issue of bad fraud detection systems and high fraud rates became so prominent that regulatory and national institutions decided to act on it and created industry-wide programs around the world to tackle this problem. Some countries set up **dedicated investigative groups**. France has an investigative body for fraud detection that provides training and certificates for fraud officers. The UK set up an Insurance Fraud Bureau. Some European countries directly **cooperate with law enforcement** as police officers are often very well equipped to detect fraudulent activities, in particular when they stem from organized crime. Maybe the most important development in fraud detection is the use of Big Data and new technologies to improve fraud detection systems. Insurance companies are increasingly making use of external databases, e.g., tax authorities' data. National authorities are supporting this, for example, the UNESPA, the national insurance association of Spain, which provides **two common databases** of all motor and property insurance claims which can be used to train and improve fraud detection models. Similar networks with shared data across the industry exist in the UK, Slovenia, Italy, and other countries. Thinking this through to the end, a modern, digitalized insurance company must **employ machine learning** to best make use of the Big Data available. The largest Belgian insurance company did exactly that and created an integrated solution based on ML for its fraud detection model. Insurance Europe, the European insurance federation, recommends making use of Big Data and artificial intelligence in fraud detection and making it a board-level issue (insurance europe 2019).

3 Use Case: Fraud Detection with Machine Learning on Car Insurance Claims

3.1 Data Collection and Preparation

The analysis in the paper is based on the public dataset from Kaggle (Kaggle 2018) including 1000 insurance claim samples, where nearly a quarter of them are fraudulent. The data is slightly imbalanced and the minority class (fraud class) is the one that we are interested in identifying. As introduced in (Liermann et al., Mathematical Background of Machine Learning 2019), imbalanced data is a common problem in classification where the classes are distributed unequally in the dataset. This affects model training and causes underfitting, where the model can recognize patterns from the majority class but ignores the minority class. In this article, we will use the oversampling technique to adjust the class distribution by duplicating the minority class (Fig. 1).

39 attributes are included in the dataset where the attribute "fraud_reported" is binary and shows whether the claim is fraudulent or not. The attribute "fraud_reported" will be the "label," i.e., the information the model is aiming to predict. The other 38 attributes are called features. Some attributes contain numerical values, and some are categorical. Examples are given in the following figures. Note that the data attributes are all considered numeric, although they are discrete, since they are measurements and have a mathematical meaning (Tables 1 and 2).

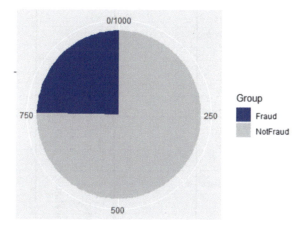

Fig. 1 Imbalanced dataset (© ifb SE)

Before we start to train the model, the data needs to be cleansed according to the following two steps:

Remove the identity attributes

Some attributes, such as identification number, are unique per claim and should not be used for training the model. In our dataset, we discovered two columns: policy_number and incident_location.

Remove the missing value

The attributes containing missing values should be removed. In more advanced cases, the missing value should be fulfilled by using average values or sampling methods. We only discovered one attribute X_c39, therefore it makes sense to ignore it.

In the more general case, we should take some further steps to clean the data, such as removing duplicate observations, removing attributes with very few unique values, and standardization for numerical values.

The following analysis is implemented by using the R and machine learning open-source platform H2O (H2O.ai 2019).

3.2 Model Selection

As a supervised learning model, the algorithms usually learn on a labeled dataset and the label is the target that needs to be predicted. In our example, the data samples are already labeled as "Fraud" or "Regular Claim." In contrast, labeling is not necessarily required for unsupervised learning models. In this case, the algorithms assume that most of the claims are not fraudulent and learn to inherit structure from the normal data. The anomalies/outliers,

Table 1 Numeric attributes (© ifb SE)

months_as_customer	age	policy_bind_date	policy_deductable	policy_annual_premium
umbrella_limit	capital.gains	capital.loss	incident_date	incident_hour_of_the_day
number_of_vehicles_involved	bodily_injuries	total_claim_amount	injury_claim	property_claim
vehicle_claim	auto_year			

Table 2 Categorical attributes (© ifb SE)

policy_number	policy_state	policy_csl	insured_zip	insured_sex
insured_education_level	insured_occupation	insured_hobbies	insured_relationship	incident_type
collision_type	incident_severity	authorities_contacted	incident_state	incident_city
incident_location	property_damage	witnesses	police_report_avaliable	auto_make
auto_model				

which are suspicious by differing significantly from the normal structure, are identified as anomalous. In the following sections, we will provide experiment results for both supervised and unsupervised learning models and compare them by listing the pros and cons in Table 5. In addition, we suggest an advanced ensemble model, which combines the supervised and unsupervised learning in section Fehler! Verweisquelle konnte nicht gefunden werden. As a result, we verify that the model performance is getting better, where AUC (area under the curve), precision, and recall are selected as evaluation indexes. For more details about model evaluation, we refer the reader to (Liermann et al., Mathematical Background of Machine Learning 2019).

3.2.1 Supervised Model

For the supervised model, we chose a random forest where the number of trees is set to ten and the maximum depth of trees is set to ten. The cross-validation performance result is given as follows, where 10 folds are used (Table 3).

We extract the variable importance of the above random forests. Recalling method article, variable importance shows the contribution of a feature for making accurate prediction on label. The more a model relies on a feature to make predictions, the more important it is for the model. In the following figure, the first ten significant features are illustrated (Fig. 2).

Reading from the Fig. 2: Variable importance, the features "incident_severity" and "insured_hobbies" have the most significant influence on the prediction of fraud. We are also able to verify this by illustrating "insured_hobbies" against "Fraud." As shown in Fig. 3: Insured_hobbies vs. label, the insured parties who like playing chess and watching movies have a much higher probability of making fraudulent claims. As a comparison, we illustrate the "insured_education_level" against "Fraud" in Fig. 4: Insured_education_level vs. label. It is not hard to see that education level has nearly no influence on the claim being fraudulent or not.

Table 3 Random forests: performance (© ifb SE)

AUC (area under the curve)	Precision	Recall
0.8439	0.6242	0.7950

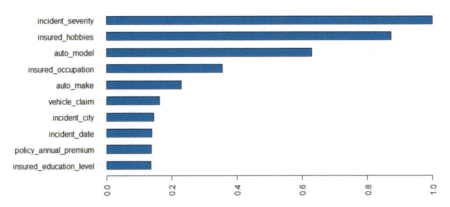

Fig. 2 Variable importance (© ifb SE)

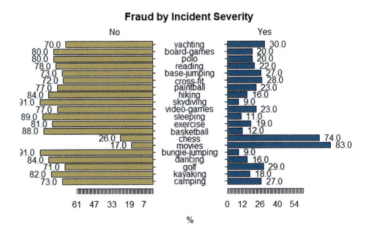

Fig. 3 Insured_hobbies vs. label (© ifb SE)

3.2.2 Unsupervised Model

Similarly to (Liermann et al., Batch processing—Pattern recognition 2019), we use autoencoders, which are classic artificial deep networks and capable of performing unsupervised learning tasks. They are targeted by learning an efficient representation/reconstruction of the input data within the network structure. The reconstruction error is used to quantify the probability of an anomalous sample, in other words, a large reconstruction error value indicates an anomaly. For more details about autoencoders, we refer the reader to (Liermann et al., Batch processing—Pattern recognition 2019).

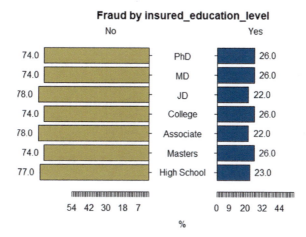

Fig. 4 Insured_education_level vs. label (© ifb SE)

Table 4 Autoencoder: performance (© ifb SE)

AUC (area under the curve)	Precision	Recall
0.6508	0.4424	0.7449

We chose an autoencoder with three hidden layers and 20, 30, 20 hidden nodes, separately, where the Tanh function is set as an activation function. The ten-cross-validation result is given as follows (Table 4).

We illustrate the reconstruction error against label in Fig. 5: Reconstruction error vs. label. It is not hard to see a sharp separation between normal and fraudulent samples at a reconstruction error of around 0.065.

In comparison to supervised learning models, autoencoders target identifying the anomaly according to the reconstruction error. Some normal samples (the points on the top right-hand side of Fig. 5) are suspicious as an anomaly, but incorrectly identified as fraudulent samples (false positive). This leads to lower precision. We summarize the pros and cons of both learning models in the following table (Table 5).

3.2.3 Ensemble Model

In the last part of this section, we provide an algorithm which combines both supervised and unsupervised learning approaches. The intuition is illustrated in the following figure, where the reconstruction error of the unsupervised method is taken as an additional feature for random forests (Fig. 6).

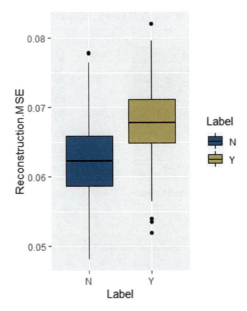

Fig. 5 Reconstruction error vs. label (© ifb SE)

Table 5 Pros and cons of supervised and unsupervised learning (© ifb SE)

Supervised learning	Unsupervised learning
• Labeling necessary	– Labeling not necessary
– Good explainability (variable importance)	• Black box
– Efficient detection of existing patterns in the past	• Risk of high false negative (anomaly ≠ fraud)
• Not sensible for new fraud	– Able to recognize new anomaly/fraud pattern

By adding this additional feature, we can improve the model learning performance by extracting a further finer correlation between anomaly and fraud. For example, which anomalous samples have a higher probability of being fraudulent and which are just normally anomalous. The ten-cross-validation result is presented in Table 6.

Recalling Tables 3, 4, the validation performance is significantly better in comparison to each single approach. The AUC (area under the curve) increases from 84 to 88.5%, which shows that the ensemble models can learn more sufficiently. In addition, we verify this by illustrating the variable importance of ensemble models. Not surprisingly, the reconstruction error (Reconstruction.MSE) has taken Rank 4, which indicates that the influence of anomaly on the prediction of fraud should not be ignored (Fig. 7).

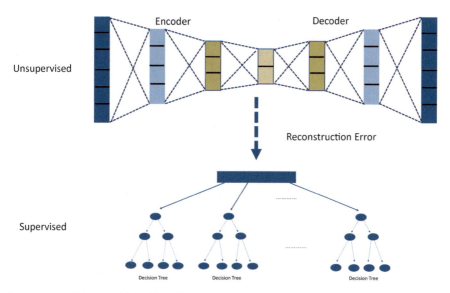

Fig. 6 Ensemble model (© ifb SE)

Table 6 Combined model: performance (© ifb SE)

AUC (area under the curve)	Precision	Recall
0.8858	0.6915	0.8787

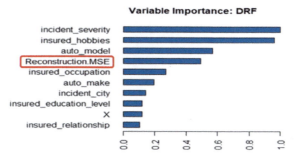

Fig. 7 Variable importance (© ifb SE)

3.3 Model Calibration

When carrying out the model calibration, the business owner first must think about the goals of the new model. In our approach like in many statistical models, there is a natural inverse relationship between the rate of fraud cases the model can predict correctly (recall) and the efficiency with which the prediction can take place (precision). Therefore, it is wise to think about these numbers in the very early stage of a fraud detection project, also because the calibration can have a drastic effect on the process design in claims handling and the model must be accepted by the claims department. A more efficient model needs more care in checking the stability of the unpredicted fraud cases (random sampling), while a model focused more on the fraud detection rate needs more process steps to weed out the false positives (Fig. 8).

The calibration of the model also has an effect on the business case, which should be made before the project is even budgeted. A model focused on the fraud detection rate will have more savings from avoiding paying wrongful claims while a more efficient process frees up more employees for other tasks. The model is calibrated by changing the threshold from which a particular claim is classified as a fraud case. This threshold is set on the fraud probability, which is an interim result in the classification model. This will be elaborated more in 4.Process Design. The model calibration can then be read and is set like this.

"A claim is classified as a fraud case if the estimated fraud probability exceeds 95%" means the threshold is set at 95%

"The model correctly predicts 93% of all fraud cases" means recall of 93%

"For every 4 true fraud cases a claims handler will have to look into 1 falsely predicted claim" means the efficiency (precision) of the model is 80%. For

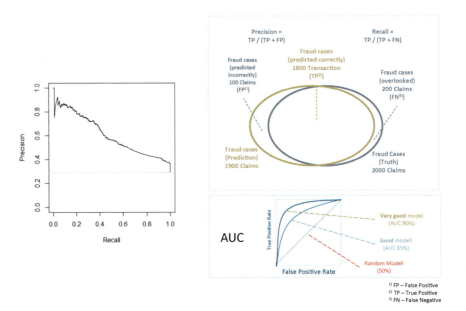

Fig. 8 Calibration statistics (© ifb SE)

more details on recall, precision, and model calibration in machine learning models see (Hartung and Führer 2021).

4 Process Design

A key insight into adopting machine learning can be drawn from experience in the medical field: when doctors have the right amount of data and sufficient time, they are currently still able to keep up with success rates of AI-based solutions. HBR cites a study in which 99% of treatments suggested by the doctors were also suggested by the AI solution. But the assumptions from lab tests are usually not fulfilled in reality. Doctors are not always able to request all diagnostics and do not have the time to analyze everything in detail. Therefore, in reality, success rates are often lower. This shows the potential for fraud detection: a synergetic approach to AI selection and expert approval. This will also lead to a much more satisfying approach in claims handling as the responsible parties will mostly look at true frauds. The study also indicates that AI-based solutions are on the verge of beating humans at diagnostics as they are just able to consume much more information. In this case, the AI solution merely suggested treatments based on papers the doctors had not read yet. The same is possible for fraud detection: the engine will be able to take into account all available information and if implemented correctly even tells the fraud expert how it came to the conclusion of a fraud indication. Now we will show how to set up an AI-based process.

The fraud detection process usually designed follows the process steps detection, investigation, prevention. The task of setting up an efficient machine learning-based fraud detection process can be divided into two pillars: (I) An ML classification engine that categorizes new claims into risk buckets based on fraud patterns in the past (II) A process that searches for new fraud patterns in the "no fraud bucket" and identifies false positives. In addition to this, a feedback loop is required to feed the results into the model training process (Fig. 9).

Let us first look into the fraud classification engine. This engine will be based on the methodology described in Part III. The resulting estimate of the machine learning algorithm provides a probability for each claim that, given the history of detected frauds, it belongs to a particular fraud cluster. Using this, claims will be categorized into risk buckets. The number of buckets depends on client-specific needs and affects the granularity of the process. The minimum requirement is a two-bucket process with a fraud and no-fraud bucket for claims. This can easily be extended to a traffic light (three buckets)

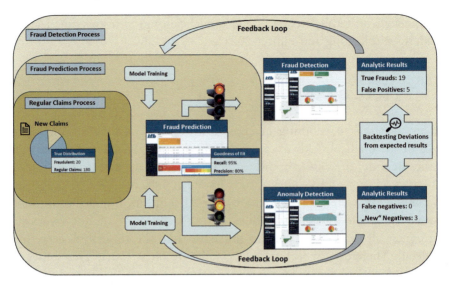

Fig. 9 Target operating model fraud (© ifb SE)

approach. In both cases, the classification is based on thresholds/boundaries for the estimated fraud probabilities. A traffic light approach could use the following boundaries for the classification: Green light: Fraud probability < 70%; Yellow light: Fraud probability 70–90%; Red light: Fraud probability > 90%. The last category should be calibrated such that it remains feasible to check every claim in that bucket. In particular, the threshold for the highest risk bucket will determine the quality of the classification. The lower the threshold, the higher the share of true fraud detected by the algorithm. This is indicated by the derived recall measure—when recall is at 95% this means that 95% of all true frauds will be in the highest risk bucket. The threshold also has a second implication, which is precision. The precision of the process will increase with the level of the threshold, which means that the higher the fraud probability threshold is set, the higher the share of true frauds in the fraud classification bucket, but also the higher the number of missed fraud cases in the lower risk buckets. Therefore, insurance companies need to take into account the share of true frauds they want to have in the highest risk bucket when redesigning the process. In addition, the middle-risk bucket(s) can be set up with a leaner process or a random sampling approach to increase the overall recall and retain a high precision in the top bucket. It might be that recall of the highest risk bucket is 90%, but the overall recall of the two combined risk categories is 98%. Identifying these eight additional percentage points will be much tougher though due to the lower precision and the resulting (far) lower proportion of true frauds in the analyzed claims. The process design is therefore key when deciding on a multi-bucket approach.

Now let us look into the second pillar. When setting up processes as mentioned above, two things need to be clear and cannot be forgotten. Firstly, the algorithm described in section three only relies on past observation. It will inherently be biased toward the past. Therefore, it is crucial to always analyze your lower risk buckets for new fraud patterns. Secondly, the minute an insurer goes live with an ML-based classification system, the algorithm will only be trained with the true frauds detected through the clustering. This will to some degree be countered by the analysis of the lower risk categories mentioned above. Nevertheless, it is recommended to include a sample in the process that is analyzed in an expert-based process. Feeding this data into the algorithm increases the quality of the classification and combats the risk of historical bias.

5 Implementing an AI-Based Fraud Detection System

Most insurance companies will have a claims management system in place. Also. data will probably be extracted to carry out fraud analysis. To implement an ML-based KI classification, an open-source solution is strongly recommended. Insurance companies tend to have more experience with R, so the displayed implementation shows a setup based on an R architecture. Nevertheless, the same can be done using Python. For the target architecture, an interface of the claims management system to R should be established. This can easily be established using microservices or other open-source solutions to keep costs low. The models should be pretrained in the implementation of the architecture and updated regularly, but not too often to keep the process efficient. Once a month is a recommended frequency, but this depends on the inflow of new claims. ifb is using the R package shiny as a user interface (UI). The UI usually has two components: one for the data science team to train and calibrate the model and one for the claims handling department. The second dashboard will be the main supporting pillar for the fraud detection team.

A dashboard should also offer other supportive information to help the claims handler choose the best next step, e.g., which information to ask for, such as which features were most important in classifying the particular claim as fraudulent (Fig. 10).

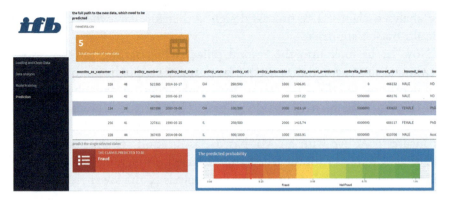

Fig. 10 Example setup of fraud detection dashboard (© ifb SE)

One challenge in implementation can be the maintenance of an open-source architecture. As it is not standard software, there is no vendor with maintenance responsibility. On the other hand, there are no license fees and millions of users worldwide are carrying out maintenance by developing new content and ensuring the compatibility of different packages with one another. The second big challenge is data cleaning. For the algorithm to work well, features need to be defined in a consistent format. Also including new data sources needs to be considered in PoCs in the implementation phase (Hartung and Führer 2021).

6 Summary

All in all, it is clear that machine learning is the future of fraud detection for insurance companies. The transition point is just a matter of data availability, budgets, and tackling the resistance of, for example, the claims department to changing current processes. When it comes to the implementation, data cleaning and introducing new external data sources into the process are key to get the results in terms of recall and precision that are needed to set up an efficient process. Finally, it is important to start small but think big. Start the project with PoCs and prototypes, but when the decision for implementation of the productive process is made, think about whether to use a common data store for the ML architecture. Every AI solution will benefit from large data availability, so do not restrict yourself with short-sighted architecture decisions. Open-source microservices can help a lot with setting this up without encountering the past pitfalls of failed central data platform projects.

Literature

Hartung, Sören and Manuela Führer. 2021. "AI for Impairment Accounting." In *The Digital Journey of Banking and Insurance, Volume I—Disruption and DNA*, edited by Volker Liermann and Claus Stegmann. New York: Palgrave Macmillan.

H2O.ai. 2019. *h2o.ai Overview*, January 29. Accessed September 29, 2020. http://docs.h2o.ai/h2o/latest-stable/h2o-docs/index.html.

insurance europe. 2019. *Insurance Fraud: Not a Victimless Crime*. Brussels: Insurance Europe aisbl, November.

Kaggle. 2018. *Auto Insurance Claims* Data, August 20. Accessed September 27, 2020. https://www.kaggle.com/buntyshah/auto-insurance-claims-data.

Liermann, Volker, Sangmeng Li, and Norbert Schaudinnus. 2019. "Batch Processing—Pattern Recognition." In *The Impact of Digital Transformation and Fintech on the Finance Professional*, edited by Volker Liermann and Claus Stegmann. New York: Palgrave Macmillan.

Liermann, Volker, Sangmeng Li, and Norbert Schaudinnus. 2019. "Mathematical Background of Machine Learning." In *The Impact of Digital Transformation and Fintech on the Finance Professional*, edited by Volker Liermann and Claus Stegmann. New York: Palgrave Macmillan.

McKinsey & Company. 2015. *Claims Management: Taking a Determined Stand Against Insurance Fraud*. Germany: Munich.

Velauthapillai, Jeyakrishna and Johannes Floß. 2021. "Special Data for Insurance Companies." In *The Digital Journey of Banking and Insurance, Volume III—Data Storage, Processing, and Analysis*, edited by Volker Liermann and Claus Stegmann. New York: Palgrave Macmillan.

Use Case: NFR—HR Risk

Harro Dittmar, Arne Schmüser, and Farah Skaf

1 Introduction

It can take years to establish a business reputation, but one employee who acts unprofessionally can harm all these efforts and ruin the reputation and/or the turnover of the company. For this reason, appropriate HR risk management is very important to keep these risks in view and counteract them if necessary, before the business is damaged. Therefore, a measurement and reporting system must be defined and introduced, so that the situation can be identified based on a few indicators and appropriate measures taken. In this way, grievances can be uncovered before they lead to major problems. The basis for this is not the individual monitoring of employees, rather a summary of general information and metadata.

In the following section, we will be describing the taxonomy of non-financial risks up to the risk of resignation and why we have specifically chosen to talk about this risk category. The concepts of impact graphs and

---

H. Dittmar (✉) · A. Schmüser · F. Skaf
ifb SE, Grünwald, Germany
e-mail: Harro.Dittmar@ifb-group.com

A. Schmüser
e-mail: Arne.Schmueser@ifb-group.com

F. Skaf
e-mail: Farah.Skaf@ifb-group.com

indicators are also included.[1] In Sect. 3, we explain how the corresponding key indicators can be developed, measured, and converted into a scoring system. This scoring system forms the basis for risk management. In Sect. 5, we use an example to illustrate the possibilities of AI and machine learning in this area. A summary and an outlook will conclude the article in Sect. 6.

2 Resignation Risk: A Fraction of Non-financial Risk

Non-financial risks can be described as a variety of risks that can damage the company's operations and/or reputation. These risks can be allocated to different categories,[2] for example:

- Strategic risk
- Political risk
- Environmental, social, governance (ESG) risk
- Cyber risk
- Legal risk
- Regulatory risk
- HR risk
- …

In this article, we will focus on a significant risk category: human resources risk (HR). The actions and behavior of employees can have either a positive or a negative impact on the company. To keep track of these risks and to react to them before they harm the organization, appropriate HR risk management is essential.

2.1 Taxonomy of the Risk Category HR Risk

All risks caused directly or indirectly by the behavior, communication, or characteristics of employees are summed up in the category HR risk. We can categorize them into the following sub-risk categories:

---

[1] For even more details of impact graphs and Indicator, see also Liermann et al., Breaking New Grounds in Non-financial Risk Management (2021).

[2] A full NFR taxonomy is introduced (Liermann et al., Breaking New Grounds in Non-financial Risk Management 2021).

(a) **Change and run risk**: This risk is primarily caused by the workload or the qualifications of the employees. It is related to a skills risk, for example, where the employee lacks the technical or professional know-how to accomplish a task or to execute a change.
(b) **Communication risk**: The occurrence of this risk may impede the understanding of the exchange of messages or information between people. It can be a semantic issue, for example, when the same terms can be understood differently within the company/the departments. Communication channels can be another possible issue if the exchange of information is difficult because of the complexity and/or the capacity of the communication system.
(c) **Conduct risk**: This behavioral risk can be associated with the way organizations and their employees interact with customers and the surrounding financial markets. An example of such a risk is an inappropriate complaints management system or when employees act in an unprofessional way to each other or to the customers.
(d) **Risk of dissatisfaction in the office**: This risk can be understood as to how the employees feel about the organization, department, and team. Dissatisfaction lowers the productivity of employees and teams and—the most obvious consequence—can lead to resignation.

The risk category dissatisfaction in the office is particularly important, since there are many interdependencies with the other sub-risk categories. A dissatisfied employee could communicate inappropriately with customers and must therefore be considered a trigger for conduct risk. Conversely, inadequate communication within a team can trigger dissatisfaction in the office.

An obvious consequence of dissatisfaction is resignation. This should be avoided if possible, because it can lead to restrictions in business operations and other significant problems, such as skill risks. Most obvious to quantify are the costs incurred by recruiting and training new employees—the team cannot work efficiently without a (key) player. But there are also many consequences that are difficult to quantify, for example, the loss of know-how, reduction of network effects, etc.

This is one of the reasons why the risk of resignation must be considered further.

2.2 Position of the Resignation Risk in the HR Taxonomy

The resignation risk cannot be clearly associated with a single sub-risk category in the taxonomy presented. The reasons for resignation can be so varied that it must be carefully analyzed to capture it as completely as possible. A detailed analysis of the abovementioned HR sub-risks shows that all of them can also occur as a trigger for resignation (see Fig. 1). For example, an employee who lacks the technical know-how to accomplish their task within a project (skill risk) can be unsatisfied and may quit the job for another one. This example clarifies the complexity of HR risk: a combination of sub-risks often occurs. Here, change and run risk and risk of dissatisfaction. This applies in particular to all events that lead to a resignation. Resignation risk therefore plays a central role in HR risk management. You therefore cannot avoid managing resignation risk, if you want robust NFR management ().

To manage the resignation risk, a situation analysis and measurement methods must be introduced. Experienced HR managers have their own methods, adapted to the respective institute, to determine which employees are likely to resign. It is obvious that the reasons that lead an employee to terminate their employment are usually individual and personal. However, they are often based on the work environment. A combination of an analysis of the work field and the knowledge of the reasons for resignation can be used to define indicators that can be a good basis for measuring and controlling the risk of resignation throughout the company. In the next section, we

Fig. 1 Connection between HR sub-risks and resignation risk (© ifb SE)

will illustrate how impact graphs can be helpful to obtain these indicators. Also, we explain how scoring these indicators helps with the quantification and measurement of the resignation risk.

3 Impact Graph and Indicators of Resignation Risk

Knowing the indicators or drivers of resignation is helpful. In order to be able to assess the risk adequately, one must be able to measure these indicators quasi scientifically and compare them with defined threshold values. We will demonstrate that this challenge is feasible below.

We will begin with an introduction to impact graphs and derivation of indicators.

3.1 Impact Graph

An impact graph is a presentation of the interaction between events, vulnerabilities, risk events, risk types, and materializing risks. A combination of an event and a vulnerability can result in a risk event, which leads to a materializing risk for the company. In this way, a risk to be averted can be attributed to specific causes. If identified vulnerabilities are eliminated, the resulting risk event can usually be completely averted.

There are two ways to create impact graphs:

- Ex-Ante based on expert estimations, where the experts envision the possible scenarios and their effects.
- Ex-Post based on a damage analysis, where the causes of the damage and the connections between them are reconstructed.

This can be helpful to find out which events trigger the risk we are confronted with or which we will be confronted with, and to clearly identify to which risk types it belongs (Fig. 2).

Once we had successfully identified all parameters and transformed them into impact graphs, the next step is to merge them to obtain a graphical representation as one graph. This extensive graph is shown in Fig. 3 in a non-readable form. The details are described in Sect. 4 *Measure Resignation Risk*.

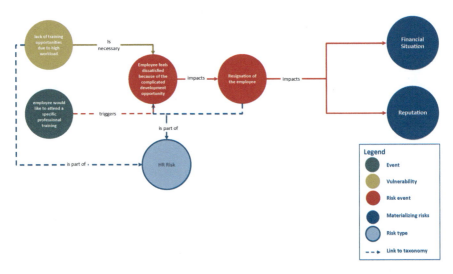

Fig. 2 Example of impact graph with one resignation trigger (© ifb SE)

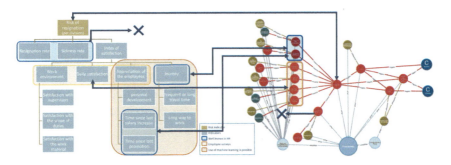

Fig. 3 Comparison of the tree of indicators and impact graph (© ifb SE)

3.2 Indicators

After generating all the impact graphs which lead or can lead to risk, we can derive indicators, which helps us to have a consolidated view of the threat situation. This is a profound assessment of the probabilities of its occurrence and the source of this risk. The essential feature of an indicator is its measurability. Only based on these measurements can the management of the risk and its changes be done seriously. Indicators that react quickly to changes are particularly practical for management.

To assess the risk of resignation, we have considered the following indicators:

- Resignation rate: This rate can either be department-specific or for the entire company. If there is a high fluctuation rate, one must also be prepared for more resignations. This information is collected by any trustworthy HR management system.
- Sickness rate: Rising sickness rates are of course a bad sign. If the workload of individual employees increases too much it can lead to resignation. This rate is easy to compute and is often collected monthly by HR.
- Satisfaction index: This rate is very helpful to analyze whether employees are satisfied or if something is going wrong, so we can try to change the situation before it is too late. Employee surveys can provide more information.

We can notice that some of the essential statistics are already known to HR management. They only need to be evaluated or transferred into a score value with algorithms. The other numbers are obtained through (regular) employee surveys and are not an insurmountable obstacle.

A closer look at the satisfaction index and a subdivision into further indicators is given in Sect. 4.1 and Fig. 3.

3.3 Relationship Between Impact Graphs and Indicators

A comparison of the model of indicators and the consolidated impact graphs is shown in Fig. 3. This graph indicates the limits and possibilities of our approach. It helps us to see whether we have adequately considered all the events which may happen or raise the risk of resignation.

At the same time, it illustrates that only the combination of both views guarantees completeness. There are indicators that have no counterpart in the impact graph. On the other hand, there are risk events for which changes in the probability of occurrence are not measurable—at least not with current methods.

In the following, we will restrict ourselves to measurable indicators.

4 Measure Resignation Risk

It is undisputed that there are measurable indicators for the risk of resignation. There are always new concepts as to which are the most important indicators, for example, the readiness to recommend one's own company as an employer. By conducting a regular survey of a large group of employees, it could be proven that this indicator decreases massively months before a resignation (peakon 2020). But this is information you usually do not have.

It is important to recognize that a change in behavior occurs weeks or months in advance. This makes a sophisticated risk model even more desirable. As described above, we use a combination of the events, vulnerability, and risk events from the impact graph and the respective indicator. To give another example: the vulnerability "*The supervisor is a micro manager*" and event "*Employee would like to be accountable for some tasks*" result in the risk event "*Conflict with the management style*", which leads to the employee feeling dissatisfied. We can cluster these in the indicator "*Satisfaction with the supervisor*".

4.1 Scoring Resignation Indicators

Now it is time to demonstrate how we can get the data to quantify this indicator so we can measure the probability of the risk occurrence. Therefore, it is appropriate to use a categorization of these aspects according to their data source. Either the data is obtained through employee surveys or it is already available to HR management.

I. Use of surveys and their interpretation:

In order to quickly identify changes in the risk of resignation and to be able to assess the development, a simple measurement of daily satisfaction is recommended. For this purpose, it is enough if a large number of employees anonymously document their satisfaction at the end of the working day. This could be done by a simple query at the workstation or computer. This can be easily evaluated in digital form and serves as an indicator. The evaluation of the situation and its transformation into a score is only possible and reasonable with an expert estimation. Of course, the evaluation of this measurement must first be calibrated over a longer time period in order to establish a reliable causality to the risk of resignation.

Further aspects can only be assessed with suitable interviews. The evaluation of the situation and its transformation into a score is only possible and reasonable with an expert estimation. The interviewer must be trained and instructed accordingly to quantify the dissatisfaction of the employee. The clearer the dissatisfaction, the higher the risk score. The time scale must also be considered: if an employee repeatedly denounces shortcomings without changing the situation, the weight of the dissatisfaction must be higher.

Indicators and examples of aspects for which we can collect data through employee surveys:

- Conflict with the management style, e.g., the supervisor is a micromanager.
- The tasks given are not challenging, e.g., the employees have monotonous work tasks, or the tasks do not require them to make use of their education.
- Poor working conditions, e.g., ineffective workplace technology.

II. Appropriate use of data we collect through HR management:

HR management has access to a large amount of employees' data, which can be very helpful for the measurement of the resignation risk. These aspects are easy to quantify and can be automatically evaluated if the data is recorded and stored accordingly (e.g., time between salary increases, or even between the expressed wish for and the execution of further training). Furthermore, we can identify dependencies and seasonal effects if we compare the assessment results to the thresholds and document a progression over a period of time.

The scale of each scoring system depends on the situation. Certain aspects may need to be subdivided more finely than others. And when comparing or merging different scores, weighting may be necessary.

Example of aspects for which we can collect data through employee surveys:

- No possibility for advanced training, e.g., employees have no time for training due to workload.
- Long journey to work or lots of business travel, e.g., over one hour daily.
- Employees feel unappreciated, e.g., employee gets good (performance) ratings without corresponding salary increase or title change.

A summary of the indicators and their data sources is given in Fig. 4. This shows which indicators can be summarized for reporting purposes. The report for the top management focused on changes in the risk of resignation. This aggregates the outcome of indicators from the other layers, which are used for targeted analysis.

Furthermore—in preparation for Sect. 5—the figure highlights for which data interpretations machine learning algorithms should be used.

Other indicators are conceivable but will not be discussed here. They are either not measurable (e.g., poaching attempts by competitors) or difficult to reconcile with privacy agreements (e.g., internal communication behavior).

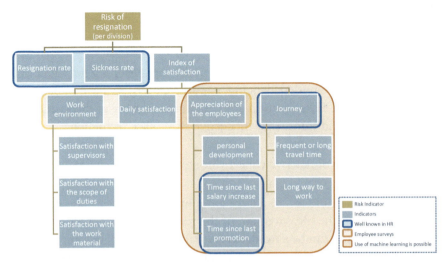

Fig. 4 Indicator tree for resignation risk (© ifb SE)

4.2 Merging Score Values

The approach shown so far is characterized by a high degree of modularity. As the edges and nodes of the impact graph can receive specific weightings, individual departmental weightings can be considered. This is important for adequate risk reporting, as it can be customized easily. How exactly the resignation triggers influence each other depends on many personal and cultural factors. In a work area where travel is part of the job description, the frequent travel time may not be evaluated as negative. The reporting will become more refined as the knowledge of the specific situation increases.

Nevertheless, a procedure for merging values must be started. An initial, effective approach is shown in Fig. 5. Therefore, we use a scoring system with a value between zero (low risk) and ten (high risk) and all indicators are equally weighted.

Three problem areas and their triggers are listed there. The impact graph must be read from left to right. There are certain vulnerabilities (golden) that either occur (score = 1) or do not occur (score = 0). Furthermore, there are associated events (turquoise) with a score between one and ten. This score represents the probability of occurrence. It is advisable to design a general tree that is as extensive as possible and to switch the respective vulnerabilities/preconditions on or off individually.

Multiplying the incoming edges results in a score for a possible resignation trigger. For example, growing dissatisfaction due to lack of opportunities for further training: the employee wishes to attend specific further training and

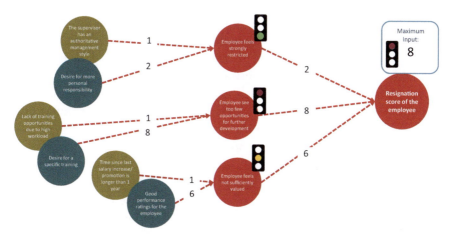

Fig. 5 Example calculation for resignation score of an employee, along an impact graph (© ifb SE)

so far this wish could not be granted due to the workload in the department. Since the employee has already requested this further training several times, the score was considered high. This leads to a red traffic light—as an indication that action is needed. If the employee's request can be granted, the score for this trigger drops to zero, since the precondition no longer applies. The scores of the other triggers are calculated in the same way.

When merging the scores, the maximum score should at least be maintained. This is ensured in the example by transmitting the maximum value. In a more complicated case, the other scores should be included in the calculation. Three or more amber traffic lights are usually an indication that action is needed (i.e., a red light is a result). These and other calculations can easily be implemented in a reporting system.

The resignation score of individual employees is relevant information for their managers. For example, enabling regular working from home increases the satisfaction of employees with long commuting distances. In order to determine a resignation risk score for a company or department, the findings must be summarized and weighted as far as possible. A simple average employee satisfaction value may suffice. It is deceptive, however, if the productivity of a team depends on certain individuals. In such a case, the evaluation of the key person must be given a higher weighting. To estimate the score of an entire department, a comparable impact graph can be used. This has the characteristic that the weighted averages mentioned are located on the edges (connections). In order to determine the score of an entire company, the scores of the individual departments are taken and used to form a weighted average. Such scores can be formed for each risk event, so that a drill-down analysis can be performed at any position in the graph. A drill down becomes useful if the scores overwrite certain thresholds. Then it can be helpful to distinguish in which departments the main drivers are located, in order to initiate the appropriate countermeasures.

Over time, one will gain enough experience to adapt the algorithms to the employer's individual circumstances. Machine learning algorithms can be helpful here, as we will explain in the next section.

The limitations of the approach presented are visible in the illustrations of impact graphs: the dependencies between indicators or events are not considered in the illustrations because they are difficult to estimate. In order to get the best interpretation from the collected data, the use of artificial intelligence or machine learning is necessary. The possibilities are discussed in the next section.

5 Use of Machine Learning

Before we discuss machine learning (ML) in the specific context of resignation risk, the main characteristics of such algorithms are briefly explained. A more detailed discussion of model families can be found in Liermann et al., Mathematical background of machine learning (2019), and in the hands-on e-books of Jason Brownlee (2020) among numerous other sources that are freely available. ML algorithms can learn complex patterns and nonlinear relations that exist in static and dynamic data and use them to perform classifications and predictions of future events. They can perform useful and efficient abstractions of complex and big data streams, be it from visual, audible, or other sources of digital information. Computers have the power to perceive, filter, analyse, and relate tirelessly much more data than humanly possible. They perform "data mining" much more efficiently and with a comprehensive, scalable view of the available data.

5.1 Training Machine Learning Algorithms: General Considerations and Preliminaries

Models that are capable of **deep unsupervised learning** can identify abstract relations in data which have not been labeled or explained to them beforehand, for example, the existence of concepts like "grammar" or "language" in a text (Young and Hazarika 2018), the identification of characteristic items in images (Liu et al. 2017), or the behavioral patterns of people (Rabinowitz et al. 2018). Such **descriptive models** help data scientists to analyze more data, understand and utilize what computers can see, and evaluate the importance and possible causal relations between variables. The data scientist must define a suitable model complexity that reflects the information content of the training data. By parameterizing the model, one defines the level of abstraction, how data-hungry the model will be, and what can eventually be learned from the data. The model should be just complex enough that overfitting is possible, which is no trivial task. In many cases, the availability of training data limits the operable depth or intelligence that a model can achieve. Another manual task is the definition of the processes by which information from several data sources, scales, or domains is combined.

Typical economic applications of **supervised machine learning** involve the categorization of people. Their goal is the recognition of patterns and distinguishable clusters, based on which the prediction of behavioral patterns and risk events become possible. Such **predictive models** depend on "supervised learning" that requires the knowledge and/or systematic definition of the actual values of the target variable in the training data. It is important to note that any automatic categorization reflects the prejudice suggested by the training data, which, in turn, should represent the events of interest adequately. The initial supervised training and the following regular calibration of an economic model to the latest trends, habits, or seasonal fluctuations depend on the continuous availability of informative data. Some trends might even compete with the development of reliable predictive models, especially in the context of fraud prediction. This is the main reason for secrecy and the fact that data has become so valuable in the information age. Based on the recognition of patterns in historic data, one should always expect that predictions get worse as the learned patterns come of age: most models expire as culture and environmental conditions evolve dynamically in the real system. Naturally, a model that is trained with observations, which can only mirror a limited perspective for a limited time window, cannot be expected to reproduce the full evolutionary complexity of the underlying real system. Nevertheless, outdated datasets are useful at the early stages of the model development, i.e., to test models and to rank their performances.

Preprocessing is an essential part of model development, as it reduces possible "distractions" from the training by noisy, irrelevant, or outdated pieces of the raw data. It enables the data scientist and the computer to make optimal use of limited information. It should be mentioned that the techniques used for preprocessing, such as principal component analysis or auto-encoding, are diverse and important, but reviewing them would go far beyond the scope of this article. Briefly speaking, the successful development and application of any deep learning method depends on:

- the availability of current, complex, reliable, high-quality training data with enough observations of the interesting events or classes that are to be predicted (stochastic convergence),
- a judicious choice of methods to preprocess and sample relevant data (e.g., to impute data gaps, balance the populations of the target categories, or homogenize information densities),
- the judicious choice of a suitable model family and limitation of complexity,
- the performance metrics that are used for model evaluation and the avoidance of overfitting,
- and compliance with data safety regulations and ethical rules.

Once a model has been trained and its transferability to unseen data has been validated, new data samples can be classified rapidly. Autonomous driving is one example that illustrates how trained algorithms can interpret images in real time, as required to steer the vehicle.

5.2 Drafting an Example Model: Resignation Risk

Instead of designing calculation sequences as illustrated in Fig. 5 manually from scratch, **modern open-sourcesoftware packages** for pattern recognition provide tools to automatically generate model ensembles, optimize hyperparameters in predefined ranges and offer a variety of metrics to determine the model with the largest predictive power. The Python packages "sklearn" and "tensorflow", and the R packages "mlr" and "h2o", for example, are open-source machine learning frameworks that contain model builders for distributed random forests, neural networks, and gradient boosting machines. Such software packages accelerate the development and implementation of a robust model considerably.

In the previous sections, we defined what kind of data could potentially be used to estimate resignation risk. The prediction of whether an employee will resign within a fixed period can be treated as a binary classification problem (either the resignation is highly probable, or not), which can be approached with machine learning algorithms. Companies that are strongly involved in the development of machine learning and that collect a lot of data from clients and employees support their HR management with such AI algorithms. IBM made headlines in April 2019 claiming that its AI system *WATSON* identified employees who want to quit with 98% accuracy (cnbc 2019). Below, we demonstrate an application of supervised machine learning based on the mentioned software packages h2o[3] and a public dataset that was synthetically produced and published by IBM for the purpose of testing simple models (Swaminathan and Hagarty 2019). This dataset has also been used for methodical scientific publications and in various demonstrations (kaggle 2019).

The data contains 1470 records (observations) that describe employees. Each of these individual records consists of 33 features and the binary target label "Attrition", which indicates whether an employee has eventually quit or not. The column names and the first five observations are listed in Table 1. We found that excluding any of the features did not improve the model performance significantly, likely due to the polished and academic, synthetic nature of the dataset and the absence of typical data quality issues like missing (or interpolated) values. Therefore, we could skip the typical effort for preprocessing and merely use this data as a basis of a proof of concept.

To evaluate the performance of a model without bias, one must **split the data** into a set that is used for the training and a set that is to be used to test the model. We split the data into 50% training data and 50% test data, the latter of which remained "unseen" during the training and optimization of the hyperparameters. For the optimization itself, another nested split of the training data was used to enable 10-fold **cross-validation** of the compared parameterizations. As a performance metric, we used the area under the receiver operating characteristic curve (AUC-ROC) (Hanley and McNeil 1982), which is the default for binary classification problems. It quantifies the correct distinction of the two target classes of a binary classification with a scalar value that ranges from 0.5 for arbitrary labeling to 1.0 for perfect classification. A comprehensive review of **performance metrics** for classification and regression problems has been published by Alice Zheng (2015).

Another simple performance metric is the accuracy, the ratio of correctly classified samples over the total number. It is important to note that absolute accuracy values do not allow direct, immediate conclusions about how useful the model is. The reason for this is that their meaningful range depends on the possible **class imbalance** that is typical for the prediction of undesirable rare events. The meaningful AUC values, on the other hand, always range from 0.5 to 1.0, and class imbalance merely affects the error of these values. To give an example: in the dataset that is used here, only 237 observations are labeled as "Attrition" = yes. Therefore, even the undistinctive generalization that "all observations are non-attrition" would yield a mean

---

[3] h2o cluster version: 3.32.0.1; R version 3.6.3 (2020-02-29).

Table 1 Overview of the 28 employee features of the example dataset that can be utilized as possible predictors for the binary classification of the attrition tendency (© ifb SE)

quasi-continuous numeric features	ordinal categorical features	nominal categorical features
Age	Education	Department
DailyRate	EnvironmentSatisfaction	EducationField
DistanceFromHome	JobInvolvement	Gender
HourlyRate	JobLevel	JobRole
MonthlyIncome	JobSatisfaction	MaritalStatus
PercentSalaryHike	RelationshipSatisfaction	Overtime
TotalWorkingYears	StockOptionLevel	
TrainingTimesLastYear	WorkLifeBalance	
YearsAtCompany	BusinessTravel	
NumCompaniesWorked		
YearsInCurrentRole		
YearsSinceLastPromotion		
YearsWithCurrManager		

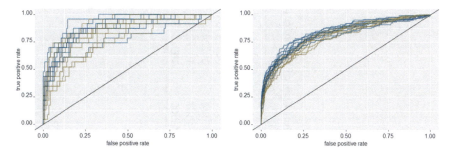

Fig. 6 ROC curves for 10 trials with independent splits of the data into training set and test set. The curves correspond to a 90:10 split ratio on the left and to a 50:50 split ratio on the right. The blue curves were obtained for a generalized linear model and the golden curves for a gradient boosting tree (© ifb SE)

accuracy of $237/1470 = 83.9\%$. In many use cases, the class imbalance is even higher, and one must choose a performance metric that is sensitive toward the interesting minority class.

Figure 6 shows the ROCs that correspond to 10 independent data splits and trainings, illustrating the uncertainty of the model performance, and how it depends on the split ratio. The shape of an ROC gives some detailed insight into the quality of the predictions of both classes, while the average AUC quantifies the performance in a single value. The AUC is slightly larger for the blue curves that were obtained for the generalized linear model. One can clearly see that a split ratio for which the test set gets very small leads to a higher uncertainty of the AUC performance measure.

5.3 Strategies to Find the Best Model and Enable Systematic Improvements

The h2o package also provides an **automated comparison** of models of different families, including generalized linear models, gradient boosting machines, distributed random forests, and some default neural networks (details can be found in the h2o docs under "AutoML"). This facilitates the search for an adequate model that is just complex enough. Table 2 shows the results of this automated model comparison. In our case, a generalized linear model was ranked highest according to its AUC. The generalized linear model (GLM) is a generalization of logistic regression and can be thought of as an elastic net that separates the feature space into regions that can be attributed to the different target classes. It uses continuous representations of all predictor variables to perform a regression. Within the error of the

Table 2 Summary of different model families (and their ensembles) that were compared with the AutoML function of the h2o R package. The AUC measure is highlighted as the performance metric that was used to rank the models (© ifb SE)

Model	AUC	Logloss	aucpr	mean_per_class_error	rmse	mse
StackedEnsemble_AllModels	0.8429545	0.3056523	0.6375340	0.2548533	0.2979359	0.08876582
StackedEnsemble_BestOfFamily	0.8428261	0.3065255	0.6345194	0.2409734	0.2991510	0.08949133
GeneralizedLinearModel	0.8395427	0.3193002	0.6310390	0.2352038	0.3037124	0.09224120
GradientBoostingMachine	0.8074762	0.3462017	0.5579690	0.2709918	0.3181567	0.10122367
DistributedRandomForest	0.8060646	0.3949995	0.5314601	0.2750470	0.3244000	0.10523539

AUC performance metric, the GLM performed just as well as the computationally more demanding ensemble methods. This illustrates that, depending on the use case, more complex or deeper machine learning methods may be outperformed by simpler ones. As an analogy, one can think of insects that perform certain tasks better and more efficiently than humans: they do not have a brain, but they also do not have to learn as much. The "intelligence" of models makes them more versatile, which, however, should not be misinterpreted as universal applicability. The comparison was carried out based on a single cross-validation of the entire dataset, because we were only interested in the ranking at this point. For the evaluation of the actual performance of a chosen model, however, the optimization of hyperparameters should be carried out in a nested cross-validation mentioned in the previous section. The trend stays the same, but the maximum AUC drops to about 0.81 as soon as 50% of the data is reserved for an outer validation.

Another important step in the evaluation of alternative models is the analysis of the so-called "**feature importance**" values. As the name suggests, they quantify how much influence a variable has on the prediction of a model, and they can be used to guide data collection efforts in a productive direction. Because generalized linear models use regression, it is possible in principle to interpret the absolute values of the coefficients of this regression as the importance of individual variables. A more generally applicable measure that enables direct comparisons between different model families is the so-called "permutation feature importance". This quantifies how much the error of the predictions increases if a feature is shuffled (and its information thereby ignored). If such important values turn out to be consistently high for different model families, this is a strong indication that the feature is not only important for the individual model predictions, but also "truly important" in the real system. Figure 7 shows which features have the highest influence on our classification example. One can see that the feature "Overtime" is decisive, and that the "JobSatisfaction", "DistanceFromHome", and "JobRole" have also proven to be useful predictors in both models. However, with the real data that companies collect from their employees and customers, the interpretation of the results could go deeper, and one might find that satisfaction or a short journey to work is actually more important than expected coming from a preliminary model that has been trained with limited data. A more detailed description of this analysis has been published by Brad Boehmke (Boehmke 2018).

Figure 8 shows the relation between the binary predictor "Overtime" and the predicted classes of the binary target "Attrition": among the employees who quit their job (right side), there are 19% more who do Overtime,

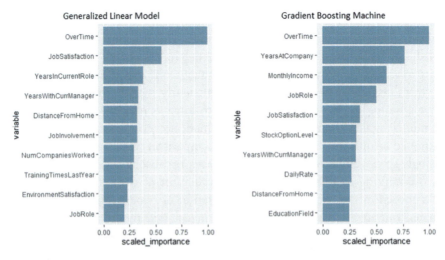

Fig. 7 Relative importance of the 10 most important variables for the predictions of the GLM (left) and the GBM (right) (© ifb SE)

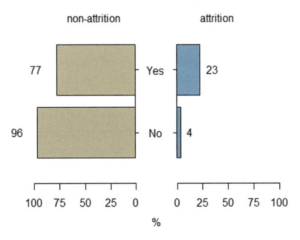

Fig. 8 Attrition by Overtime (yes/no) for the GLM predictions in percent (© ifb SE)

meaning that there is still a considerable overlap of the Overtime values of both target classes, even though it is the most decisive predictor. Obviously, high relative feature importance does not allow direct conclusions as to which features can be ignored. Nevertheless, it facilitates the systematic reduction of noise in the training data.

The synthetic dataset on which these sample calculations are based only represents the situation at the time of its creation. Also, it is not very large. If a similar algorithm is used in HR management, it improves as more historic data becomes available. Therefore, the benefits of machine learning for the management of resignation risk can be exploited by medium and large companies especially with access to large datasets. Small companies typically lack the amount of current data needed to train such a model. Also, generalizing statistical measures against attrition are less likely to work if not applied to a large workforce for which one can assume a temporally stable average behavior.

6 Summary

The management of non-financial risk is increasingly important. As part of this, the management of HR risk will become even more important than it already is. Due to its quantifiability and comparatively easy implementation, the risk of resignation must be considered the most elementary component of HR risk.

We were able to show that the risk of resignation can be assessed without having to establish many new processes for data collection. Above all, the existing data must be appropriately combined so that it can be interpreted accordingly. Non-established data collections, such as a daily satisfaction inquiry, can be implemented without much effort. For the interpretation of the data, it is advisable to program an algorithm that corresponds to the best practice approach. If the data quality is high enough, the use of machine learning is best suited to improve the analysis. Which ML models are used depends strongly on the data basis and the research question? In this article, we have shown that even with a small database a reliable differentiation into the groups "quits"/"does not quit" can be realized with simple methods. A more differentiated assessment than that presented in this article is possible, however, not on the given data basis.

As we become more aware of the situation, the parts of the impact graphs that we have only touched upon here can also be included in the reporting: quantifying the effects of resignations. With such knowledge, it is possible to simulate and estimate the costs or damages to reputation that could result from certain resignations.

If the management of resignation risk is established, further sub-risk categories of the HR risk can be quantified with identical procedures. The procedure presented here (impact graphs—hierarchy of indicators—use of ML) can be applied to most non-financial risks.

Literature

Boehmke, Brad. 2018. *IML: Machine Learning Model Interpretability and Feature Explanation with IML and H2O.* August 13. Accessed September 20, 2020. https://www.business-science.io/business/2018/08/13/iml-model-interpretability.html.

Brownlee, Jason. 2020. *machinelearningmastery.com.* Accessed September 20, 2020. https://machinelearningmastery.com.

2019. cnbc. Accessed September 23, 2020. https://www.cnbc.com/2019/04/03/ibm-ai-can-predict-with-95-percent-accuracy-which-employees-will-quit.html.

Hanley, James A., and Barbara J. McNeil. 1982. "The Meaning and Use of the Area under a Receiver Operating Characteristic (ROC) Curve." *Radiology* 143: 29–36 (April).

2019. *kaggle.* Accessed September 24, 2020. https://www.kaggle.com/pavansubhasht/ibm-hr-analytics-attrition-dataset.

Liermann, Volker, Nikolas Viets, and Davin Radermacher. 2021. "Breaking New Grounds in Non-financial Risk Management." In *The Digital Journey of Banking and Insurance, Volume I—Disruption and DNA*, edited by Volker Liermann and Claus Stegmann. New York: Palgrave Macmillan.

Liermann, Volker, Sangmeng Li, and Victoria Dobryashkina. 2019. "Mathematical Background of Machine Learning." In *The Impact of Digital Transformation and Fintech on the Finance Professional*, edited by Volker Liermann and Claus Stegmann. New York: Palgrave Macmillan.

Liu, Qing, Ningyu Zhang, Wenzhu Yang, Sile Wang, Zhenchao Cui, Xiangyang Chen, and Liping Chen. 2017. "A Review of Image Recognition with Deep Convolutional Neural Network." In *Intelligent Computing Theories and Application*, edited by V. Bevilacqua, P. Premaratne, P. Gupta, and D. S. Huang, 69–80. Cham: Springer.

2020. *peakon.* Accessed September 22, 2020. https://peakon.com/heartbeat/reports/the-9-month-warning-identifying-quitters-before-its-too-late/.

Rabinowitz, Neil, Frank Perbet, Francis Song, Chiyuan Zhang, S. M. Ali Eslami, and Matt Botvinick. 2018. "Machine Theory of Mind." *deepmind.com.* Accessed September 21, 2020. https://deepmind.com/research/publications/machine-theory-mind.

Swaminathan, Saishruthi, and Richard Hagarty. 2019. *developer.ibm.com.* January 29. Accessed September 20, 2020. https://developer.ibm.com/patterns/data-science-life-cycle-in-action-to-solve-employee-attrition-problem/.

Young, T., and D. Hazarika. 2018. "Recent Trends in Deep Learning Based Natural Language Processing." *Computational Intelligence Magazine* 13 (3): 55–75.

Zheng, Alice. 2015. *Evaluating Machine Learning Models.* 1005 Gravenstein Highway North, Sebastopol, CA: O'Reilly Media, Inc.

Sentiment Analysis for Reputational Risk Management

Daniel Schröder and Marian Tieben

1 Introduction

1.1 Reputational Risk

Only those who measure reputation can manage it! But reputation is much more difficult to put into numbers than revenues or working hours. Reputation is determined by a lot of influencing factors: economic performance, corporate governance, sustainability, product quality, as well as trends and other factors. It is not the actual, factual performance in these areas that is directly decisive for the company's reputation, but how it is perceived by stakeholders.

While financial institutions have well-developed credit, market and liquidity risk management frameworks in place, there is growing acknowledgment of the need to manage non-financial risk as well. In this article we present a framework to manage reputational risk as one of the risk categories in non-financial risk assessment. The first step in handling the institution's reputation is to find a way to measure it. Possible solutions to achieve this

---

D. Schröder (✉) · M. Tieben
ifb SE, Grünwald, Germany
e-mail: Daniel.Schroeder@ifb-group.com

M. Tieben
e-mail: Marian.Tieben@ifb-group.com

might be found in a population-representative market research survey as well as in a survey which covers the relevant stakeholders. An alternative or supplementary approach, which uses modern techniques of data science, is to perform a sentiment analysis on a mass of already existing text data, provided the organization is present in media coverage.

1.2 Sentiment Analysis

Sentiment analysis—also called opinion mining—is a field of study that aims to extract opinions and sentiments from natural language text using computational methods. (Liu 2015)

Sentiment analysis refers to certain techniques for automatic evaluation of human-written texts in order to identify expressed attitude or sentiment. As almost 99% of all research on sentiment analysis has been published since 2004 (Mäntylä et al. 2018), it is considered a relatively young and dynamic field of research. Nowadays, sentiment analysis is widely used to examine textual content from the Internet, e.g. social media, blogs, news articles, forums, reviews or comments. Since human-written documents usually convey a perception, attitude or simply a sentiment, we recognize these contents as a suitable basis for measuring an organization's reputation. By applying sentiment analysis techniques, we can investigate the polarity (positivity or negativity) of text documents written about the organization concerned.

1.3 General Approach

In this article, we want to present a straightforward and easy-to-implement approach which could serve as a first step in measuring an organization's reputation, and hence could be used to manage reputational risk.

To achieve this, we split the process into two main parts: Facing the mass of available data in media coverage, first we need to be able to identify to what extend a previously unseen text mentions the organization. We describe a method based on word embeddings and topic modeling in Sect. 2. Secondly, we demonstrate how to apply sentiment analysis to the text data labeled as relevant using a dictionary approach in Sect. 3. Based on our approach, building a working reputational risk management framework is feasible, which additionally can be utilized to produce labeled data for further state-of-the-art machine learning techniques (Fig. 1).

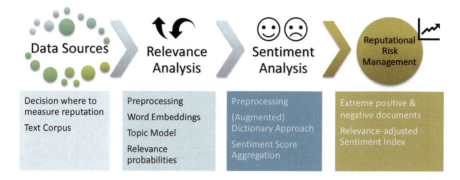

Fig. 1 Approach overview (© ifb SE)

By applying our discussed approach to a large corpus[1] of text documents, we end up with two different numeric labels per document: the first label is a relevance probability representing the likelihood that each and every sentence in the document is solely written about the organization concerned. The second label is an aggregated sentiment score, which reflects the total polarity of the document. In this context, a document denotes a container of textual data, which can be defined in different ways: it may represent a whole newspaper article, a paragraph or even a single sentence. We decided to treat each article as a document for the analysis.

1.4 Management of Reputational Risk

The evaluation of relevance and sentiment by the process described saves a lot of time compared to a situation where humans have to constantly read, label and filter for relevance all the available documents. This also guarantees that we comprehensively capture the organization's media coverage due to the large number of articles we can analyze.

To manage reputational risk, we can consider different aspects. Extremely negative or positive articles should be subjected to further detailed examination by responsible employees, because it is important to consider the content and the underlying arguments.

In addition, we can calculate a relevance-adjusted sentiment index over time. More precisely, this means calculating an expected average sentiment score for each time period. For this purpose, we calculate the probability of each possible relevance scenario and the corresponding mean sentiment value.

---

[1] In natural language processing a collection of text documents is often denoted as *(text) corpus*.

Table 1 Example calculation of expected mean sentiment for three documents (© ifb SE)

	Doc 1	Doc 2	Doc 3				
Relevance Probability	0.2791	0.4744	0.3328				
Sentiment Score	-0.2691	0.6177	0.2294				
Scenario that …	Probability Calculation				Mean Sentiment Calculation		
					No. Documents	Sum Sentiment	Mean Sentiment
… no Document is relevant	0	0	0	0.2528	0	0.0000	0.0000
… only Doc 1 is relevant	1	0	0	0.0979	1	-0.2691	-0.2691
… only Doc 2 is relevant	0	1	0	0.2282	1	0.6177	0.6177
… only Doc 3 is relevant	0	0	1	0.1261	1	0.2294	0.2294
… only Doc 1 & Doc 2 are relevant	1	1	0	0.0883	2	0.3486	0.1743
… only Doc 2 & Doc 3 are relevant	0	1	1	0.1138	2	0.8471	0.4236
… only Doc 1 & Doc 3 are relevant	1	0	1	0.0488	2	-0.0397	-0.0199
… all Documents are relevant	1	1	1	0.0441	3	0.5780	0.1927
Expected Mean Sentiment							0.2147

Finally, the resulting mean sentiment values are weighted with their respective probability of occurrence.

Table 1 illustrates the procedure using a fictitious example with three documents. However, this computation is quite expensive in real applications, since the number of scenarios grows exponentially with the document count.[2] But a sufficiently good approximation can be achieved using Monte Carlo simulation. This method allows us to compute the relevance-adjusted sentiment score by randomly sampling N scenarios to calculate the mean sentiment values for. The average of these calculated values then provides the approximation for the expected mean sentiment score.

Figure 2 illustrates how a relevance-adjusted sentiment index can look and how it could reveal the dynamics of sentiment in media coverage over time. The size of the time buckets depends on the scope of media coverage of the organization. This can be further differentiated by the source of interest (newspaper, social media, specialist literature). Additionally, we are able to visualize the average sentiment of relevant benchmarks like the banking industry as a whole, specific bank groups or single competitors and compare it with our sentiment (depicted as benchmark).

These insights provide a suitable foundation to determine the reputation drivers. We can identify time periods of increasing or decreasing sentiment scores as well as differences compared to the benchmark. This information can be used to figure out what happened in these time periods. Furthermore, we can determine the need for action when the reputational score is decreasing. In addition, we have the foundation to quantify the effects of actions taken, for example, campaigns. Lastly, forecasts of reputation based

---

[2] In general, if there are n documents to consider, the total count of possible scenarios adds up to 2^n.

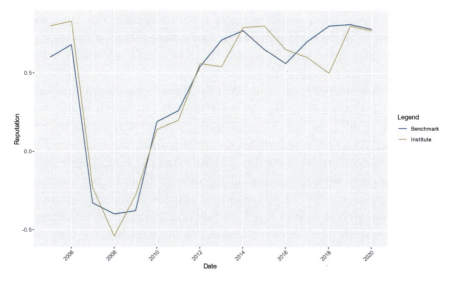

Fig. 2 Graphical representation of reputation over time (© ifb SE)

on prediction models could deliver the basis for necessary future measures to mitigate reputational risk in advance (Liermann et al. 2021).

2 Relevance Analysis

In this section, we demonstrate the use of text mining tools to explore a large corpus of unseen text documents. The universe of Python and R packages contains a variety of useful open-source toolkits such as spaCy (Honnibal and Montani 2017), an industrial strength natural language processing (NLP) framework, which comes with powerful pre-trained linguistic models to perform preliminary tasks, e.g. tokenization,[3] part-of-speech tagging,[4] named-entity recognition[5] or lemmatization.[6]

To illustrate the procedure, we downloaded the "all-the-news" dataset from Kaggle (Thompson 2017), which consists of 143,000 articles from 15 American publications. The following explanations will demonstrate how to reveal the most relevant articles together with a probabilistic measure of the relevance of each document regarding the mentioning of one organization, the

---

[3] *Tokenization* refers to the parsing of text documents into atomic units like words and punctuation.
[4] *Part-of-speech* or *POS tagging* is a method to detect a word's grammatical group.
[5] *Named-entity recognition* (NER) is a method to mark clearly identifiable elements (e.g. persons, organizations).
[6] *Lemmatization* aims to transform inflectional forms of words to their base or dictionary form.

European Central Bank in our example case. As it turns out later, we will have to identify all the various mentions and replace them with a single proxy search term. But unfortunately, we do not know exactly what different forms of mentioning are present in the data.

A first intuitive approach would be to perform a case-insensitive full text search within the whole corpus, using a short list of search terms. Natural search term candidates are the organization's name and its corresponding abbreviation. As we are searching for documents about the European Central Bank, this list consists of *European, Central, Bank* and *ECB*. To reduce the dataset's volume, we can remove all documents that do not contain any of these four terms. To be less exclusive on this initial classification, we apply fuzzy word comparison based on the Levenshtein distance (Levenshtein 1966). Thereby, the term *bank* will also match the term *banking*, for example.

In a second step, we ought to train a word embedding model[7] on the remaining text data subset. This will allow us to use cosine similarity to query the corpus' vocabulary for the most similar words with respect to the search terms and thereby to reveal the hidden forms of the organization's mentioning. These can be replaced by a single proxy search term afterward. Lastly, we will apply a widely used topic model to calculate the probabilistic measure of relevance. As upfront preparation, we discuss the basic concepts of preprocessing and how to query word embedding models.

2.1 Preprocessing

Preprocessing is usually considered the first step in any text mining task. Vijayarani et al. (2015) provide a discussion on various frequently used preprocessing techniques. Nevertheless, there is no universal preprocessing recipe. Instead, the procedure is highly dependent on the objective and the particular text mining tool in use. As the objective is to find all the different forms of similar mentions, we ought to transform all the words to lowercase and apply lemmatization as well. We also consider stop word[8] removal, so the skip-gram window can capture a wider range of non-frequent words. In addition, we apply a concept called phrasing, to put groups of related words into phrases.

---

[7] *Word embedding* is a technique to map words to vectors of real numbers. We refer to a model which represents words in a multidimensional semantic vector space where similar words are located close to each other (see Liermann et al. 2019).

[8] *Stop words* are very common words, such as articles, prepositions or pronouns, which usually do not contribute to the semantic message but rather worsen the model accuracy.

Phrasing is an important preprocessing technique for our classification task. The best way to explain the basic concept is to examine an example text:

The European Central Bank (ECB) announced on Friday that it will start conducting experiments to decide whether to launch a digital euro. In a report setting out the pros and cons of launching a digital euro, the ECB said that it 'could support the Eurosystems objectives by providing citizens with a safe form of money in the fast-changing digital world.' Unlike private digital currencies like Bitcoin or Facebook's Libra, the digital euro would be a central bank liability and would complement the current offering of cash and wholesale central bank deposits.

The single words *European, central* and *bank* can all appear in very different contexts all over the documents in the entire corpus. But tied together, these words form a phrase that names a specific organization, the European Central Bank. For further illustration, we analyzed the example text using spaCy's pre-trained natural language processing model. The string was decomposed into tokens and fed to a pipeline mechanism, which contains part-of-speech tagging, lemmatization and named-entity recognition. Table 2 shows a cutout of the applied lemmas and part-of-speech tags at token level. Table 3 displays the output of the applied NER module, which is beyond token level.

The example illustrates that spaCy's NER module was able to correctly recognize that the sequence "European Central Bank" stands for an organization and the same result applies to the abbreviation ECB. This new understanding of tagging motivates a sense-disambiguated word embedding model suggested by Trask et al. (2015). The so-called Sense2Vec model comes with a powerful phraser that identifies n-grams[9] based on provided tags, especially POS tags and NER tags, and concatenates these word sequences into one phrasal token. In addition, to disambiguate the sense, the corresponding tag is appended to the phrasal token as well. As a benefit for us, this procedure will transform the tri-gram *European Central Bank* into a unigram, namely *European_Central_Bank|ORG*.

2.1.1 Training the Word Embedding Model

The Sense2Vec model does not directly enhance the way a neural network is trained to learn word embeddings. Rather, it targets the preprocessing step where the model input is prepared in the previously described manner. Based

---

[9] In the fields of computational linguistics and probability, an n-gram is a contiguous sequence of n items from a given sample of text or speech.

Table 2 Token level results of spaCy's NLP pipeline showing lemmatization and POS tagging (© ifb SE)

Index	Token	Lemma	POS tag	POS tag explanation	Alpha	Stop	Punct
0	The	the	DET	determiner	True	True	False
1	European	European	PROPN	proper noun	True	False	False
2	Central	Central	PROPN	proper noun	True	False	False
3	Bank	Bank	PROPN	proper noun	True	False	False
4	(	(	PUNCT	punctuation	False	False	True
5	ECB	ECB	PROPN	proper noun	True	False	False
6	)	)	PUNCT	punctuation	False	False	True
7	Announced	announce	VERB	verb	True	False	False
8	On	on	ADP	adposition	True	True	False
9	Friday	Friday	PROPN	proper noun	True	False	False
10	That	that	SCONJ	subordinating conjunction	True	True	False
11	It	-PRON-	PRON	pronoun	True	True	False
12	Will	will	VERB	verb	True	True	False
13	Start	start	VERB	verb	True	False	False
14	Conducting	conduct	VERB	verb	True	False	False
15	Experiments	experiment	NOUN	noun	True	False	False
16	To	to	PART	particle	True	True	False
17	Decide	decide	VERB	verb	True	False	False
18	Whether	whether	SCONJ	subordinating conjunction	True	True	False
19	To	to	PART	particle	True	True	False
20	Launch	launch	VERB	verb	True	False	False
21	A	a	DET	determiner	True	True	False
22	Digital	digital	ADJ	adjective	True	False	False
23	Euro	euro	NOUN	noun	True	False	False
24			PUNCT	punctuation	False	False	True

on this preprocessed data, any established word embedding algorithm, like GloVe (Pennington et al. 2014) or FastText (Bojanowski et al. 2016), can be used to calculate the actual word vectors. The latter was used to calculate word vectors for the following analysis, but a comparison of these two algorithms, with respect to the relevance measuring task, is still subject to future discussion.

2.1.2 Querying the Vocabulary

In applications, cosine similarity is widely used as a metric to determine similarity between word vectors (Singhal 2001). The metric only considers orientation of vectors while their magnitude is completely irrelevant. Based

Table 3 Span level results of spaCy's NLP pipeline showing results of named-entity recognition (© ifb SE)

Index	Phrase	Start	End	NER tag	NER tag explanation
0	The European Central Bank	0	25	ORG	Companies, agencies, institutions, etc
1	ECB	27	30	ORG	Companies, agencies, institutions, etc
2	Friday	45	51	DATE	Absolute or relative dates or periods
3	ECB	213	216	ORG	Companies, agencies, institutions, etc
4	Eurosystems	249	260	ORG	Companies, agencies, institutions, etc
5	Bitcoin	396	403	ORG	Companies, agencies, institutions, etc
6	Facebook	407	415	ORG	Companies, agencies, institutions, etc

on the cosine of the angle between two vectors, this method applies a similarity score of 1 to parallel vectors, a score of 0 to perpendicular vectors and a score of −1 to diametrically opposed vectors.

We can apply cosine similarity to query the most similar words in terms of context, within the vocabulary compared to the now phrased search terms *european_central_bank|ORG* and *ecb|ORG*. We can also apply Levenshtein similarity to find the most similar words in terms of spelling. Tables 4, 5, 6, and 7 display the results of these queries on the newspaper dataset.

Discussing Tables 4, 5, 6, and 7, we first recognize an unsurprising result: the two phrased search terms are highly related to each other,

Table 4 Ten most similar word vectors by **cosine similarity** with respect to search phrase "**european_central_bank|ORG**" (© ifb SE)

Idx	Sence2Vec phrase	Similarity
0	'ecb|ORG'	0.9043
1	'bundesbank|ORG'	0.8930
2	'mario_draghi|PERSON'	0.8823
3	'a_week|DATE'	0.8820
4	'european_central_bank's|ORG'	0.8813
5	'march_10|DATE'	0.8810
6	'shave|VERB'	0.8687
7	'hint|VERB'	0.8667
8	'60_billion_euros|MONEY'	0.8657
9	'embark|VERB'	0.8643

Table 5 Ten most similar word vectors by **cosine similarity** with respect to search phrase "**ecb|ORG**" (© ifb SE)

Idx	Sence2Vec phrase	Similarity
0	'bundesbank|ORG'	0.9180
1	'european_central_bank's|ORG'	0.9175
2	'march_10|DATE'	0.9067
3	'european_central_bank|ORG'	0.9043
4	'taper|VERB'	0.8970
5	'setter|NOUN'	0.8890
6	'quantitative|ADJ'	0.8887
7	'easing|NOUN'	0.8880
8	'80_billion_euros|MONEY'	0.8804
9	'embark|VERB'	0.8800

Table 6 Ten most similar word vectors by **Levenshtein similarity** with respect to search phrase "**european_central_bank**" (© ifb SE)

Idx	Sence2Vec phrase	Similarity
0	'european_central_bank|ORG'	0.9500
1	'european_central_bank's|ORG'	0.9500
2	'european_central_bank's_governing_council|ORG'	0.9000
3	'european_central_bank_governing_council|ORG'	0.9000
4	'european_investment_bank|ORG'	0.6900
5	'euro|GPE'	0.6800
6	'central|ADJ'	0.6600
7	'u._s._central_bank|ORG'	0.6500
8	'central_bank|ORG'	0.6500
9	'u._k._central_bank|ORG'	0.6500

Table 7 Ten most similar word vectors by **Levenshtein similarity** with respect to search phrase "**ecb**" (© ifb SE)

Idx	Sence2Vec phrase	Similarity
0	'ecb|ORG'	0.9000
1	'the_ecb|WORK_OF_ART'	0.9000
2	'ecb_vio|ORG'	0.9000
3	'ecb_qe|ORG'	0.9000
4	'ecb|PROPN'	0.9000
5	'ecbwatch|ORG'	0.9000
6	'symantec|ORG'	0.6800
7	'sec|ORG'	0.6800
8	'say|VERB'	0.6000
9	'economy|NOUN'	0.6000

showing a cosine similarity score of 0.9043. Moreover, the queries identified further, similar terms, like *european_central_bank's|ORG* or *european_central_bank_governing_council|ORG*. The reason why the latter term is not shown in Table 4 is because it only appears once in the entire corpus.

To take these findings into consideration, manual adjustments are necessary. As it is advantageous to only identify the relevant documents by one proxy search term, we can use the results of this analysis to implement special mapping rules during the preprocessing step. Table 8 shows an overview of the mapping rules which can be derived from the former analysis.

Another interesting result is found in Tables 4 and 5: unsurprisingly, large amounts of money, such as '*60_billion_euros|MONEY*' or '*80_billion_euros|MONEY*' often appear in the context of ECB-related documents. As we do not intend to disambiguate the actual amounts, we can additionally implement a simple regular-expressions-based rule to map these amounts to a proxy term as well (see Table 9).

With these new mapping rules in place, we can run the preprocessing again and calculate a new set of word vectors. Then, we query again for the search terms and repeat the analysis to check whether it brings up new noteworthy findings or not.

Table 8 Special mapping rules to be applied in preprocessing (© ifb SE)

Index	Input	Output
0	'ecb|ORG'	'ecb|ORG'
1	'european_central_bank|ORG'	'ecb|ORG'
2	'european_central_bank's|ORG'	'ecb|ORG'
3	'european_central_bank's_governing_council|ORG'	'ecb|ORG'; 'governing_council|ORG'
4	'european_central_bank_governing_council|ORG'	'ecb|ORG'; 'governing_council|ORG'
5	'the_ecb|WORK_OF_ART'	'ecb|ORG'
6	'ecb_qe|ORG'	'ecb|ORG'; 'quantitative|ADJ'; 'easing|NOUN'
7	'ecb|PROPN'	'ecb|ORG'
8	'ecbwatch|ORG'	'ecb|ORG'; 'watch|NOUN'

Table 9 Special mapping rules for large amounts of money (© ifb SE)

Index	Input	Output
0	'60_billion_euros|MONEY'	'billions_of_euros|MONEY'
1	'80_billion_euros|MONEY'	'billions_of_euros|MONEY'

2.1.3 Interim Summary

Based on the former analysis, we can describe a binary classification process: instead of performing a fuzzy full-text search, we can now use the proxy search term *ecb|ORG* to search for relevant documents within the preprocessed text data. Each document that contains the proxy search term can be classified as relevant, while the remainder can be classified as irrelevant.

However, this binary classification does not provide any information on *how* relevant a document is with respect to the organization of interest. Therefore, we could calculate a term frequency of *ecb|ORG* for each document. This is the total count of the proxy search term in the document (Manning et al. 2008). In any case, the following section will introduce a more sophisticated and unsupervised topic modeling technique, which uses the idea of term frequencies to result in a probabilistic relevance measure.

2.2 Topic Modeling

In the field of natural language processing, topic modeling comprises all types of statistical models for discovering the hidden thematic structure within a collection of text documents. A topic model is a text mining technique that is able to connect words with very similar meanings, make distinctions between uses of words with several meanings and reveal groups of words that frequently occur together (co-occurrence). The central idea behind topic modeling is the intuition that words like "loans," "finance" and "payment" will appear more frequently in texts about banking than in texts about tennis.

Sharma (2017) provides a discussion about recent evolutions in topic modeling. They also outline how latent Dirichlet allocation (LDA) has been dominating the field since its introduction into machine learning in 2003. The model is widely used in applications and suitable for our task of measuring the relevance of documents.

2.2.1 Latent Dirichlet Allocation

Latent Dirichlet allocation is a generative statistical model proposed by Pritchard et al. (2000) in the context of population genetics and was applied to machine learning by (Blei et al. 2003). At this point, we would like to refer to the original papers for a formal definition and further discussion of inference techniques. Instead of listing all the details of this quite complex mathematical model, we decided to explain the model by illustrating a simple but specific example.

Figure 3 provides a general overview of the LDA model: the uppermost box represents the input of $M = 6$ documents. In this case, each document m consists of $N_m = 4$ words. In real applications, of course, the number of words within a document will vary. Here, the entire corpus' vocabulary consists of $N = 16$ words. The red box is called document-term matrix, this is a $(M \times N)$-matrix which captures the total count of each word within each document. The total number of topics is a model hyperparameter[10] and thus can be chosen freely. For illustration purposes we have chosen the minimum of $K = 2$ topics.

Topics are illustrated by the box below the document-term matrix. The topics themselves are model parameters[11] and considered a probabilistic composition of all words in the vocabulary. This means each topic is represented by a categorical distribution over all words. We say topic-word distribution (vector) $\vec{\varphi}_k$ when referring to topic k.

More model parameters are illustrated on the right side of the document-term matrix: each document is considered a probabilistic composition of all topics. We say document-topic distribution (vector) $\vec{\theta}_m$ when referring to document m.

2.2.2 Relevance Probability

Now, we show how to combine the concepts of latent Dirichlet allocation and word embeddings. Furthermore, we make use of the probabilistic nature of LDA to derive a probabilistic measure of how relevant a document is. After we have applied the LDA model to our formerly preprocessed documents, we can calculate an expected topic vector representation for each topic k.

In vector representation, the vocabulary V can be written as $(E \times N)$-matrix, with E denoting the dimension of the word embeddings vector space[12] and N denoting the total count of words in the entire corpus' vocabulary. Therefore, each column in this matrix represents a word in the vocabulary. For each topic, the topic-word distribution vector $\vec{\varphi}_k$ is an N-dimensional vector of probabilities. Therefore, we can multiply each word

---

[10] **Model hyperparameters** can be thought of as settings for a machine learning algorithm that are tuned by the data scientist before training.
[11] **Model parameters** can be thought of as what the model learns during training, such as the weights for each word in a certain topic.
[12] The dimension of the resulting vector space is a hyperparameter in the word embedding model and commonly set to 300.

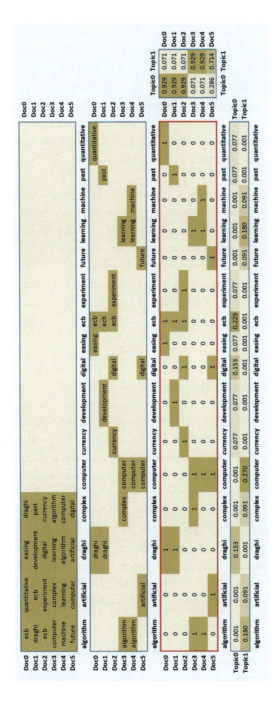

Fig. 3 Latent Dirichlet allocation example and overview (© ifb SE)

vector by its corresponding probability and then make the sum to calculate the expected topic-word vector representation $E(\vec{t}_k)$. This mathematical procedure can be written in the notation of matrix–vector multiplication as follows:

$$E(\vec{t}_k) = V \cdot \vec{\varphi}_k \tag{1}$$

Equation 1: Expected topic-word vector representation

This calculation must only be made once for each topic k and the resulting vectors are very unlikely to be present in the vocabulary V. Afterward, the resulting K expected topic vectors can be written together as $(E \times K)$-matrix denoted as $E(T)$, which we call the expected topic matrix. Note that, for each document, the document-topic distribution vector $\vec{\theta}_m$ is a K-dimensional vector of probabilities. Therefore, the expected document-word vector representation $E(\vec{d}_m)$ can be written in the notation of matrix–vector multiplication as follows:

$$E(\vec{d}_m) = E(T) \cdot \vec{\theta}_m \tag{2}$$

Equation 2: Expected document-word vector representation

Again, the resulting word vector is very unlikely to be present in the vocabulary V. But, calculation of cosine similarity between these document vectors $E(\vec{d}_m)$ regarding the proxy search term vector $\vec{s}$ is still possible. However, the application of cosine similarity results in relevance scores in the interval $[-1, 1]$ rather than probabilities as desired.

So far, we have not pointed out that the latent Dirichlet allocation, as a generative statistical model, is based on Bayesian inference for calculating the model parameters. This means the document-topic distribution vectors are actually random vectors. Therefore, the distribution of each random vector $\vec{\theta}_m$ is given by a Dirichlet distribution with an estimated hyperparameter vector $\vec{\alpha}_m$. This is stated in short notation as $\vec{\theta}_m \sim D(\vec{\alpha}_m)$.

Furthermore, we can calculate the most suitable vector $\vec{\alpha}_0$, which fits best regarding the expected topic matrix $E(T)$ and the proxy search term vector $\vec{s}$ under the metric of cosine distance:

$$\vec{\alpha}_0 := \underset{\vec{\alpha}}{\operatorname{argmin}}\left[\operatorname{cosine\ distance}(E(T) \cdot \vec{\alpha}, \vec{s})\right] \tag{3}$$

Equation 3: Most suitable vector

We define the random vector $\vec{\theta}_0$ to be Dirichlet distributed with hyperparameter vector $\vec{\alpha}_0$ and we say: the more similar the probability distributions of $\vec{\theta}_m$ and $\vec{\theta}_0$, the more likely document m is considered relevant regarding our search term vector $\vec{s}$. Finally, we can define a probabilistic measure of relevance as follows:

$$P\left(\vec{d}_m \text{ is relevant regarding } \vec{s}\right) := \operatorname*{argmax}_{0 \leq p \leq 1}\left[P\left(\left\|\vec{\theta}_m - \vec{\theta}_0\right\| \leq 1 - p\right) \geq p\right].$$

Equation 4: Probabilistic measure of relevance

(4)

2.3 Interim Summary and Outlook

Based on preprocessed data, where all the mentions of the organization of interest were replaced by a proxy search term, we illustrated how to combine latent Dirichlet allocation and word embeddings to compute a probabilistic measure of relevance for each document. Both models are trained on exactly the same set of preprocessed data, but independently of each other.

For further improvement, the recently proposed models LDA2Vec (Moody 2016) or Gaussian-LDA (Das et al. 2015) should be considered. While LDA2Vec trains both word embeddings and LDA simultaneously, at very high computational costs, Gaussian-LDA modifies the LDA model so that the underlying statistical model works on word vectors instead of document terms. This modification changes the model's prior distribution from Dirichlet to multivariate Gaussian distribution, which is why the naming was chosen accordingly.

3 Sentiment Analysis

From a top-level view, sentiment analysis can be split into dictionary approaches and machine learning approaches, whereby the latter can be seen as state of the art. However, there is a huge variety of models as well as fast progress in the development of neural networks, which reflects implementational complexity. Furthermore, well-suited data for model training is essential but usually not available, except for product and movie reviews. If we focus on measuring reputation by newspaper articles, the performance of pre-trained neural networks might be poor. Therefore, we illustrate an easy-to-implement dictionary approach which does not need training data.

We start by presenting the traditional bag-of-words approach, where several unigrams or bigrams get their respective sentiment score from the dictionary. Afterward, an augmented dictionary approach is presented, where preceding and following words can influence the polarized word. Therefore, we can partially consider word order in sentences.

3.1 Dictionary-Based Approach

One way to analyze the sentiment of our relevant documents is to consider the text as a combination of its individual words, and the sentiment of the whole text as the sum of the sentiment of the individual words. Our goal is to obtain one sentiment label per document.

To implement this approach, we need dictionaries with words and their sentiment scores which we can aggregate at document level. We use already existing dictionaries in our target language which are built and maintained by linguistical research teams. The assigned sentiment labels could be discrete like *positive*, *negative* or *neutral* or more granular categories from *very negative* to *very positive*. The discrete categories can be expressed by strings, as in the above example, or numbers. Another possibility is to determine the sentiment with a continuous numeric scale, e.g. in a range of $[-1, 1]$, where -1 describes the most negative words, $+1$ the most positive words and, accordingly, sentiment scores in between describe less positive or less negative words. Furthermore, dictionaries can be distinguished by whether they consist of domain-specific or rather general-purpose words.

Two popular examples for English general-purpose lexicons are the Bing (2004) and AFINN (Nielsen 2011) dictionary. The former categorizes words in a binary way into positive and negative categories and the latter assigns words integer scores between -5 and 5, with positive scores indicating a positive sentiment.

An example of a general-purpose dictionary for the German language is the SentimentWortschatz (Goldhahn et al. 2012), or SentiWS for short, which expresses the sentiment of words in a continuous interval of $[-1, 1]$ as described above. The current version of the SentiWS contains about 1650 positive and 1800 negative basic forms and their corresponding part-of-speech tag. Including the various inflectional forms, a total of about 16,000 positive and 18,000 negative word forms are covered. SentiWS contains not only adjectives and adverbs, but also nouns and verbs that are carriers of sentiment. An alternative general-purpose German dictionary is the German-PolarityClues lexicon (Waltinger 2010), which determines sentiments in a binary fashion, positive or negative. In comparison to the SentiWS, it offers an extra of 2064 positive and 4421 negative terms.

3.1.1 Preprocessing and Sentiment Score Calculation

To obtain a sentiment score for each document, we must join the words with their respective scores and aggregate them at document level. However, we must preprocess our data in advance. This procedure differs to the formerly illustrated preprocessing for relevance analysis and depends strongly on the dictionaries used.

Preprocessing

Stop words, for example, articles, prepositions or pronouns like *I, we, the* or *a*, will be removed. These words are usually non-semantic and provide less sentiment contribution but rather worsen the analysis accuracy. However, in sentiment analysis it is crucial not to remove stop words which are part of negations (e.g. *not, no, nobody*) and adversative conjunctions (e.g. *however, but, whereas*).

When analyzing social media data, we convert emojis and emoticons to words. Afterward, we apply stemming or lemmatization. The goal of both is to reduce inflectional forms to a common base form. The necessity depends on whether the dictionary has only base forms or the respective inflectional forms as well.

Furthermore, we add corresponding part-of-speech tags to the words. This is important because the *conjunction like*, for example, has no sentiment, whereas the *verb like* surely expresses a positive attitude. The usefulness of part-of-speech tags depends on whether the dictionary provided them as well. Afterward, we convert the text to lowercase and tokenize the text into n-grams.

Unigram Sentiment Score Calculation

As the first step, we split our preprocessed documents into unigrams. After assigning the dictionary's sentiment labels to the words of one document, we must aggregate the scores to one sentiment score of the document. In practice this is achieved in several ways: when the sentiment score is numeric,[13] we can calculate the mean sentiment score of all words or alternatively the difference of positive words and negative divided by the total number of words. This way, we obtain one numeric sentiment score per document.

3.1.2 Challenges

The word-level dictionary approach is intuitive and easy to implement. However, there are some aspects to keep in mind to avoid oversimplification:

First, language and the connotation of words can be highly context dependent, which means that domain-specific dictionaries should be used to maximize the accuracy.

Secondly, irony and negation are key challenges. Satire, irony, dark humor and the like are almost impossible to consider with the dictionary-based approach, because it is strongly heterogeneous. Indeed, negation can be captured by considering at least some grammatical rules of language. To capture negation, we must tokenize the text into consecutive sequences of length greater than one.[14] One common approach is to parse the text into bigrams. Hence, we can assign bigrams like *not good* a negative sentiment, whereas a unigram-based analysis only would have wrongly detected the word *good* with a positive sentiment. This means that we must search for typical negation terms and reverse the sentiment of the word that got a sentiment label from the dictionary (polarized word) within the bigrams.[15] Non-negation bigrams with two polarized words receive an averaged sentiment of the underlying two labels. This significantly increases the accuracy, while still not considering more complex negations.

Thirdly, to increase precision of the analysis we should take the effect of amplifiers and de-amplifiers, like *really* or *barely*, into account. Hence, the numeric sentiment label of the polarized word within the bigram should be adjusted. That can be done using lists of amplifiers/de-amplifiers where amplifiers have values above 1 and de-amplifiers lower than 1. The corresponding amplification value is then multiplied by the sentiment score of the respective polarized word.

---

[13] When the sentiment is given in strings, we must convert them to numeric. For example, in a binary classification, negative to -1 and positive to $+1$.
[14] The tokenization of the sentence *word1 word2 word3 not good* works as follows: the bigram tokens would be (word1 word2), (word2 word3), (word3 not), (not good); the trigram tokens (word1 word2 word3), (word2 word3 not), (word3 not good) and so on. Hence, negation patterns can be preserved.
[15] The GermanPolarityClues lexicon, for example, offers negation control with 290 bigrams to capture selected negation patterns.

The extension from unigram to bigram analysis enhances the accuracy significantly. But how can we handle something like *not really good*? We could extend the token size to trigrams and consider bigram amplifier/de-amplifier or negation patterns. Nevertheless, this points out that the decision about the size of the n-gram is rather a heuristic procedure and it is always difficult to find the right window. An empiric approach to determine ideal size seems appropriate.

Through the consideration of negations, as well as amplifiers/de-amplifiers, the analysis of bigram or trigram tokens usually performs better than the oversimplified unigram approach.

3.1.3 Augmented Dictionary Approach

To deal with more sophisticated patterns, we present a powerful augmented dictionary approach in the following. Up to now, we have not mentioned the consideration of double negation, conjunctions, as well as adversative conjunctions like *however, but* or *whereas*. The latter overrules the previous clause containing a polarized word.

I like it but it's not worth it.

This example sentence should have a negative sentiment, since the adversative conjunctions *but* overrules the positive sentiment of the verb *like*. Negations, amplifier/de-amplifier, conjunctions and adversative conjunctions are also called valence shifters.

To consider more sophisticated valence shifters, the augmented approach differs from the n-gram procedure because it tokenizes the text into sentences which are then broken into an ordered bag of words. The words of one sentence get their numeric sentiment score from the dictionary as shown above. The crucial difference happens afterward. The algorithm looks at the words around the polarized words whereby the default is four words before and two words after, a parameter that can be adjusted by the user. The polarized word together with the words around it build a context cluster, which is the bag of words that determines the sentiment of the polarized word.

If the algorithm detects amplifiers, the score increases. Amplifiers become de-amplifiers if the context cluster contains an odd number of negators (e.g. *not really*, where *really* correctly becomes a de-amplifier due to one negator). De-amplifiers reduce the sentiment score of the polarized word. Negations act on amplifiers/de-amplifiers as described and reverse the sentiment. Double negation, as well as more complex forms, are captured by raising -1 to the

Table 10 Examples of sentence classifications (© ifb SE)

Sentence	Challenge	Sentiment score
Sentiment analysis is powerful	Positivity	0.375
Sentiment analysis is useless	Negativity	−0.375
Sentiment analysis is really powerful	Amplifier	0.6037384
Sentiment analysis is not really powerful	De-amplifier	−0.06123724
It doesn't mean that sentiment analysis isn't good	Double negation	0.265165
Sentiment analysis is really powerful but it's not worth it	Adversative conjunction	−0.1539239
It would be optimal if it would be more precise	Conjunctive	−0.3288769
This is neither good nor amazing	Limitations	0.5103104
I do not love it but i hate it	Limitations	0.56225

power of the number of negators in the context cluster. The underlying idea is that two negatives are equal to a positive, while three negatives remain negative, and so on. Typical conjunctive patterns as *would be* or *should have* are captured through direct negative scores. Finally, an adversative conjunction before a polarized word raises its sentiment score and reduces the score if the adversative conjunction is located behind the polarized word. Furthermore, an adversative conjunction reverses the sentiment of the previous word. For example, *it is tasty but unhealthy* with the adversative conjunction *but* gets a negative sentiment because *tasty* is down-weighted and *unhealthy* is up-weighted and the positive sentiment of *tasty* is overruled.

The adjusted sentiment scores of the polarized words are summed up and divided by the square root of the word count leading to an unbound polarity score for each sentence. Finally, the sentiment scores of the sentences will be aggregated at document level. The augmented dictionary approach is implemented in the R package sentimentr (Rinker 2019). Although the package is equipped with English words only, it is open source and can easily be extended to further languages.[16]

Table 10 shows the augmented dictionary approach's potential in capturing several typical pitfalls of sentiment analysis. The accuracy of binary sentiment classification tested on three datasets of product reviews lies between 71 and 77 percent. This is notable because product reviews are rather short documents which are more vulnerable to misclassification. Additionally, the

---

[16] For more German dictionaries not mentioned here as well as lists of German amplifiers/de-amplifiers and negations see the website of IGGSA, the Interest Group on German Sentiment Analysis.

accuracy is comparable to a famous deep learning model that was also tested on the same datasets.[17] Table 10 also shows two examples of a wrong classification. The phrase *This is neither good nor amazing* is classified as strongly positive because the two negators *neither* and *nor* cancel each other out. The second misclassification occurs due to the fact that *but* in this context is rather an amplifier of the negative sentiment than an adversative conjunction reversing the negative sentiment of *not love*. These limitations can be partly worked around by adding further rules.

The (augmented) dictionary approach has pitfalls and challenges. The definition of the context cluster/n-gram is a rather heuristic process and must be tested empirically. Furthermore, there are limitations in finding very sophisticated negations, amplifier/de-amplifier patterns, irony, broader context dependency or more subtle patterns on top of grammatical structures. It also depends on the presence of suitable dictionaries to correctly consider word ambiguity and domain-specific words and their correct sentiment. This can lead to misclassification at sentence level.

Ordinal comparison of different continuous sentiment scores can be misleading. Sentiment labeling is a challenging task, even different humans would assess the sentiment of documents differently because of human biases. Hence, the overall validation of sentiment analysis is demanding since the sentiment label is not an objective unit. We can reach a good deal of human agreement when it comes to the extremes of sentiment, but there are a lot of tricky cases and gray areas. However, the augmented dictionary approach works quite well at aggregated document level and is straightforward to implement.

3.2 The NLP-Based Approach and Outlook

Machine learning models can enhance the quality of sentiment classifications. This class of models is capable of considering more complex valence shifters than the rule-based augmented dictionary approach implemented. However, the accuracy depends strongly on well-suited training data with lexical similarity to documents of interest. Therefore, we need human sentiment information on these documents, which we then use to train a machine learning classifier. To achieve this, we suggest additionally labeling the documents we are collecting during the implementation of our presented approach. This task can be performed by a team of employees, as part of a review process

---

[17] For more information see https://github.com/trinker/sentimentr.

or alternatively by paid services.[18] To reduce subjectivity, it is recommended that the sentiment classification of at least two different persons is considered. To accelerate the process, the labeling persons can rather override the given labels from the dictionary approach instead of determining new independent ones.

Transformer models like BERT are state of the art in sentiment analysis (Devlin et al. 2019). For this approach, we need a numeric representation for each word which refers to the term word embedding. The contextualized word embeddings learned by BERT represent words in a multidimensional semantic vector space whereby similar words are close to each other. Hence, non-trivial relationships of language can be considered. Word embeddings are even more powerful for the task of sentiment classification when they are constructed with data lexically similar to our labeled data for the classifier training. This is ensured when we train both our word embeddings and our classifier with the collected data. The implementation of word embeddings and sentiment classification can both be applied by the BERT model, which in turn can be implemented, for example, with Python and the corresponding toolkits. Hence, we could replace our dictionary sentiment classifier with the BERT model in an already established workflow of reputational risk management.

Literature

Blei, David M., Andrew Y. Ng, and Michael I. Jordan. 2003. "Latent Dirichlet Allocation." *Journal of Machine Learning Research* 3: 993–1022. https://doi.org/10.1162/jmlr.2003.3.4-5.993.

Bojanowski, Piotr, Edouard Grave, Armand Joulin, and Tomas Mikolov. 2016. "Enriching Word Vectors with Subword Information." *arXiv.* http://arxiv.org/abs/1607.04606.

Das, Rajarshi, Manzil Zaheer, and Chris Dyer. 2015. "Gaussian LDA for Topic Models with Word Embeddings." *Proceedings of the 53rd Annual Meeting of the Association for Computational Linguistics and the 7th International Joint Conference on Natural Language Processing.* Association for Computational Linguistics: 15–1077. http://www.aclweb.org/anthology/P15-1077.

Devlin, Jacob, Ming-Wei Chang, Kenton Lee, and Kristina Toutanova. 2019. "BERT: Pre-Training of Deep Bidirectional Transformers for Language Understanding." *Google AI Language*, May.

---

[18] For example, Amazon Mechanical Turk: https://www.mturk.com.

Goldhahn, D., T. Eckart , and U. Quasthoff. 2012. "Building Large Monolingual Dictionaries at the Leipzig Corpora Collection." *Proceedings of the 8th International Language Resources and Evaluation (LREC'12)*.

Honnibal, Mathew, and Ines Montani. 2017. *spaCy: Natural Language Understanding with Bloom Embeddings, Convolutional Neural Networks and Incremental Parsing*. http://github.com/explosion/spaCy. http://github.com/explosion/spaCy.

Levenshtein, Vladimir I. 1966. "Binary Codes Capable of Correcting Deletions, Insertions, and Reversals." *Soviet Physics Doklady* 10: 707–710.

Liermann, V., S. Li, and N. Schaudinnus. 2019. "Deep Learning: An Introduction." Chap. 4.4 in *The Impact of Digital Transformation and Fintech on the Finance Professional*, edited by V. Liermann and C. Stegmann, 331–335. New York: Palgrave Macmillian.

Liermann, Volker, Nikolas Viets, and Davin Radermacher. 2021. "Breaking New Grounds in Non-Financial Risk Management." In *The Digital Journey of Banking and Insurance, Volume I—Disruption and DNA*, edited by Volker Liermann and Claus Stegmann. New York: Palgrave Macmillan.

Liu, Bing. 2015. *Sentiment Analysis: Mining Opinions, Sentiments, and Emotions*. Cambridge University Press.

Manning, C., P. Raghavan, and H. Schütze. 2008. "Scoring, Term Weighting, and the Vector Space Model." Chap. 6 in *Introduction to Information Retrieval*, edited by C. Manning, P. Raghavan and H. Schütze, 100–123. Cambridge: Cambridge University Press. https://doi.org/10.1017/CBO9780511809071.007.

Mäntylä, Mika, Miikka Kuutila, and Daniel Graziotin. 2018. "The Evolution of Sentiment Analysis—A Review of Research Topics, Venues, and Top Cited Papers." *Computer Science Review*, February: 16–32.

Minqing Hu, Hu, and Bing Liu. 2004. "Mining and Summarizing Customer Reviews."

Moody, Christopher E. 2016. "Mixing Dirichlet Topic Models and Word Embeddings to Make lda2vec." *arXiv*. http://arxiv.org/abs/1605.02019.

Nielsen, Finn Årup . 2011. "A New ANEW: Evaluation of a Word List for Sentiment Analysis in Microblogs."

Pennington, Jeffrey, Richard Socher, and Christopher D. Manning. 2014. "GloVe: Global Vectors for Word Representation." *Proceedings of the 2014 conference on empirical methods in natural language processing (EMNLP)*. pp. 1532–1543. http://nlp.stanford.edu/pubs/glove.pdf.

Pritchard, J. K., M. Stephens, and P. Donnelly. 2000. "Inference of Population Structure Using Multilocus Genotype Data." *Genetics* 155: 945–959.

Rinker, Tyler W. 2019. *Calculate Text Polarity Sentiment*. version 2.7.1. Buffalo, New York

Sharma, Deepak. 2017. "A Survey on Journey of Topic Modeling Techniques from SVD to Deep Learning." *International Journal of Modern Education and Computer Science* 9: 50–62. https://doi.org/10.5815/ijmecs.2017.07.06.

Singhal, Amit. 2001. "Modern Information Retrieval: A Brief Overview." *IEEE Data Engineering Bulletin*: 35–43. http://singhal.info/ieee2001.pdf.

Thompson, Andrew. 2017. *All the News: 143,000 Articles from 15 American publications.* http://www.kaggle.com/snapcrack/all-the-news/metadata, 08/20. http://www.kaggle.com/snapcrack/all-the-news/metadata.

Trask, Andrew, Phil Michalak, and John Liu. 2015. "sense2vec—A Fast and Accurate Method for Word Sense Disambiguation In Neural Word Embeddings." *arXiv.* http://arxiv.org/abs/1511.06388.

Vijayarani, S., J. Ilamathi, and Nithya. 2015. "Preprocessing Techniques for Text Mining—An Overview." *International Journal of Computer Science & Communication Networks* 5: 7–16.

Waltinger, Ulli. 2010. "A Lexical Resource for German Sentiment Analysis." *Proceedings of the Seventh International Conference on Language Resourcesand Evaluation (LREC).*

Use Case: NFR—Using GraphDB for Impact Graphs

Volker Liermann and Marian Tieben

1 Introduction

1.1 Connected World

We live in a connected world. On the macro level, globalization has been driving the connectedness of the business processes (supply chains) and markets. On a micro level, the progressing digitalization—by means of making information (data) available electronically—helps us to understand the dependencies already existing. This opportunity to analyze and (sometimes) understand how things interact can be overwhelming.

Seeing the connections is the first step in the journey of managing the complexities. The major step is to communicate and discuss the matter with others. The common (and old fashioned) way is to simply write the interrelationships using a word processor (like Microsoft Word) or to document them in a list (maybe using an oversized spreadsheet like Microsoft Excel). Both approaches just document the matter, but do not offer a lean and easy way to analyze and get deeper insights.

V. Liermann (✉) · M. Tieben
ifb SE, Grünwald, Germany
e-mail: Volker.Liermann@ifb-group.com

M. Tieben
e-mail: Marian.Tieben@ifb-group.com

Graphs are an outstanding tool to model connected environments. The two key points differentiating graphs from text or lists in terms of documenting connected matters are the opportunity to (A) visualize and to (B) analyze. There is no need to discuss how visualizations help us in communicating things. Pictures support us in memorizing things. Analyzing graphs in mathematics (graph theory) has a long history and starts with the paper published by Euler on the "Seven bridges of Königsberg" problem (1736). Graph theory offers lots of analyses and algorithms to work and understand the structure of a graph. Graph theory has many applications in natural sciences, computer science, social sciences and linguistics (see Bajer et al. 2021). When attributes are assigned to a graph (or its components: edges and vertices) the term network science is often used (see Enzinger and Grossmann 2019).

1.2 Non-financial Risk Management

Non-financial risk management is structured by a taxonomy to break the high complexity down into more easily manageable pieces (see section in Liermann et al. 2021). Practice in non-financial risk management has proven that the risk categories of such a taxonomy are still interconnected, and one of the main challenges in non-financial risk management is how to bring transparency into the different risk categories and compose a bank-wide connected view of the various non-financial risk categories.

Impact graphs are among the best tools to cover this essential requirement in the context of NFR. Risk events are the key element to good non-financial risk management. Even if it is difficult to estimate a probability (for the event to happen) and the financial loss amount, the risk event can help to analyze and manage the threat level (see section in Liermann et al. 2021). An example of how to quantify a threat level is described in (Schmüser et al. 2021) in the context of person risk.

With the toolset of graphs, the connection and interaction of risk events can be documented, analyzed and managed.

1.3 Structure of the Chapter

The chapter starts with an example from the ESG[1] context in Sect. 2. In Sect. 3, an introduction to the graphs and the functions that can be applied to them is offered. Section 4 recaps the traditional approach in dealing with operational risk (which is a subset of non-financial risk).[2] How graphs can support non-financial risk management in communication and analysis is described in Sect. 5. The chapter closes with a summary in Sect. 6.

2 Example ESG Risk

ESG is a topic with a tremendous impact on the financial sector. The long-term influence comes with a multifaceted risk profile. ESG risk management aims to cover these risks. Although we see ESG risk as a non-financial risk category, even the single letters can be broken down into sub-risks. One way to structure the ESG risk is to divide the environmental risks into physical risks and transition risks. The social risks are subdivided into core compliance risk and risk coming with (non-regulatory) standards and social norms. The two parts of governance risk are risk to governance (RtG) and the risk of governance (RoG).

In our example, we will focus on the transition risk and the social norm risk.

2.1 Business Setting

The example impact graph discussed in this section analyzes the influence of the changed perception of gray finance[3] (or more precisely the carbon-intensive industry). When analyzing the impact of the changing perception the key element is the risk event.[4] A risk event is assigned to a non-financial risk category[5] and is the link between the taxonomy and the impact graph. By

---

[1] Environmental, Social, Governance.

[2] Operational risks must be covered by capital and are therefore distinguished from non-financial risk. Operational risks are a subset of the non-financial risk.

[3] Gray finance is the term used by the United Nations for financing environmentally polluting industries (Carbon.intensive or gray industries).

[4] Vulnerabilities have a similar level of importance in the framework.

[5] Each node should be assigned to a risk category.

connecting the risk events with an impact graph, the interaction and dependencies are illustrated. In addition, the analysis opportunities arise from the graph-based documentation.

2.2 Impact Graph

Figure 1 shows an example impact graph in the ESG context. The impact graph illustrates the influence of the changed perception of gray finance with the starting points (in terms of graph theory in a directed graph—sources) social change and the questioning of the carbon-intensive industry model. The institute suffers a loss of reputation and a loss in its bond portfolio, but only if the institute-specific vulnerability "Investment concentration in carbon-intensive finance" is active.

The nodes in the directed graph are divided into five node types: risk events (red), events (blue green), vulnerabilities (gold), negative effects[6] (dark blue) and non-financial risk categories (light blue). Additionally, the edges are attributed the following keywords: "impacts", "triggers", "is required" and "is part". The edges "impacts", "triggers" and "is required" connect risk events, events and vulnerabilities, while "is part" connects the aforementioned non-financial risk categories (and therefore bridges the taxonomy and the impact graph).

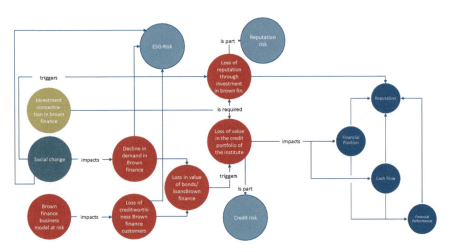

Fig. 1 Impact graph ESG (© ifb SE)

---

[6] Components of the PCP situation and reputation (PCP stands for financial position, cash flows and financial performance).

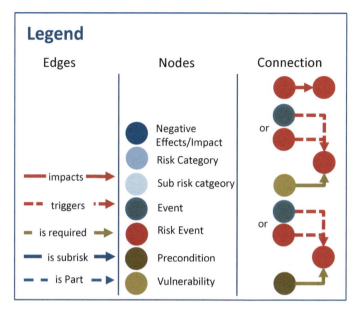

Fig. 2 Symbols in an impact graph (© ifb SE)

Figure 2 gives an overview of the different types of edges and nodes in the impact graph context. More detailed discussion of these edge and node types can be found in Sect. 2.4 in Liermann et al. (2021).

3 Graph Functions

In order to draw conclusions based on impact graphs, we present a framework to store and analyze them descriptively in the following.

3.1 Storage and Query in Graph Databases

To store impact graphs, we need graph databases. One popular vendor we use is Neo4j, which offers free access to build your own local or remote databases.

One characteristic of graph databases is the storage of connections between nodes. This aspect as well as the syntax of the query language of Neo4j (called Cypher) enables us to query highly connected data in a straightforward and intuitive way. In SQL queries, we must define the connections with join statements, which is usually more challenging and takes more time. Table 1 illustrates the elegance of Cypher.

Table 1 Comparison between SQL and Cypher from (Neo4J, n.d.) (© ifb SE)

SQL	Cypher
SELECT p.ProductNameFROM Product AS pJOIN ProductCategory pc ON (p.CategoryID = pc.CategoryID AND pc.CategoryName = "Dairy Products") JOIN ProductCategory pc1 ON (p.CategoryID = pc1.CategoryIDJOIN ProductCategory pc2 ON (pc2.ParentID = pc2.CategoryID AND pc2.CategoryName = "Dairy Products") JOIN ProductCategory pc3 ON (p.CategoryID = pc3.CategoryIDJOIN ProductCategory pc4 ON (pc3.ParentID = pc4.CategoryID)JOIN ProductCategory pc5 ON (pc4.ParentID = pc5.CategoryID AND pc5.CategoryName = "Dairy Products");	MATCH (p:Product)-[:CATEGORY] ->(l:ProductCategory)-[:PARENT*0..]- (:ProductCategory {name:"Dairy Products"})RETURN p.name

3.2 Descriptive Analysis Functions in the Impact Graph Context

The dynamic dashboard is implemented with R and enables a querying of data from the graph database with Cypher, as well as a transformation and visualization of the data.

In order to comprehensively analyze several non-financial risks and their connections, we build many different impact graphs that lead to one large, connected global graph. To reduce complexity, we can assign specific nodes to scenarios, which we can in turn visualize separately as illustrated in Fig. 3.

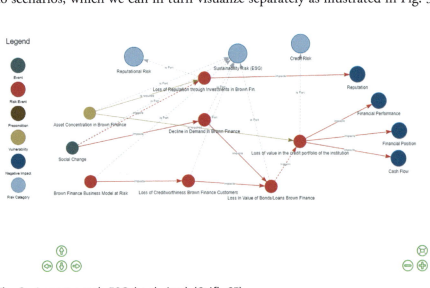

Fig. 3 Impact graph ESG (tool view) (© ifb SE)

This allows a focused view of specific impact graphs if desired.

Furthermore, we can assign nodes of scenarios to different granularity levels and visualize them separately. This enables visualizations of compact impact graphs for management representations or rather granular impact graphs, e.g. specialist departments.

3.2.1 Predecessor and Successor Analysis

The impact graphs are usually large and complex. In order to facilitate the following of specific paths, the tool highlights the nearest neighbors of one node after it is clicked on. We have specified that the degree is the maximum and that both directions are visualized.

The algorithm identifies the clicked-on node as well as the connected nodes in both directions, which are on the same paths. As illustrated in Fig. 4, the clicked-on node is visualized in blue and its name is written in bold. The other relevant nodes and their corresponding edges are still visualized with the original colors whereas the irrelevant nodes and edges, which are not on the paths, are transparent and gray. This functionality is especially useful in larger scenarios as well as in the global graph.

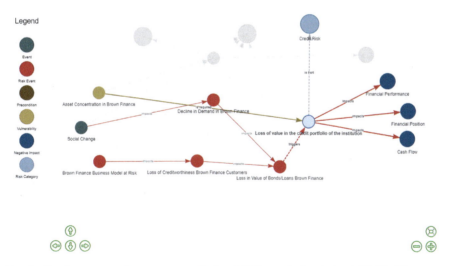

Fig. 4 Predecessor and successor analysis of ESG graph (tool view) (© ifb SE)

3.2.2 Risk Driver (Sources)

Every impact graph has its starting points. As we are designing impact graphs from left to right, they are usually the farthest left nodes and only have outbound edges. These nodes are initially triggering following nodes and are therefore of particular importance and can be seen as risk drivers. Additionally, vulnerabilities are preconditions for nodes to trigger successor nodes. This class of nodes only has outbound edges and correspondingly belongs to risk drivers, too.

3.2.3 Impacted Nodes (Sinks)

The final nodes of impact graphs only have inbound edges and can be seen as final consequences. In many cases, impact graphs end in the four nodes of the category negative impact: reputation, financial position as well as financial performance and cash flow.

3.2.4 Graph Aggregation

As mentioned above, the sources and sinks have a special role in impact graphs. Additionally, we assign nodes to risk categories to consider connections of risk categories within and between different scenarios. Hence, we implemented an algorithm which aggregates this important information.

The algorithm identifies the clicked-on node and traverses the paths forward and backward until the sinks and sources are found. Furthermore, all risk categories that are assigned to nodes located on the relevant paths are identified and visualized. This algorithm can be applied to the global graph as well as to scenarios.

Figure 5 illustrates the output of the algorithm which considers all the relevant aspects for management aggregation: the clicked-on node in the middle, risk driver to the left, final consequences to the right and the affected risk categories above.

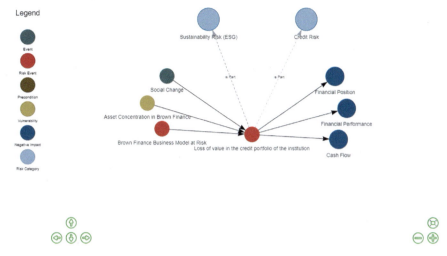

Fig. 5 Management aggregation of ESG graph (tool view) (© ifb SE)

4 Traditional Oprisk Approach

Impact graphs have long been known as a tool in the context of operational risk management. As operational risk has its origin[7] in Basel II, Basel II (and the following initiatives) aim to encourage banks to hold sufficient capital to avoid financial misalignment by taking too much risk. Hence, the framework is designed to calculate potential losses (or make a statistical description of the potential losses, e.g. a loss distribution).

This approach is not feasible for all risk events and all risk categories (HILFE[8] problem). Despite this fact, a solution for how to cover events, the probability and impact of which are hard to quantify, will be delivered in Sect. 0.

While nonetheless non-financial risk management can go the same way, we will briefly introduce one variant of this approach.

---

[7] Although approaches to operational risk existed before the consultation paper to Basel II, regulatory demand accelerated the development as an independent risk category.
[8] HILFE—High-impact low-frequency events make the estimate extremely challenging, because there is normally no historical data available.

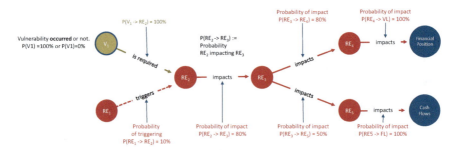

Fig. 6 Expected values of the probabilities of occurrence—numerical example (© ifb SE)

4.1 Abstract Example

In Fig. 6, an abstract example is shown. On the left side we start with a conditional vulnerability and a risk event. In this stage example, we only place the probabilities on the edges, which allows us to calculate the probabilities of the different paths in the graph.[9] In the middle, risk events impacting one after the other are shown and on the right side the negative impacts (financial position represented by the balance sheet, and cash flow situation represented by the cash flow statement) are placed.

The calculation is straightforward and can be expressed in the following equations:

$$P(RE_1 \to FP) = \left(\prod_{i=1}^{N_1} P(RE_i \to RE_{i+1})\right) \cdot P(RE_{N_1} \to FP)$$

Equation 1: Path probability—risk event 1 to financial situation

$$P(RE_1 \to CF) = \left(\prod_{i=1}^{N_2} P(RE_i \to RE_{i+1})\right) \cdot P(RE_{N_2} \to CF)$$

Equation 2: Path probability—risk event 1 to cash flows

N_1 and N_2 are the length of the considered paths.
Taking these formulas, a calculation gives the following results:

$$P(RE_1 \to FP) = 10\% \cdot 80\% \cdot 80\% \cdot 100\% = 6.4\%$$

---

[9] There are many ways to assign attributes to nodes and edges.

and

$$P(RE_1 \rightarrow CF) = 10\% \cdot 80\% \cdot 50\% \cdot 100\% = 4\%$$

More important than the probability of a risk event is the financial loss it could cause (always given there are data and methods available to make an estimation). In Fig. 7, this idea is implemented on the left-hand side where an impact graph with loss amounts attributed to nodes is shown. When we further assume, we draw random numbers based on the risk events occurrence, we get the loss distribution on the right-hand side. The loss distribution gives us a clearer picture of the risk (loss potential) of the considered impact graphs and the corresponding risk events.

In Fig. 8, the risk modeling is taken a step further: we assume here that we have an uncertainty[10] in the loss amount coming with the different risk events.

This approach works quite well for some risk situations (especially high frequency[11] and even more if the impact is low). But the challenges in non-financial risk lie more in the space of low-frequency events with a huge impact.

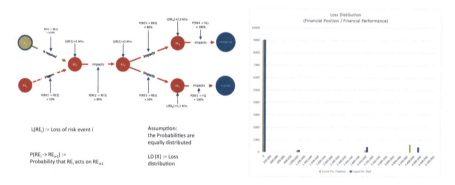

Fig. 7 Distribution of losses—numerical example (© ifb SE)

---

[10] We assume a 10% variance for the loss amount.
[11] With high frequency normally comes reliable data, which can be used to build models.

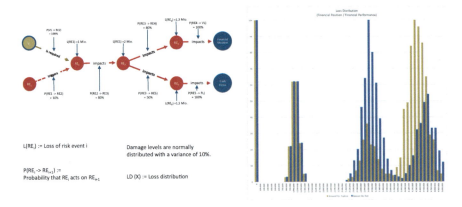

Fig. 8 Distribution of losses—numerical example—normally distributed damage amounts (© ifb SE)

5 NFR Approach—Estimation of the Threat Situation

5.1 General Idea

Good risk management is not only about exact estimation of loss amounts. It is important to discover the impactful events and manage them. If the impact of an event is approximately half of the equity of an institute it does not matter if it is 45 or 55% of the equity, it has the potential to kill the institute.

In many situations, the risk cannot be mitigated at reasonable cost. Then, taking the risk is the least costly strategy. In this situation, management of the risk becomes even more important.

To manage a risk, measurement procedures are required. The major point in good and practicable risk management is what you measure. In these situations, the past has shown that trying to estimate the financial loss will fail. But good risk management can be established by trying to describe (and quantify) the threat level. This section gives an example approach from the context of HR risk.

5.2 Example HR Risk

To consider threat situations, we can assign risk indicators (RI) and key risk indicators (KRI) to impact graphs which are not based on probabilities and loss amounts. An intuitive example of termination risk of employees is described in Sect. 4 in Schmüser et al. (2021). HR risk is of particular interest since the assigned nodes are often risk drivers and trigger subsequent nodes of other risk categories.

The basic idea is to collect data from surveys or data that is already available through HR management. The collected RIs can be expressed in rates or scores and are assigned to their corresponding edges. Several risk indicators finally lead to one KRI where the overall risk situation is aggregated.

To assess threat situations based on RIs/KRIs, we define thresholds. This framework is implemented in the tool with traffic lights and is illustrated in Fig. 9.

The three green events on the left are risk drivers of the threat situation which can be quantified with scores in the interval [0,10], whereby zero means low risk and ten high risk. A good source for the score calculation can be provided by employee surveys. The corresponding vulnerabilities are risk drivers too and either active (score = 1) or inactive (score = 0). In Fig. 9, all three vulnerabilities are active, which means that all three RIs on the edges from the events (green nodes) trigger the subsequent risk events. In the graph tool, the score information is visible through a mouseover, which means that the scores are not available in the figure.

The traffic lights are determined by the scores and the thresholds, which can be seen in the legend on the left in Fig. 9. We visualize threat situations with three colors: green = low risk, orange = intermediate risk, red = high

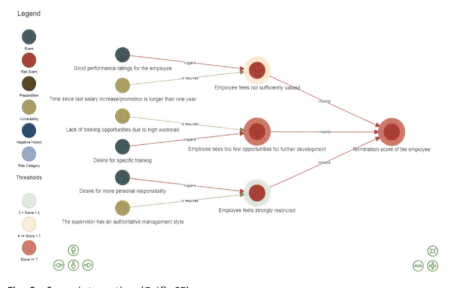

Fig. 9 Score integration (© ifb SE)

risk and need for action. The number of categories can be customized to capture more granular differences if desired.

The node "Termination score of the employee" represents the KRI node in this scenario since several previous RIs ultimately lead to this node. The traffic light color of the KRI node is based on the maximum value of all three incoming scores since simple mean or median averaging would be misleading. For example, if all incoming scores are zero except one with a significant threat situation and correspondingly a score above seven, a mean/median would not always capture the need for action. However, the aggregation logic can be customized differently if desired. In Fig. 9, the total risk of termination is significantly driven by the fact that the employee sees too few opportunities for further development. Consequently, the KRI node is marked with a red border.

5.2.1 Change Activity Status

Assuming the organization has removed vulnerabilities of threat situations through corresponding actions, the tool is equipped to capture this. In Fig. 10, the vulnerability "Lack of training opportunities due to high workload" is no longer active. Paths that are not relevant anymore are visualized as more transparent and grayer. Additionally, the general threat situation has decreased through this action as visible in the orange traffic light color of the

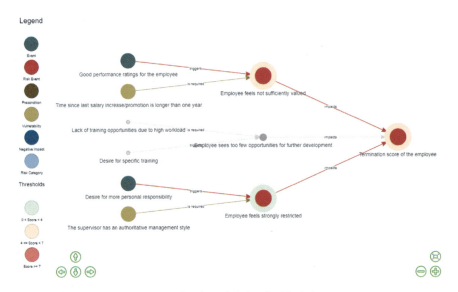

Fig. 10 Change activity status of vulnerabilities (© ifb SE)

KRI node, because the maximum valid score now lies in the intermediate range.

5.3 Reporting

The risk event is the key element of the approach to develop a reasonable risk management framework for non-financial risk. Reporting has two aims: (A) describing and illustrating the threat level of a risk event (and if possible, estimating the loss amount and probabilities of the risk event),[12] (B) embedding the risk event in the context of its surroundings (the other risk events).

The other risk events can be assigned to the same risk category but can also come from another risk category. By connecting the risk events through an impact graph, we can break out of the silo of a single risk category and can deliver a holistic institute-wide view of all non-financial risks.

This reporting approach is illustrated in Fig. 11. The three upper right boxes show the connection of the risk events in the reported risk category. First, the triggering risk categories are shown (the connection is derived from the associated nodes). The middle box shows the status of the risk events directly assigned to the risk category. The box on the right shows the further linked risk categories (again derived from the risk events).

A more detailed discussion of non-financial risk reporting can be found in Sect. 5 in Liermann et al. (2021) and in Schmüser et al. (2021).

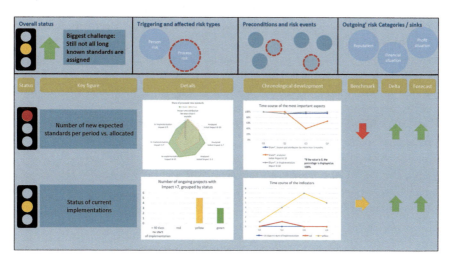

Fig. 11 Example reporting (© ifb SE)

---

[12] This is only possible in a small number of relevant events.

6 Summary

The opportunity for visualization and the structured way of documenting the connections and interactions between the risk events make the impact graphs a highly effective tool in the context of non-financial risk management.

The risk event is the starting point for the analysis and documentation of the things that can go wrong. As highlighted in Sect. 0, the best way to manage risk is not only by making estimates for loss amounts (because it is just impossible to do so with a minimal amount of certainty). Therefore, the estimation, documentation and communication of the threat level for a risk event can be a more powerful tool than getting lost in statistics without any empirical evidence or any explanatory power for the future.

Impact graphs and the embedded nodes are the eye-opener for the risk situation in the context of non-financial risk.

Literature

Bajer, Krystyna, Sascha Steltgens, Anne Seidlitz, and Bastian Wormuth. 2021. "Graph Databases." In *The Digital Journey of Banking and Insurance, Volume III—Data Storage, Processing, and Analysis*, edited by Volker Liermann and Claus Stegmann. New York: Palgrave Macmillan.

Enzinger, Philipp, and Stefan Grossmann. 2019. "Managing Internal and External Network Complexity." In *The Impact of Digital Transformation and Fintech on the Finance Professional*, edited by Volker Liermann and Claus Stegmann. New York: Palgrave Macmillan.

Liermann, Volker, Nikolas Viets, and Davin Radermacher. 2021. "Breaking New Grounds in Non-Financial Risk Management." In *The Digital Journey of Banking and Insurance, Volume I—Disruption and DNA*, edited by Volker Liermann and Claus Stegmann. New York: Palgrave Macmillan.

Neo4J. n.d. *Neo4J Developer Guide*. Accessed December 17, 2020. https://neo4j.com/developer/cypher/guide-sql-to-cypher/.

Schmüser, Arne, Farah Skaf, and Harro Dittmar. 2021. "Use Case—NFR—HR Risk." In *The Digital Journey of Banking and Insurance, Volume II—Digitalization and Machine Learning*, edited by Volker Liermann and Claus Stegmann. New York: Palgrave Macmillan.

High-Performance Applications

The subject of high-performance applications is a wide-open space, and this part covers only a few topics of this universe. Cloud computing and the architectural pattern used by Hadoop perform computation on a computer cluster. Hadoop and the different distributions and derivations like Cloudera and Databricks allow computer clusters composed of more or less standard hardware to be built up and managed. Intelligent load distribution provides organizations with computational power at a relatively low price. Cloud computing helps to cut costs from another angle: the usage of the cluster. Without cloud computing, a department needs to buy a server if the tasks require a certain computational power. However, most of the day the server remains unused because, for example, risk calculation may only be performed over night from 10:00 pm until.

4:00 am and the server may remain unused for 75% of the time. Only really big companies could provide a reasonable load balancing across departments and servers. Cloud providers are able to provide this load balancing and offer this pay-as-you-use service to the clients. Pay-as-you-use in combination with server management tools (like Cloudera) can provide an affordable and conditioned access to computational power.

The first chapter (Liermann et al. "Distributed Calculation Credit Portfolio Models" 2021) picks up the important task of credit portfolio risk models and shows in practical examples how to parallelize an existing R package for the well-known CreditMetrics credit portfolio model and how to deploy it to a Hadoop cluster using R sparks.

The next chapter (Liermann and Dittmar "BSDS—Balance Sheet Dynamics Simulator [Implementation ABM in Cloudera/Simudyne]" 2021) also shows an implementation on a Hadoop cluster of computational purposes. The chapter describes an agent-based model implemented in Simudyne. The model is the Balance Sheet Dynamics Simulator (see volume I of this series [Liermann and Dittmar "BSDS—Balance Sheet Dynamics Simulator [Implementation ABM in Cloudera/Simudyme]" 2021) used for projecting the institute's balance sheet into the future and analyzing its impact on the institute's stability using the Financial Navigator (see Thiele 2021).

The third chapter (Liermann and Li "Dynamic Dashboards" 2021) introduces dynamic dashboard technology. The chapter proves the appropriateness of Kahneman's concept of fast and slow thinking (see Kahneman 2011). It lines up some tools for implementing dynamic dashboards and analyzes several use cases to explore the readiness of the technology.

Another high-performance application is presented in the last chapter of the part: breaking passwords. Hashes are a widely used technique to secure passwords or provide cryptographic security like in Bitcoin or other distributed ledger frameworks. The chapter (Bogomolec "High-Performance Applications" 2021) briefly explains the idea of hashes and shows a practical application in a specific case for how to break them.

Literature

Bogomolec, Xenia. 2021. "High-Performance Applications." In *The Digital Journey of Banking and Insurance, Volume II—Digitalization and Machine Learning*, edited by Volker Liermann and Claus Stegmann. New York: Palgrave Macmillan.

Kahneman, Daniel. 2011. *Thinking, Fast and Slow*. New York: Farrar, Straus and Giroux.

Liermann, Volker, and Harro Dittmar. 2021. "BSDS—Balance Sheet Dynamics Simulator (Implementation ABM in Cloudera/Simudyme)." In *The Digital Journey of Banking and Insurance, Volume II—Digitalization and Machine Learning*, edited by Volker Liermann and Claus Stegmann. New York: Palgrave Macmillan.

Liermann, Volker, and Sangmeng Li. 2021. "Dynamic Dashboards." In *The Digital Journey of Banking and Insurance, Volume II—Digitalization and Machine Learning*, edited by Volker Liermann and Claus Stegmann. New York: Palgrave Macmillan.

Liermann, Volker, Sangmeng Li, and Johannes Waizner. 2021. "Distributed Calculation Credit Portfolio Models." In *The Digital Journey of Banking and Insurance, Volume II—Digitalization and Machine Learning*, edited by Volker Liermann and Claus Stegmann. New York: Palgrave Macmillan.

Thiele, Markus. 2021. "Financial Navigator—A Modern Approach to Analytical Banking." In *The Digital Journey of Banking and Insurance, Volume I—Disruption and DNA*, edited by Volker Liermann and Claus Stegmann. New York: Palgrave Macmillan.

Distributed Calculation Credit Portfolio Models

Volker Liermann, Sangmeng Li, and Johannes Waizner

1 Introduction

Credit risk is still one of the most important financial risks. The COVID-19 pandemic in the year 2020 has proven that forward-looking credit risk management secures the long-term profitability of an institute (see Liermann and Viets, Predictive risk management 2019).

Other challenges like ESG will drive the number of calculation runs. The long-term impact of changes to the economy introduced by ESG must be monitored continuously. Different credit portfolio development scenarios (parameter and transaction scenarios) must be evaluated on a recurring basis scaling up the number of calculation runs.

All these requirements generate a high demand for computational power at reasonable cost. This chapter will present an approach to cover this challenge.

V. Liermann (✉) · S. Li · J. Waizner
ifb SE, Grünwald, Germany
e-mail: Volker.Liermann@ifb-group.com

S. Li
e-mail: Sangmeng.Li@ifb-group.com

J. Waizner
e-mail: Johannes.Waizner@ifb-group.com

1.1 Initial Situation

Many credit portfolio models are quite intensive in terms of computing demands. In recent years, the trend is heading more and more toward Monte Carlo simulations, because in a model based on Monte Carlo simulations extensions are easily integrated. Examples of model extensions are spread movements in rating classes or dynamics in collateral values (see Liermann et al., Immobilienrisiken präventiv analysieren 2018).

The cost-efficient implementations of these extensions are an important subject for risk managers. In addition, cloud providers like Azure, AWS or Google Cloud allow a demand-sensitive pricing of server infrastructure with the "pay as you use" model.

1.2 Structure of the Chapter

In Sect. 2 of this chapter a brief overview of credit portfolio models is given. The implementation of the distributed calculation on a Hadoop cluster (using Spark and R) is presented in Sect. 3. The final Sect. 4 provides a summary and an outlook.

2 Credit Portfolio Models

2.1 Overview of the Common Types of Credit Portfolio Risk Model

The so-called classical credit portfolio models were mostly developed in the mid-90s. The models can be classified as asset-based models(CreditMetrics[1] and KMV[2]) and intensity-based models (CreditRisk+[3] and CreditPortfolioView[4]). Very early in the year 1998 there was a well-known comparison and summary (see Koyluoglu et al. 1998; and a later analysis Crouhy et al. 2000).

All these models have variants used in practice. CreditMetrics, KMV and CreditPortfolioView are all Monte Carlo simulation models by design, and

---

[1] See Gupton et al. (1997).
[2] See Kealhofer (1998).
[3] See Wilde (1997).
[4] See Wilson, Portfolio credit risk (I) (1997) and Wilson, Portfolio credit risk (II) (1997), The German Savings Banks Association (DSGV) has developed a specific model variant.

some variants of CreditRisk+[5] are implemented as a Monte Carlo simulation as well.

The power of Monte Carlo models lies in the flexibility to implement extensions of an existing model. In analytical or closed form models, extensions or changes in the general setting (like a distribution assumption) can cause massive changes in the formulas and sometimes, depending on the extensions, the model cannot be described in a closed form.

2.2 Short Introduction to CreditMetrics

The CreditMetrics model is well known, and many variants of the original model are discussed in scientific literature and used in daily risk management routines.

Figure 1 shows a high-level flow of the calculation in the original model. The process described now will loop over the different simulation runs.[6] For illustrative purposes, in Fig. 1 it is assumed that we calculate a portfolio of 4000 clients (M is the number of clients), which are associated with specific sectors out of a possible set of 50 sectors (S is the number of possible sectors). Further, we assume that at least 1 million runs (N is the number of simulation runs) are performed.

In the first step for each sector, a correlated set of index changes is drawn. In addition to the sector value changes, for each client an idiosyncratic value

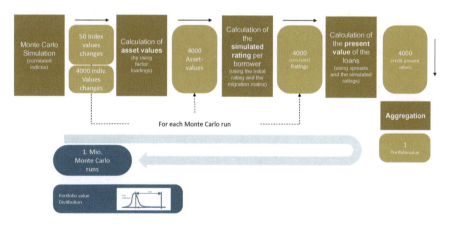

Fig. 1 Overview CreditMetrics (© ifb SE)

---

[5] CreditRisk+ is a closed formula model, which is a solved algorithm (e.g. by using Fourier transformation).

[6] The convergence of Monte Carlo simulation is a widely discussed topic in science (see xx).

change is drawn. In the second step, the asset value changes are calculated by incorporating factor-loadings. The factor-loadings are the weights that define the impact of the assigned sectors to the individual client.[7]

$$\Delta A_i = \underbrace{b_{i,1} X_1 + \ldots + b_{i,N} X_s}_{\text{"systematic risk"}} + \underbrace{\left(\sqrt{1 - \sum_{k=1}^{S} b_{i,k}^2} \right) \varepsilon_i}_{\text{"individual risk"}}$$

Equation 1: Factor-loadings (© ifb SE)

ΔA_i are the changes in enterprise value (asset returns) of the i-th client, X_i are the systematic factors (normally distributed and independent), ε_k are the individual factors (normally distributed and independent), $b_{i,j}$ are the weights of the systematic factors (factor-loadings) of the i-th client and S is the number of systematic factors.

$$\Delta A_i = \rho X + \varepsilon_i \sqrt{1 - \rho}$$

Equation 2: One-factor variant (© ifb SE)

ΔA_i are again changes in enterprise value (asset returns) of the i-th client, and ρ is the correlation between the macroeconomic factor X and the idiosyncratic factor ε_i.

Next, the asset value changes are mapped into rating changes by using the probabilities in the migration matrix. In the penultimate step of a loop, the present value of the client's cashflow is calculated by assuming the simulated rating development. At the end of a loop, the simulated portfolio is the aggregation of all the client's present values. The whole procedure is carried out for N runs, so that the N simulated portfolio values can be viewed as a discrete distribution. This discrete distribution can be used to calculate the key risk indicators like VaR[8] and expected shortfall.[9]

To summarize the main model parameters in CreditMetrics, an overview is given in Fig. 2. The sector correlations are high-level parameters, influencing the portfolio dynamics as a whole. Factor-loadings are client specific and help to map the sector dynamics to each client. The migration matrix translates the

---

[7] In practical implementations, only in rare situations do more than three factor-loadings not equal zero. These three main factors usually cover the main impact of the economy on the client. In some implementations, the factor-loadings are restricted to one factor (representing the whole economy, e.g. GDP).
[8] Value at risk (see Jorion 2006).
[9] Expected shortfall (see McNeil et al. 2005).

Fig. 2 Parameter CreditMetrics (© ifb SE)

simulated asset values into ratings. Credit spreads and the LGD are used for the valuation of the client's transactions given a simulated rating (including default).

All these parameters must be available to the calculation nodes that perform the parallel and distributed calculation.

2.3 Parallel Computing—Business-Driven Angle

An important aspect of implementing a parallel and distributed calculation of a business problem is how to divide the business entities into packages without crushing potential dependencies of the calculation flow. In the given problem of the credit risk portfolio calculation with the CreditMetrics model, the task is manageable.

In Fig. 3, the calculation steps are mapped and split into parts that can be parallelized and those that are the waiting points where the calculation queue

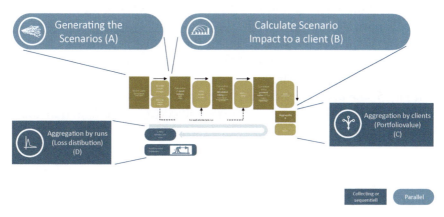

Fig. 3 Overview of the parts to be parallelized (© ifb SE)

must wait to collect the results from the parallel blocks. In the first step, the scenarios (sector changes and idiosyncratic changes) need to be generated (A). This task can be parallelized itself by the scenarios. The next block is the calculation of the impact on the value of the client transactions (B). The following block (C) is to collect the results (vector of value changes by run or vector of value changes by client)[10] and aggregate the result vector. In the last block (D), the portfolio value changes are, for each run, condensed in a discrete loss distribution, which is the foundation for the VaR calculation (determine the quantile value).

In the following section, we describe different splitting approaches for the calculation of the scenario impact on the client transaction value (B). The chosen approach has an impact on the way the aggregation is performed in block (C).

2.3.1 Natural Splitting and Block Building

The structure provided by the model offers two natural ways to build the calculation blocks. These two ways are illustrated in Fig. 4. On the left side, the calculation is distributed by N individual calculation runs (Variant A). The whole portfolio (all clients, i.e. all transactions and their simulated present value) is calculated for one simulation run or scenario (sector changes and idiosyncratic changes). If no further analysis on a client level is required,[11] then the client transaction value can be aggregated on a portfolio level. The simulated portfolio value can be provided to the P&L distribution. On the right side of Fig. 4, the separation is performed by the M clients (Variant B). Here, for one client (and their transactions), all simulations/scenarios are calculated in one block. The vector of the client's values for each scenario must be transferred back and can only be aggregated when the whole portfolio is returned.

As long as there is no demand for further client-level analysis, the separation by runs offers some simplification in collecting the data out of the calculation performed in parallel.

In Fig. 5, the queuing and distribution over a four-node cluster is shown for Variant A. The illustration clarifies that all client-related (and transaction-related) data must be transferred to the calculation node. As long as the raw

---

[10] See Sect. 2.3.1.
[11] One common application is the calculation of risk contributions of a single client to the portfolio VaR.

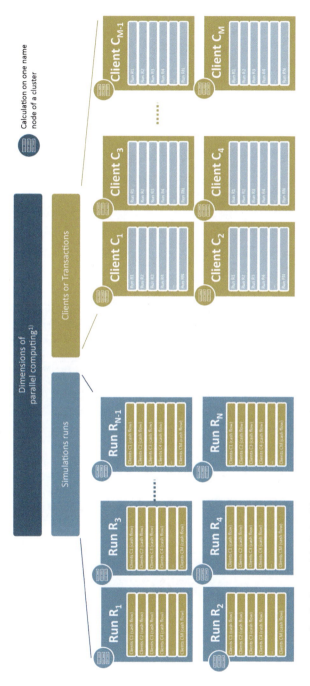

Fig. 4 Natural calculation block building—Variant A (lhs) and Variant B (rhs) (© ifb SE)

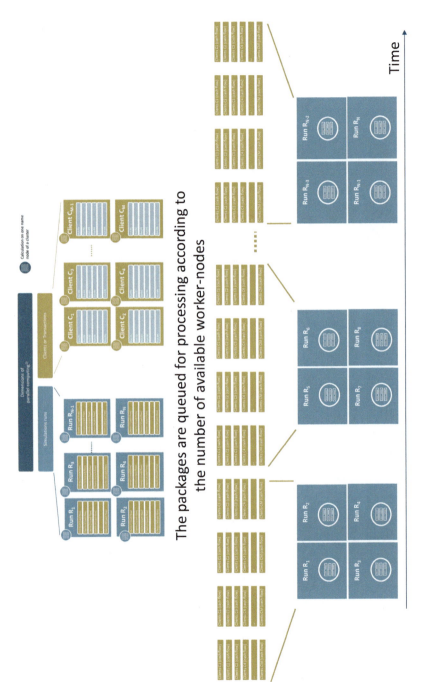

Fig. 5 Overview of queuing for the calculation blocks (© ifb SE)

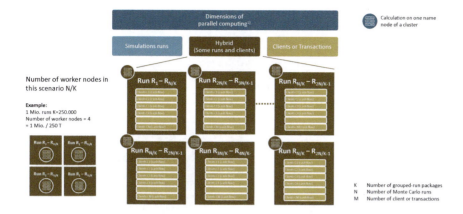

Fig. 6 Hybrid approach to designing the calculation blocks (split by runs)—Variant C (© ifb SE)

client data is the same for each run (and node), the network traffic can be significantly reduced by caching this data in the worker node.[12]

2.3.2 Hybrid Approach to Splitting and Block Building

In Fig. 6, a mixture of the two approaches (from Fig. 4) is shown (Variant C). As in the first approach, all clients are calculated in one block, but, additionally, several runs are put into one block to minimize the network traffic and parallel computational overhead. How big the chosen block can be depends on the size of the calculation node (mainly the RAM of the server).

Although, as shown in Fig. 2, the sum of parameters is of moderate size, the client/transaction-related data (especially the cashflows) can have a significant volume. Therefore, the reduction in network traffic and hence the whole hybrid model can be a key accelerator to improve the overall model (computational) performance.

In Fig. 7, the queuing and distribution of the calculation blocks is shown for the hybrid approach, i.e. Variant C. With this approach (if caching is not used) the network traffic can be reduced, because the client data can be used for multiple runs on a worker node.

The last possible variant to split clients and runs for a parallel computation is shown in Fig. 8. Here, the calculation of one client is split further by calculation runs (Variant D). Again, caching can help to improve the overall

---

[12] Worker node is a common expression in cluster architectures like Hadoop and describes the server (node) doing the bulk of the work (in terms of data or computational power); the counterpart is the master node, which is responsible for overseeing the key operations.

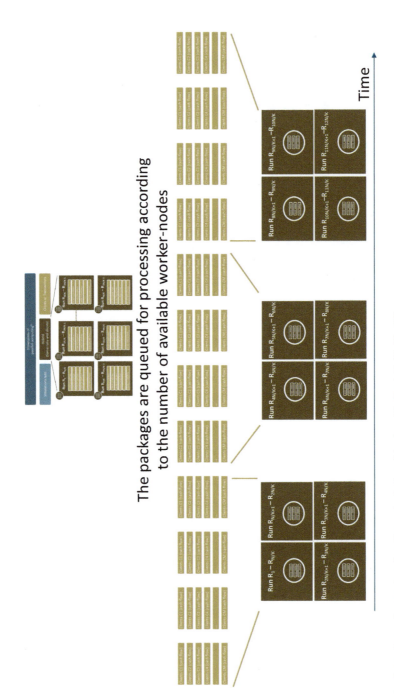

Fig. 7 Overview of queuing for the calculation blocks—Variant C (© ifb SE)

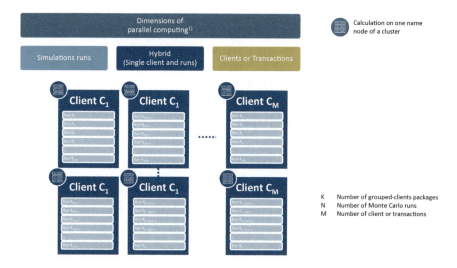

Fig. 8 Hybrid approach to designing the calculation blocks (main split by clients)—Variant D (© ifb SE)

performance of the calculation. In this variant, the run data, such as sector changes, are cached.

The approach in Variant D differs to some extent to Variant C because the clients are split into blocks with only one client and this (one-client block) is then further broken down into a set of runs. In Fig. 8, the breakdown is carried out so that one client is calculated on the full (four-node) cluster.

2.4 Comparison of the Splitting Variants

The implementation of the different splitting approaches is not rocket science. Depending on the portfolio size and the number of simulation runs, the efficiency of the approaches can differ. If the size of the split packages is too small, the cost of the Spark overhead will grow, while if the packages are too big in relation to the node (of the cluster), the cluster node becomes inefficient.

The hybrid approach (see Sect. 2.3.2) offers the highest flexibility in leveraging the computing capacities in relation to the portfolio size and the accuracy (driven by the number of runs).[13]

---

[13] Some of the more technical improvements by Spark parameters are discussed in the following section (Sect. 3.3).

```
conf <- spark_config()
conf$spark.executor.memory <- "1300m"
conf$spark.executor.cores <- 2
conf$spark.executor.instances <- 6
sc <- spark_connect(master = "yarn-client", spark_home = Sys.getenv("SPARK_HOME"), config = conf)
```

Fig. 9 sparklyr configuration (© ifb SE)

3 Distributed Calculation

3.1 Technical Environment

In this section, we provide some numerical results. All the experiments below were performed on a Cloudera server 6.1.1,[14] which hosts an Apache Hadoop distribution. As the calculation engine, we use R, since R provides a number of libraries, where various financial risk models are well implemented. In our experiment, we used the R package CreditMetrics (R Library: CreditMetrics 2015), which contains a set of functions for CreditMetrics.

To connect Spark and R, we used the R package sparklyr (sparklyr: R interface for Apache Spark 2018). This provides an R interface for Apache Spark, including building up and configuring a connection from R to Spark, running R-jobs distributed across Hadoop cluster and accessing machine learning libraries in Spark.

3.2 Configuration in Sparklyr

We need to set up a Spark configuration when connecting to Spark from R. Some of the most useful configuration parameters are listed and explained in the following section (Fig. 9).

- *Spark.executor.cores*: the number of cores to use on each executor
- *Spark.executor.instances*: initial number of executors
- *Spark.executor.memory*: required memory for each executor process

To understand how the requested configuration affected the Spark connection, two examples are provided.

In this example, 4 executors are spawned, and each executor is assigned 2 cores (Fig. 10).

In this example, 5 executors are spawned, and each executor is assigned 2 cores (Fig. 11).

---

[14] CDH 6.1.1: CDH 6.1.1 Release Notes | 6.x | Cloudera Documentation.

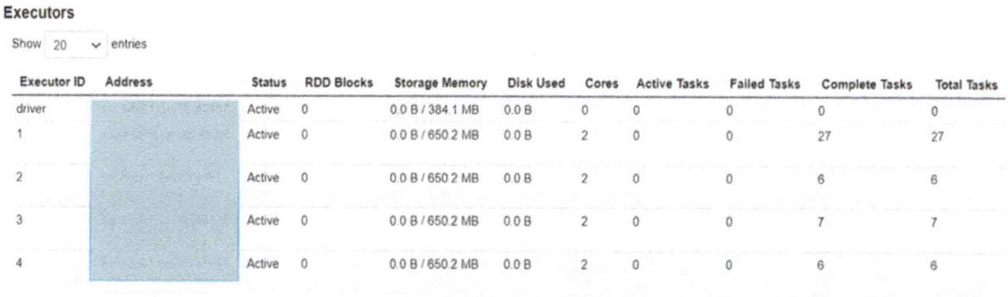
Executors

Show 20 entries

Executor ID	Address	Status	RDD Blocks	Storage Memory	Disk Used	Cores	Active Tasks	Failed Tasks	Complete Tasks	Total Tasks
driver		Active	0	0.0 B / 384.1 MB	0.0 B	0	0	0	0	0
1		Active	0	0.0 B / 650.2 MB	0.0 B	2	0	0	27	27
2		Active	0	0.0 B / 650.2 MB	0.0 B	2	0	0	6	6
3		Active	0	0.0 B / 650.2 MB	0.0 B	2	0	0	7	7
4		Active	0	0.0 B / 650.2 MB	0.0 B	2	0	0	6	6

Fig. 10 Executors in Spark UI: Spark.executor.cores = 2; Spark.executor.instances = 4; Spark.executor.memory = "1500 M" (© ifb SE)

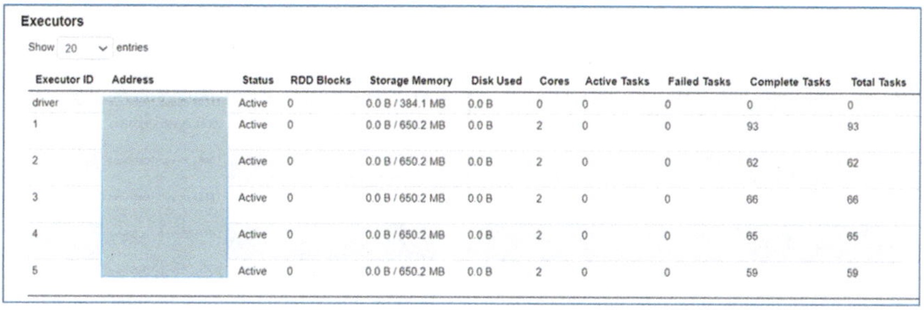
Executors

Show 20 entries

Executor ID	Address	Status	RDD Blocks	Storage Memory	Disk Used	Cores	Active Tasks	Failed Tasks	Complete Tasks	Total Tasks
driver		Active	0	0.0 B / 384.1 MB	0.0 B	0	0	0	0	0
1		Active	0	0.0 B / 650.2 MB	0.0 B	2	0	0	93	93
2		Active	0	0.0 B / 650.2 MB	0.0 B	2	0	0	62	62
3		Active	0	0.0 B / 650.2 MB	0.0 B	2	0	0	66	66
4		Active	0	0.0 B / 650.2 MB	0.0 B	2	0	0	65	65
5		Active	0	0.0 B / 650.2 MB	0.0 B	2	0	0	59	59

Fig. 11 Executors in Spark UI: Spark.executor.cores = 2; Spark.executor.instances = 5; Spark.executor.memory = "1500 M" (© ifb SE)

Note that only 650 Mb are assigned to each executor instead of 1500 Mb requested. This is due to the fixed Spark memory fraction and memory reserved for overhead.

3.3 Data Repartition

When copying a data object into Spark, Spark will partition the data, so it can be distributed within the Hadoop cluster. The number of partitions can be determined by the *repartition* parameter in the function *sdf_copy_to.*

```
# copy data into Spark
mc_tbl <- sdf_copy_to(sc, RunIDs, repartition =12, overwrite = TRUE) #Memory
```

We performed some experiments with a different number of partitions where configuration settings are fixed. Comparing the CPU usage, it is not hard to note that the number of partitions should be chosen appropriately to optimize the CPU distribution. In the examples (a) and (b) shown in Table 1,

Table 1 CPU usage (© ifb SE)

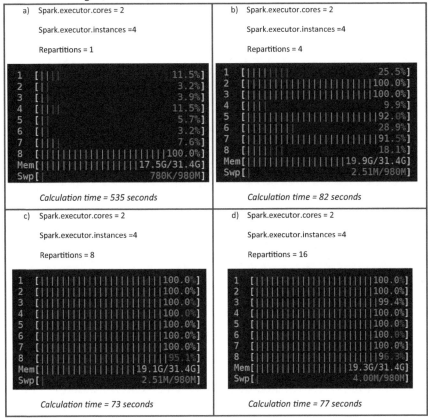

only 1 and 4 CPUs are fully utilized, although 8 cores are allocated (2*4 = 8). The reason for this is the lack of partitions. In contrast to that, there are more partitions than the allocated cores in example (d). Due to the large overhead, the calculation time is longer than in example (c) where the data is partitioned optimally.

3.4 Experimental Result

As we discussed above, we need to set the configuration parameters appropriately to distribute R jobs across the Hadoop cluster optimally. We simulate 10,000 Monte Carlo scenarios for a portfolio of 200 clients under different configuration settings and compare the calculation time against the number of used cores. Note that the calculation time decreases almost linearly and reaches its minimum at around 10 cores (Fig. 12).

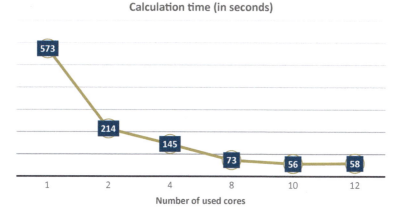

Fig. 12 Calculation performance comparison (© ifb SE)

Table 2 Comparison of splitting variants (© ifb SE)

Splitting Variant	Calculation Time
Variant A	3600 seconds
Variant B	227 seconds
No split/No parallelization	>4000 seconds

In the following table, we compare the two splitting variants introduced in Sect. 2.3, where a portfolio with 16,000 clients is taken and 10,000 Monte Carlo simulation runs are performed for each client.

Recalling Sect. 2.3, the calculation is split by the amount of single Monte Carlo simulation runs in Variant A and by a number of clients in Variant B. The third Variant did not perform any parallel computing. Variant B has the best performance compared to the other two variants, where large overhead is mainly responsible for the additional costs in Variant A, since the whole portfolio has to be "handed over" to each Spark worker (Table 2).

4 Summary

The implementation of a distributed calculation is a feasible task, given the available technology and a smart parallelization.

In credit risk management, the paradigm is shifting from a one-year risk horizon to a multiple-year view (see Liermann and Viets, Predictive risk management 2019). Risk management focuses increasingly on scenario analysis and stress tests as an important risk management method and a tool to handle the uncertainty, complexity and ambiguity (and volatility—VUCA). Giving the method of scenario analysis further growth potential, more and more efficient computing power is required. A Hadoop-like computing cluster—maybe provided by a cloud provider—offers a solution here.

The method of simulation and scenario analysis will become even more feasible with the quantum computer on the horizon (see Nonnenmann und Bogomolec 2021).

Literature

Crouhy, M., D. Galai, R. Mark. 2000. "A Comparative Analyis of Current Credit Risk Models." *Journal of Banking, Finance* 24: 59–117.

Gupton, Greg, Christopher Finger, and Mickey Bhatia. 1997. *CreditMetrics—Technical Document*. New York: J.P.Morgan & Co. Inc.

Koyluoglu, H., Andrew Ugur, and Hickman. 1998. "Reconcilable Differences." *Risk* (Risk), October: 56–62.

Jorion, Philippe. 2006. *Value at Risk: The New Benchmark for Managing Financial Risk* (3rd ed.). McGraw-Hill.

Kealhofer, Stephen. 1998. *Portfolio Management of Default Risk*. San Francisco: KMV Corporation.

Liermann, Volker, and Nikolas Viets. 2019. "Predictive Risk Management." In *The Impact of Digital Transformation and Fintech on the Finance Professional*, edited by Volker Liermann and Claus Stegmann. New York: Palgrave Macmillan.

Liermann, Volker, Iweel Otgontogoo, and Viets Nikolas. 2018. "Immobilienrisiken präventiv analysieren." *RISIKO MANAGER 01|2018*, January: 18–24.

McNeil, Alexander, Rüdiger Frey, and Paul Embrechts. 2005. *Quantitative Risk Management: Concepts Techniques and Tools*. Princeton: Princeton University Press.

Nonnenmann, Peter, and Xenia Bogomolec. 2021. "Quantum Technologies." In *The Digital Journey of Banking and Insurance, Volume II—Digitalization and Machine Learning*, edited by Volker Liermann and Claus Stegmann. New York: Palgrave Macmillan.

R Library: CreditMetrics. 02 2015. https://cran.r-project.org/web/packages/CreditMetrics/CreditMetrics.pdf.

sparklyr: R interface for Apache Spark. 2018. https://spark.rstudio.com/.

Wilde, Tom. 1997. *CreditRisk+ A Credit Risk Management Framework*. Zurich: CSFB.

Wilson, Thomas C. 1997. "Portfolio Credit Risk (I)." *Risk* 9: 111–117.

Wilson, Thomas C. 1997. "Portfolio Credit Risk (II)." *Risk* 10: 56–62.

BSDS: Balance Sheet Dynamics Simulator

Volker Liermann and Harro Dittmar

1 Introduction

The idea of agent-based modeling has a long history. Actor models and graph-theory-oriented algorithms that propagate complex systems of many interacting entities through time have existed for more than half a century (Hewitt 1969). Along with the concept of cellular automata, they emerged as tools for the rather esoteric field of complexity science (Conway 2000). However, this bottom-up approach stayed dormant for a while until it gained popularity in economics. This can be attributed to recent developments in distributed computation, the performance of modern computational infrastructures, the availability of large open-source programming libraries and the growing number of established model references. It is safe to say that ABMs are still the new kid on the block in the model zoo of the financial sector risk manager. Their design as actor models is suitable for a scalable bottom-up approach oriented toward the micro-states and micro-interactions of the participants in a financial system. By design, such models are very flexible regarding successive refinement of the agent behavior.

V. Liermann (✉) · H. Dittmar
ifb SE, Grünwald, Germany
e-mail: Volker.Liermann@ifb-group.com

H. Dittmar
e-mail: Harro.Dittmar@ifb-group.com

The goal of the Balance Sheet Dynamics Simulator (BSDS), the core ideas of which have been described in (Liermann and Dittmar 2021), is to simulate the balance sheet dynamics of banks in a competitive macroeconomic environment. This chapter focuses on technical details of the implementation of the BSDS as an actor-oriented model that uses the Simudyne software development kit[1] and a Hadoop environment for distributed computation.

1.1 Financial Navigator and Other Applications

The BSDS addresses the new transaction development aspects of a stress test. For this purpose, it generates scenarios of the balance sheet development that complement the analysis of risks associated with changes in the balance sheet structure. The BSDS is integrated into the Financial Navigator (see Thiele 2021), a scenario-based credit risk management framework aiming to discover the mid-term impact (3–5 years) of rating changes driven by macroeconomic scenarios on a projected portfolio[2] that has possible applications in planning and controlling.

Recent conceptual improvements in the planning process aim to make the process more dynamic to accelerate the response to changing environments. We refer to this trend as value-driver-oriented planning.[3] Value-driver-oriented planning involves the identification of drivers behind the planning volumes and making them (or more holistically the generated values for the institute) dependent on observable indicators. The first step on the road to a value-driver-oriented planning process is to establish a connection (maybe by using regression models) between the driver and the targeted transaction volume in the balance sheet. This approach is always backward looking and cannot incorporate new trends or behavioral changes. The BSDS predicts possible structural changes. From the results, impulses could be derived to adjust the mechanics connecting the value driver and the projected volumes in the balance sheet.

The BSDS is meant as a prototype for a challenger model for the estimates made by the planning process (conventional or value-driver-oriented). Another application could be asset liability management in banks, especially

---

[1] For details see Simudyne (n.d.).
[2] Actual portfolio plus the simulated new transaction generated by the BSDS.
[3] See Valjanow et al., Digital Planning—Driver-Based Planning Leveraged by Predictive Analytics (2019) and Valjanow et al. (2021).

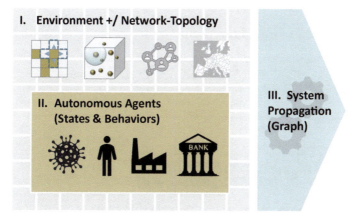

Fig. 1 ABM—essential elements (© ifb SE)

the aspect of the interest rate in the banking book[4] The BSDS presented here is a model state with a reduced functional scope for didactic purposes.

1.2 Structure of the Chapter

This chapter is structured as follows: Sect. 2 describes the basic assumptions and model components, Sect. 3 introduces the technical details of Simudyne's ABM framework and the Hadoop[5] cluster on which the simulation runs are performed, Sect. 4 discusses some preliminary results regarding the calibration of parameters and Sect. 5 gives an outlook for sensible extensions of the model.

2 Model

2.1 Recap: Elements of an Agent-Based Model

Figure 1 shows the essential ingredients that are needed to define an ABM for a specific use case. Those are the agent classes, the environmental definitions and the action sequence that defines the rules for the propagation of the system through time.

---

[4] The regulatory requirements are given by (Basel Committee on Banking Supervision, Interest rate risk in the banking book 2016) and this standard is integrated in 2021 Basel Framework (Basel Committee on Banking Supervision, The Basel Framework 2021).

[5] Hadoop is a specialized computing cluster designed to store and analyze large amounts of unstructured data (for more details see Akhgarnush et al. 2019).

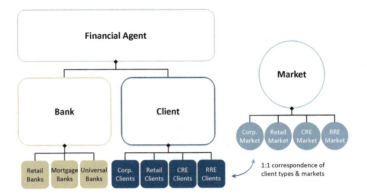

Fig. 2 BSDS—hierarchy of agents in a class diagram (© ifb SE)

Agents are defined as autonomous computational entities that interact with their environment (including other agents). From the technical viewpoint, they are instances of classes with (1) field variables, the values of which represent an agent's state and (2) algorithms that encode their possible actions (behavior). Agents interact by exchanging messages and the behavioral code reacts to those messages by updating the state of the agent. Effectively, agents thereby change states of themselves and induce state changes of other agents.[6]

Obviously, the structure that defines the possible agent interaction as exchange of messages is another essential ingredient of an ABM. It is referred to as topology of the computing graph that specifies the links over which the agents send the information to interact.

While the agent topology defines which agents can interact, the action and messaging sequence defines the order of computational tasks and communication itself. It coordinates the agents' behavior and propagates the system from one time step to the next, with synchronization of the agents' activity status at the end of each time step (see Pregel approach to graph processing [Malewicz et al. 2010]). The following subsections explain these three essential ingredients of an ABM for the specific case of the BSDS.

2.2 Agent Types

The BSDS has three major agent types: banks, clients and markets. Figure 2 shows the corresponding hierarchy of agent classes.

Banks and clients inherit common properties (but no action code) from the financial agent class, such as variables that store their type, ID and a list

---

[6] See mode details in Sect. 3 in (Liermann and Dittmar 2021).

of loan agreements. The bank and client classes differ considerably in their actions: while banks try to grow and establish a certain portfolio structure, clients merely seek a certain total amount of credit depending on individual desired debt ratios and the global macroeconomic situation.

The different subtypes of banks and clients exhibit the same behavior among their subclass, but their algorithms use different parameters: for example, retail banks have a higher contingent for retail clients in their portfolio, and corporate clients apply for loans with longer durations than retail clients.

For each of the four client types, there is one market, reflecting the simplifying assumption that clients apply for only one client-type-specific product and do not seek diversified portfolios. The markets form non-discretionary matches between the individual supplies and demands of banks and clients by combinatorial optimization. The only difference between the markets are their links to other agents, as explained in the following section.

2.3 Environmental Definitions

The environmental definitions of the BSDS do not include any spatial aspects. The topological environment of an agent is defined by the links to the agents it communicates with, as shown in Fig. 3.

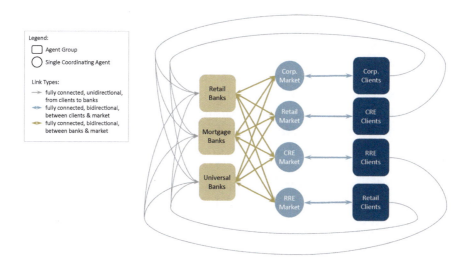

Fig. 3 BSDS—topology of directional communication links between groups of agents (© ifb SE)

The groups of different agent classes are fully connected, reflecting the simplifying assumption that no bank or client has an advantage or disadvantage during the fair and rational matching of supplies and demands that is controlled entirely by the markets. This simple topology corresponds to a world with unrestricted sharing/homogeneous availability of information. Clients and banks both interact with markets to communicate their individual credit supplies and demands, and to receive a response whether a suitable business partner has been found during the matching process (blue and golden arrows in Fig. 3). Since no rating agencies are modeled, clients communicate their current rating information directly to the banks (grey arrows).

Another environmental element is the time series of an exogenous simulation of the macroeconomy, meaning they follow their own, decoupled dynamics that are independent of the agent topology. Macroeconomic parameters can be accessed globally but remain unaffected by the agents. Individual supplies and demands only depend on the current agreements and the exogenous macroeconomy.

The number of agents and their connectivity are kept constant throughout the simulation. At this stage, we do not consider any long-term growth or network dynamic aspects of the system but assume these to be negligible on the time scale of our simulations.

Note that the market agents play a special practical role in this topology: depending on the number of bank client agents and the logic behind the market interactions, the number of messages that must be sent between actors to cover all interactions possible in principle in a fully connected network can be very large. Therefore, it is necessary to reduce this number by introducing "coordinating" agents. Having more than one market increases the efficiency of the overall action sequence by reducing the number of messages that need to be sent between the financial agents: instead of having to process individual communication between all possible ($N_{banks} \cdot N_{clients}$) pairs of banks and clients, markets cache ($N_{banks} + N_{clients}$) messages and process them in one action. In this role, the markets are referred to as "coordinating agents", as they funnel and reduce the flux of information through the system. This improves the performance, if the tasks that need to be done for each pair are not so complex or heterogeneous that they would actually benefit from being processed by financial agents in parallel threads instead of being processed sequentially by a centralized market.

2.4 Sequence of Agent Actions and Messages

The action sequence that propagates the system through time is shown in Fig. 4. It defines the course of actions that are carried out at each time step with a temporal resolution of 1 month. The sequence is repeated iteratively to generate the evolution of bank portfolios over a time span of 36 to 60 months. The colors indicate which agent groups execute the actions described. For example, dark blue action blocks are performed by all members of the four client groups in parallel. Some of the action blocks contain several numbered actions, which are performed one after the other (without needing to be triggered individually). For example, the market begins to match individual supplies and demands after having collected all loan applications and exposure reports. Action blocks are arranged as split blocks or sequence blocks. The actions of a split block start simultaneously, while the actions of a sequence block start successively from left to right.

Each time step starts with client and market actions: clients update their desired debt ratios according to the GDP growth factor and apply for loans that are calculated from this debt ratio, the running loans and their respective client size. Simultaneously, clients send their current ratings to the banks, which then update their desired total exposure and use the latest client ratings to compare their target rating structures with the actual ones according to their current portfolios and their bank-type-specific business models. The resulting exposure gaps translate to the credit supplies that are reported to the four markets. The markets match credit demands and supplies with a parameterized combinatorial optimization algorithm and send response messages

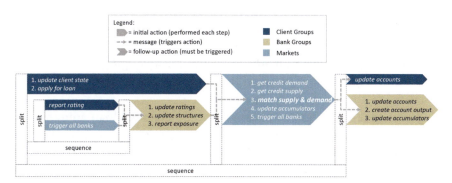

Fig. 4 BSDS—sequence of actions and messages of the actor model. The diagram shows blocks of actions that are executed by all individual members of the corresponding color-coded agent group (© ifb SE)

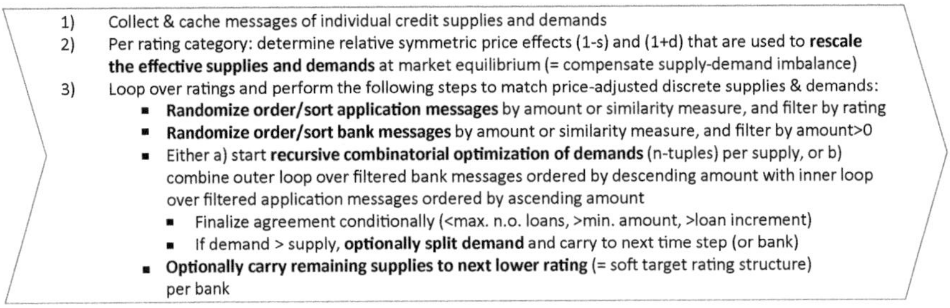

> 1) Collect & cache messages of individual credit supplies and demands
> 2) Per rating category: determine relative symmetric price effects (1-s) and (1+d) that are used to **rescale the effective supplies and demands** at market equilibrium (= compensate supply-demand imbalance)
> 3) Loop over ratings and perform the following steps to match price-adjusted discrete supplies & demands:
>   - Randomize order/sort **application messages** by amount or similarity measure, and filter by rating
>   - Randomize order/sort **bank messages** by amount or similarity measure, and filter by amount>0
>   - Either a) start **recursive combinatorial optimization of demands** (n-tuples) per supply, or b) combine outer loop over filtered bank messages ordered by descending amount with inner loop over filtered application messages ordered by ascending amount
>   - Finalize agreement conditionally (<max. n.o. loans, >min. amount, >loan increment)
>   - If demand > supply, **optionally split demand** and carry to next time step (or bank)
>   - Optionally carry remaining supplies to next lower rating (= soft target rating structure) per bank

Fig. 5 BSDS—outline of the steps performed by the matching algorithm of the markets (© ifb SE)

to the respective counterparties of successful, non-discretionary matches. The logic behind this matching routine (action "3. match supply & demand" in Fig. 4) is outlined in Fig. 5, and parameterized behavior is marked bold.

Note that credit default events are not considered in this model, and cashflows are not modeled as explicit independent action events, but only represented implicitly in pre-defined maturity structures of the exposures. Instead of generating loans in a parametric form that would specify payment schedules, they are generated as complete exposure time series with a client-type-specific static structure. Accordingly, it is instructive to think of the matching mechanism for discrete incongruent amounts as an "exposure Tetris".

2.5 Measures of the Matching Efficiency

Three time-averaged indicators are proposed as measures of the effectiveness of the matching algorithm, or the "performance of the exposure Tetris":

1. E: the total **exposure of banks** to clients in active agreements,
2. L: the average number of actual **loan agreements** per client, which must stay below the pre-defined upper bound,
3. M: the market-averaged ratio of successfully **matched loan amounts** relative to the sum over all requested amounts, ranging from 0 to 100% for complete matching and
4. I: the bank-type-averaged **incongruity of target and actual rating structures**, ranging from 0 for perfect overlap to 1 for complete incongruity.

Using the indices r for rating class, c for client, m for market (equivalent to client type), b for bank and t for bank type, the following formulas can be used to describe the respective contributions per time step:

$$L = \frac{1}{N_{clients}} \cdot \sum_c l_c$$

Equation 1: Average number of actual loan agreements

$$M = \frac{\sum_{c_m}(f_{c_m} \cdot a_{c_m})}{\sum_{c_m} a_{c_m}}$$

Equation 2: Ratio matched loan amounts

$$I = \frac{1}{3} \cdot \sum_t \left(\frac{1}{N_{banks,t}} \cdot \sum_{b_t} \left(\sum_m \sum_r |f_{b_t,m,r} - g_{b_t,m,r}| \right) \right)$$

Equation 3: Averaged incongruity of target and actual rating structures

l_c is the number of loans of client c. a_{c_m} are the individual requested loan amounts of the clients of type m. The multiplicators f_{c_m} that range from 0 to 1 represent the success of individual loan applications considering the possibility that only a fraction of the requested amount was matched as a consequence of splitting it into agreements with multiple banks. $f_{b_t,m,r}$ are the actual fractions of the banks' total exposure in one client type and rating category, and $g_{b_t,m,r}$ are the target fractions according to the bank-type-specific business model.

2.6 Limiting Conditions and Model Parameters

In general, adding complexity to a model complicates the interpretation of simulation results. The more parameters are involved, the less universal the model and the larger the calibration or balancing effort. Table 1 lists essential parameters of the model, grouped by six contexts and categorized either as fixed constants, conditions for the initial state or experimental parameters. The fixed constants correspond to fundamental model assumptions. The initial conditions are parameters that specify limiting conditions for the generation of the artificial initial state (see Sect. 4.1). The experimental parameters can be adjusted in successive experimental simulation that runs to tune the system behavior such that it exhibits non-trivial behavior and mimics trends of real systems.

Table 1 BSDS model parameters (© ifb SE)

Context	Parameter	Value	Type
Unit Conventions	temporal resolution	1 month	fixed constants
	monetary resolution (loan increment)	€1000	
Topology & System Size	number of banks	30	conditions for initial state
	number of clients	761	
	number of markets (equiv. to types of clients/loans)	1	
Credit Demands	client size distribution	GER_2014	
	client rating distribution	uniform	
	client target debt ratio	0.3	
Credit Supplies	target client structure per bank type	case specific	experimental parameters
	target rating structure per bank type		
	desired growth factor per bank type		
Product Parameters	loan duration per client type	case specific	
	payment term per client type		
	min. loan amount per bank type & client type		
Matching Algorithm	max. number of loans per client	see 4.2	
	allow splitting of demands into multiple agreements	yes	
	carry remaining supplies to next lower rating category	no	
	randomize order of individual demands during matching	yes	
	randomize order of individual supplies during matching	yes	

The abbreviation "GER_2014" refers to the income tax distribution according to the German wage and income tax statistics from 2014, which was taken from the Statistisches Bundesamt (Lohn- und Einkommensteuer 2014, Statistisches Bundesamt [Destatis], Artikelnummer: 2140710147005 2018).

3 Technical Implementation

3.1 Technical Scenario

Figure 6 summarizes the core elements of the technical scenario for running the simulations. All mandatory platform and software requirements are shown along with the numbers of compatible versions.

Simudyne offers a software development kit that facilitates the setup of agent-based models and provides a convenient browser-based graphical user interface for the control of simulation runs. Alternatively, simulation runs of a model that has been launched on Simudyne's "Nexus Server" can be controlled via calls to a REST-API. To enable the model to access input data for the initialization of the system from SAP Hana tables, we imported the JDBC source driver recommended by SAP, and to write parquet output to Hive tables, we imported the Apache Hadoop library. The model was

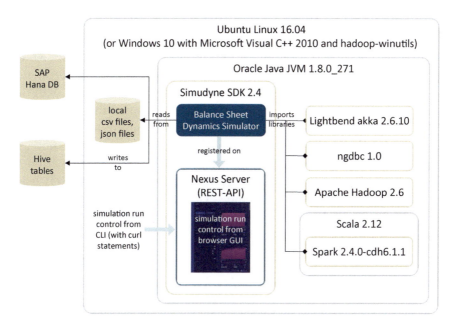

Fig. 6 BSDS—details of the technical implementation and code dependencies (© ifb SE)

programmed in Oracle Java 8 with IntelliJ IDEA that used Maven 3.6.3 for compilation.

3.2 Simudyne

The BSDS was programmed as an actor model using the Simudyne software development kit (SDK) version 2.4, which adopts the Pregel approach to graph processing (Malewicz et al. 2010) and uses Spark as a cluster management tool and Akka to coordinate the actor-based parallel computing (communication between agents). Akka relieves the user from creating the infrastructure for the actor system with the low-level code necessary to control basic behavior that is independent of the use case, such as the synchronization of messages (for further information see Lightbend [n.d.]). A detailed documentation of the Simudyne SDK is available on the website of the vendor (Simudyme n.d.). The supported Spark version depends on Scala 2.12.

3.3 Hadoop Cloudera (Distributed Calculation)

The compiled model was tested in the local Windows 10 environment, which required the installation of Microsoft Visual C++ and hadoop-winutils, and on a Hadoop cluster that runs Ubuntu Linux 16.04, is maintained with the Cloudera manager, and had access to four virtual machines that were rented on the Microsoft Azure cloud. For this article, we only tested the parallel execution of multiple instances of the model itself, which makes the sampling of multiple possible system trajectories scalable. In our continued collaboration with Simudyne we plan to distribute the model graph of the BSDS itself over several machines in the Azure cloud. This will also make the system size scalable so that it will be possible to increase the number of agents to tens of thousands and more.

4 Ergodicity and Preliminary Results

This section discusses first results for one central aspect of the calibration of parameters. When developing a bottom-up model from scratch with parameters and degrees of freedom that are based on pure intuition, it is necessary to balance their influence on the model and check whether they all add value to the model in terms of required complexity and realism. Here, we focus on the calibration of two parameters of the matching algorithm with the goal to increase the effectiveness of the matching algorithm and maintain the ergodic behavior of the system. These two parameters are the influence of the minimum offered loan amount and the maximum allowed number of loans per client. One can also think of an economic interpretation of these parameters: the lower bounds for the loan amounts represent the fact that a loan only becomes attractive once its return is significantly larger than the associated costs. Similarly, the limitation of the number of loans per client can be interpreted as the tolerance of clients toward the burden associated with the administration of multiple accounts.

4.1 Initial States

Figure 7 gives an overview of the input data that is required for the model initialization and the output data that is generated during the simulation run.

For consistency with the assumptions that we have made to simplify the portfolio, it is necessary to generate synthetic loan data that enables the initialization of the model in a corresponding simplified state. For systems

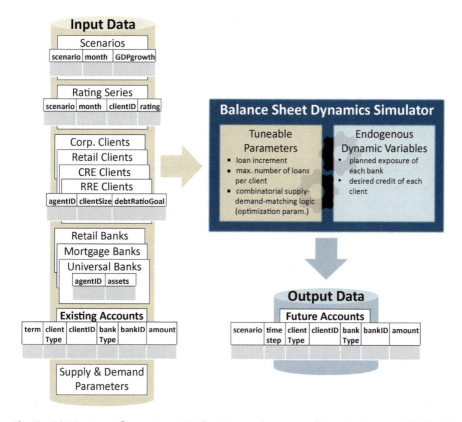

Fig. 7 BSDS—Input for system initialization and output of simulation runs (© ifb SE)

that exhibit a sensitive dependence on initial conditions, picking only one arbitrary artificial initial state might not lead to valid statistical results,[7] which is why it is important to repeat simulation runs starting from an ensemble of independent initial conditions. This gives indications for ergodic system behavior that allows a comparison of time averages instead of ensemble averages (Poitras und Heaney 2015). To compare steady states, one must meet the conditions for mixing that result in ergodic system behavior. This condition for meaningful time-averaged steady-state values also applies to the performance indicators that we use to analyze the matching efficiency.

The initial distribution of remaining terms reflects certain assumptions about the dissipation of the exposure sum over time, which should be generally reproducible by the simulation. This means that an artificial initial state that did not emerge from the model itself must be given the chance to relax to

---

[7] Since the BSDS is still in a developmental stage, we skipped the rigorous analysis of the aspect of ergodicity and merely ensured that the development of the loans "looked chaotic enough".

a steady state in a pre-run with fixed macroeconomy, client ratings and target exposures (see Sect. 4.2). Using such states as a reference, one can attempt systematic studies of stylistic macroeconomic influences on the system.

To test the matching algorithm, the model complexity was reduced by disabling all but the corporate clients. Simulation runs start from a hypothetical initial state with a total of €5.7 trillion in exposures of 30 banks that are distributed among the accounts of 761 clients in such a way that the target rating structures are perfectly matched at the start of the simulation. Accordingly, the initial values of the indicators are $L = 1$ and $I = 0$. The distribution of amounts for the artificial loan data approximates the income distribution according to the German wage and income tax statistics from 2014, which was taken from the Statistisches Bundesamt (Lohn- und Einkommensteuer 2014, Statistisches Bundesamt [Destatis], Artikelnummer: 2140710147005 2018).[8] The creditworthiness (expressed in a credit rating) of the client was taken from a uniform distribution due to the lack of real client data. Further, it was assumed that all target debt ratios lie above the initial debt ratios by 30% to start from a state of excess demand and a busy matching routine.

4.2 Simulation Runs

During the simulation, the exposure sum drops as loans mature and are not fully replaced with new ones. Several factors cause these maturing exposures to give rise to incongruent demands and supplies. Their interplay enables the matching process to introduce the **chaotic mixing of the credit amounts** that are required for aperiodic system behavior and the associated quasi-continuous shifts of exposure distributions:

1. **Asymmetric agent behavior**: There are different conditions for the messaging of loan applications and exposure reports to the markets. Thus, the sum over supplies that have been restored does not equal the sum over demands of clients who reapply with some lag.
2. **Possibility of mismatches** or sub-optimal matches of the discrete amounts per time step: The association of loan amounts with bank–client pairs changes during the simulation. Also, there is the possibility to split demands and match them with supplies from multiple banks.

---

[8] The loan amount distribution, annual return distribution and private income distribution are different things, but the reasonable assumption that their shapes have similar features suffices for a proof of concept.

3. **Discretization of loan amounts**: There is a minimum loan increment and a minimum amount below which applications are not accepted.
4. **Iterative approximation of target exposure structures**: Restored supplies are redistributed over client type and rating categories to approximate/stay near the exposure structure of the business model.

The price adjustment that is applied to compensate for the difference between total demand and total supply in each time step introduces further deviation from the initial equality of total supplies and demands. Considering all these cutting and scaling elements of one iteration, chaotic mixing seems like a reasonable assumption, underpinned by the evolution of the total exposure in the system as shown in Fig. 8.

Due to the remainder of mismatched supplies and demands, the value of E drops below its initial value and fluctuates around steady-state levels that reflect the matching efficiency. Table 2 shows how all four proposed indicators of the matching efficiency change when

Fig. 8 BSDS—evolution of the total exposure in the system in a pre-run over 500 iterations. On the left side, the number of loans per client is limited to a maximum of 5, on the right side to a maximum of 20 (© ifb SE)

Table 2 BSDS results for the efficiency of the matching algorithm (gold columns) at different combinations of parameters (blue columns). The indicators were averaged in the steady states that were reached after 250 iterations (© ifb SE)

N_{max}	A_{min} (€M)	$E(€T)$	L	M	I
5	1	4.8	5.3	100%	0.11
10	1	5.0	9.7	100%	0.10
15	1	5.4	14.0	100%	0.06
20	1	5.4	17.0	100%	0.06
50	1	5.7	17.7	80%	0.04
20	50000	5.6	14.1	80%	0.06
20	500000	5.0	4.9	50%	0.12
20	5000000	2.6	0.3	10%	0.94

A. the number of loans at which clients stop applying, N_{max}, is increased from 5 to 20 and
B. the minimum accepted loan amount, A_{min}, is increased from 1 thousand to 5 billion euros.[9]

For small N_{max}, there were not enough successful matches per time step, which prevented efficient mixing and left periodic patterns in the exposure structures that would not dissipate on a reasonable time scale (limited system size artifacts). Consequently, no steady state was established that would allow the exploration of comparably subtle effects of macroeconomic scenarios. However, allowing clients to satisfy their demands with a larger number of individual agreements eliminated this effect and the system reached a steady state within less than 250 iterations, in which the total exposure did not drop much below its initial €5.7T.[10]

The increase of A_{min} shows that a good approximation of the rating structure of the business model was still possible with clients (groups) that apply for loan amounts of at least €50000M. That means, on the stylized scales and under the assumptions of our model, it would not have an adverse effect on the portfolio planning of the banks if they were to ignore loan requests below €50000M. Increasing the minimum loan amount above this value had the undesirable effect that it excluded a significant portion of applications from the matching. Consequently, M decreased, I increased and L dropped.

When the matching did not use random combinations of demands and supplies, but performed a combinatorial optimization of successive demand triples that leave the smallest gap when filling up the supplies, a higher total exposure of €5.69T could already be reached at $N_{max} = 20$. However, this also introduced an ordering effect that caused a periodic evolution of M and a significant increase of the averaged rating incongruity I to 0.21. That means if the market uses this mechanism to yield the best coverage of the desired exposure, more banks need to be flexible to deviate from their target rating structure.

---

[9] Note that the clients' demands were scaled up to account for the unnaturally large ratio of the number of bank agents to the number of client agents that was used to boost the performance of these preliminary tests. To compensate for this imbalance, clients apply for very high loan amounts ranging from about €5M to €5B.

[10] The fraction of matched demands per time step, M, decreases to some extent, because the fluctuation of the individual amounts of supply and demand becomes larger relative to the amounts that have not been matched in previous steps.

5 Summary and Outlook

5.1 Summary

In this chapter, we presented a prototype for an agent-based model that simulates how the balance sheets of banks adapt to changes in the environment, as represented by macroeconomic parameters that are linked to client ratings. These environmental changes act as boundary conditions of a matching algorithm that re-allocates credit supplies among a constant set of clients by performing a simple "exposure Tetris". A combinatorial optimization algorithm matches individual credit supplies and demands under the influence of macroeconomic effects, causing the rating structures of the predicted portfolios to adapt.

Our results show how important it is to tune parameters in the context of simplifying assumptions. For example, for the high ratio of bank to client numbers that results from limiting the total number of agents, one also needs to allow more loans per client, N_{max}, to enter a regime in which the system behaves more naturally. A sensible economic interpretation is that we effectively consider client groups and not individual clients. The parameters of the matching algorithm define its efficiency, which could be successfully monitored by measures like the achieved total exposure in the system and the average incongruence of actual and target rating structures of the bank portfolios. Due to the small size of the system of under 800 agents, changing the parameters N_{max} and A_{min} also had a significant influence on mixing properties and thus on the fundamental system behavior. It is therefore a necessary step to make the system large enough and find regimes in which a limiting behavior with smoother amount distributions is established. This will make it possible to study more subtle aspects such as disruptive changes of client ratings.

5.2 Reasonable Model Extensions

With our future efforts we wish to reproduce real trends and aid the identification and optimization of systemic (model-level) parameters that can be used to find the best compromise between reaching the target exposure and maintaining the target rating structure in different macroeconomic scenarios. As the calibration and balancing of model parameters progresses, we hope to reproduce trends that can be expected in real bank portfolios. This will allow us to explore how different macroeconomic scenarios affect the deviation of the actual rating structures of bank portfolios from their business model, and which business models are the most resilient or competitive ones in different scenarios. Thanks to the flexibility of the ABM design, the adaptation of ideas for the elaboration of the model is straightforward to implement into the code without compromising the existing elements. Some of our planned investigations are:

- Reduce limited size effects by increasing the number of clients to ensure strong chaotic mixing that facilitates the evaluation of steady-state properties,
- Generate artificial client and account data with more realistic features regarding the distribution of ratings and loan amounts among the clients per client type,
- Define rules for partially connected network topologies with additional markets that limit the bank–client pairs that are available for matching: this will enable a better compromise between fully informed coordinating agents and high parallelization of matching processes and
- Incorporate rating models that are coupled to the system evolution and enable a dynamic client set (spawning of new competitors and deleting of defaulted client agents).

Of course, one must always consider whether such extensions of the complexity also require additional real data and complicate the calibration of parameters, and whether additional simplifying assumptions are compatible with those that have already been made.

Literature

Akhgarnush, Eljar, Lars Broeckers, and Thorsten Jakoby. 2019. "Hadoop—A Standard Framework for Computer Clusters." In *The Impact of Digital Transformation and Fintech on the Finance Professional*, edited by Volker Liermann and Claus Stegmann. New York: Palgrave Macmillan.

Basel Committee on Banking Supervision. 2016. *Interest Rate Risk in the Banking Book*. Basel: Basel Committee on Banking Supervision.

———. 2021. January 22. Accessed January 30, 2021. https://www.bis.org/basel_framework/.

Conway, John. 2000. *On Numbers and Games*. New York: CRC Press.

Hewitt, Carl. 1969. "PLANNER: A Language for Manipulating Models and Proving Theorems in a Robot." *IJCAI'69: Proceedings of the 1st International Joint Conference on Artificial Intelligence*, May: 295–301.

Liermann, Volker, and Harro Dittmar. 2021. "BSDS—Balance Sheet Dynamic Simulator (Application ABM)." In *The Digital Journey of Banking and Insurance, Volume I—Disruption and DNA*, edited by Volker Liermann and Claus Stegmann. New York: Palgrave Macmillan.

Lightbend. n.d. *Getting Started Guide.* Accessed December 15, 2020. https://doc.akka.io/docs/akka/2.6/guide/.

———. 2018. *Lohn- und Einkommensteuer 2014, Statistisches Bundesamt (Destatis), Artikelnummer: 2140710147005.* Statistisches Bundesamt.

Malewicz, Grzegorz, Matthew Austern, Aart Bik, James Dehnert, Ilan Horn, Naty Leiser, and Grzegorz Czajkowski. 2010. *Pregel: A System for Large-Scale Graph Processing.* Google.

Poitras, Geoffrey, and John Heaney. 2015. "Classical Ergodicity and Modern Portfolio Theory." *Chinese Journal of Mathematics*, February 6: 1–17.

Simudyme. n.d. *Simudyme.* Accessed December 15, 2020. https://portal.simudyne.com.

———. n.d. *Welcome to the Age of Simulation.* Accessed December 15, 2020. https://www.simudyne.com/.

Thiele, Markus. 2021. "Financial Navigatorc—A Modern Approach to Analytical Banking." In *The Digital Journey of Banking and Insurance, Volume I—Disruption and DNA*, edited by Volker Liermann and Claus Stegmann. New York: Palgrave Macmillan.

Valjanow, Simon, Philipp Enzinger, Daniel Suttner, and Maik Alexander Schmidt. 2021. "Value-Driver-Oriented Planning—Management-Oriented Design and Value Driver Identification." In *The Digital Journey of Banking and Insurance, Volume I—Disruption and DNA*, edited by Volker Liermann and Claus Stegmann. New York: Palgrave Macmillan.

Valjanow, Simon, Philipp Enzinger, and Florian Dinges. 2019. "Digital Planning—Driver-Based Planning Leveraged by Predictive Analytics." In *The Impact of Digital Transformation and Fintech on the Finance Professional*, edited by Volker Liermann and Claus Stegmann. New York: Palgrave Macmillan.

Dynamic Dashboards

Volker Liermann and Sangmeng Li

1 Introduction

1.1 Initial Situation

The frequency with which the surroundings change and sure-fire assumptions implode is at an all-time high these days. Even if we feel like we live in an ever-faster moving world, the speed of change has increased in recent years. Linear projections of the future or historical data-based continuation will fail in most circumstances. Nonetheless, in the banking and insurance sector, management without any kind of crystal ball will be even more challenging.

On the other hand, the availability of computational power and the cheap (and in the case of open source almost free) availability of software opens a window of incredible opportunities. Cloud-available computational resources and open source enable financial management departments (planning, controlling and risk management) to produce individual scenarios and their impact on the business, the business development and many aspects of

---

V. Liermann (✉) · S. Li
ifb SE, Grünwald, Germany
e-mail: Volker.Liermann@ifb-group.com

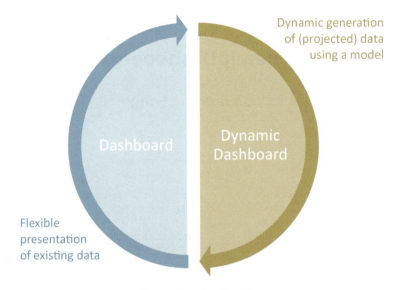

Fig. 1 Definition dynamic dashboarding (© ifb SE)

the projected future of the enterprise[1] (profits, risk situation or even the ESG state[2]).

The capabilities to visualize complex connections and links have also improved, not least due to open-source frameworks (e.g. D3[3] or others). The user appetite has moved from pure text and figures, to graphical representation, to interactive information visualization.[4]

When we put the three things above together (business needs, computational availability and new graphical representations) we end up at dynamic dashboarding. Dynamic dashboarding is another example of business requirements and technology enabling new ways for users to do things.

1.2 Definition—Dynamic Dashboarding

The term "dashboarding" is widely used in the reporting and business intelligence context. Often, the term dashboarding is used when data is sliced, diced and reorganized by the user. The accentuation here is on the fact that the user can compose the (existing or already calculated) data on the fly (Fig. 1).

---

[1] For projection of the risk situation see (Liermann and Viets, Predictive Risk Management 2019).
[2] The state in which an enterprise positions itself regarding environmental, social and governance aspects (ESG).
[3] D3 "Data-Driven Documents", see (Bostock et al. 2011) or (Bostock 2019).
[4] Which could even include AR (augmented reality) and VR (virtual reality).

We would like to establish the term "dynamic dashboarding" for the presentation of a dynamically model-based generated data (the model can be calibrated in a preceding step). Often, the data generated is a projection of future data (of key figures) based on selected scenarios.

In traditional scenario analysis, management (or the controller/risk manager) defines a set of relevant scenarios (narrative), which are then transformed[5] into the impact on key figures or the projections of key figures over time.

The precondition for a dynamic dashboard is that the whole transformation process can be implemented without any manual steps (besides parametrization). The way the model calculates the prediction is not restricted. The type can range from basic arithmetic operations (e.g. linear extension[6]), to traditional time series models (like ARIMA,[7] if the requirements for stationarity are met), to deep learning models (like RNN[8]).

1.3 Structure of the Article

Section 2 outlines the need for dynamism. In Sect. 3, example use cases are described. An overview of the technical tools is provided in Sect. 4, including a brief discussion of the advantages and challenges of the different tools. Section 5 summarizes all aspects and provides an outlook.

2 Reporting Demands in a Dynamic World

2.1 Why We Must Be Dynamic

The world is in a permanent state of change and this change is the only thing that is stable. The term describing the state of the world best is VUCA.[9] The uncertainty of our dynamic surroundings confronts us with the need to handle and reduce this uncertainty. We can try to derive and define narratives

---

[5] The transformation process often includes manual steps.

[6] Often used in planning processes, if the institute is not using value-driver-oriented planning (see Valjanow et al. 2019).

[7] Auto-Regressive Integrated Moving Average (for an introduction see Shumway and Stoffer (2017) or Box et al. (2016).

[8] Recurrent neural network (for an introduction see Sect. 3.2 in [Liermann et al., Deep Learning—An Introduction 2019]).

[9] VUCA is an acronym which stands for "volatility", "uncertainty", "complexity" and "ambiguity". The term was first used by the U.S. military—United States Army War College (USAWC) see U.S. Army Heritage and Education Center (2019).

and extrapolate their (negative) impact (this is the way good stress testing is done). If we have a good understanding of the environment, we can develop a model to predict the impact.

The changes of the world can be of two different natures: (A) the model mechanics must be adapted and (B) the dynamics in the parameter need to be adjusted.[10] The first point is always linked with structural change (which can be applied within a day or even hours if the right infrastructure is provided – > data scientist workplace and Financial Navigator). The second point can be realized within seconds, depending on the complexity of the model and the chosen computational architecture (see Liermann et al., Distributed Calculation Credit Portfolio Models 2021).

The proposed changes in the infrastructure can shift the baselines for banks and insurance companies. Today, most institutes need one day to recalculate the models with adjusted parameters, and it takes them several days (if not weeks) to adopt the model mechanics.

2.2 Risk Reporting

Daniel Kahneman introduced two ways of thinking and decision-making (see Kahneman 2011). System 1 is fast, intuitive and emotional; System 2 is slower, more deliberative and more logical. The way risk management reporting is used by senior management has certain similar patterns.

Senior management is confronted with a wide array of figures embedded in numerous reports. The reports include sensitivity analyses, historical developments and scenario-based stress tests. The challenge in good risk reporting lies beyond these topics. Sensitivity analyses are important, but in most cases one dimensional. Historical developments are by nature past-oriented and, even if they are applied to the actual portfolio,[11] they lag behind in the future projection of unseen effects (the U in VUCA). Stress tests at best have a narrative and translate the story into stressed parameters, and they calculate the impact on P&L[12] or the risk situation (expressed by KRI[13]). But stress test reporting is restricted to the narrative scenarios. Anything beyond the sensitivity analysis and the specific stress scenario needs to be extrapolated by management (in terms of Kahneman System 1 thinking). This intuitive reading between

---

[10] Sometimes, the adaptation leads to the simultaneous changing of a combination of parameters.
[11] Like in the historical simulation in the Value at Risk.
[12] Profit and loss.
[13] Key risk indicators.

the lines is fast and gives us an experience-based impression of the situation, but Kahneman has shown us the drawbacks of System 1.

How could a System 2 look for risk management reporting? Dynamic dashboarding is the answer.

When we talk about really dynamic dashboards, we have a slider where we change a parameter and see the changes to the key figures relevant to our decision immediately. Our System 1 is therefore no longer needed and is replaced by a more logical and model-based decision support.

2.3 Exploring Sensitivity and Combined Parameter Shifts

The dynamic dashboard is a well-accepted tool for visualizing complex relationships. In addition, the dynamic dashboard idea has two major achievements: (A) The opportunity to interactively explore (and to experience[14]) the sensitivity of model parameters or market data shifts. (B) The possibility to explore the model dimensions in a simultaneous shift of two or more model parameters. Both aspects leverage the fact that on top of the actual data a model is projecting data in multiple dimensions (e.g. time, transaction scenarios, market data scenarios or model parameter scenarios).

Aspect (A) focuses on the experience for a user and the haptics of the dynamic dashboard. It is a different way of exploring a model by moving sliders and seeing how the figure and graph change, or writing down the number for the first derivation of a model for a specific parameter. The latter way is more analytical and addresses analytical skilled persons. The first way offers a more intuitive access to the model.

The multi-dimensional sensitivity analysis can be performed analytically by combined derivation. But shifting a parameter might cause a different position in the model space and thus change the sensitivity (even given only two dimensions the generated figures are beyond the capabilities of figure- or graph-based reporting). By using dynamic dashboards to explore the two or more model dimensions (aspect B), this issue is solved. The sliders can move around the model space. If the user finds a situation they want to examine in more detail, they can use the various sliders to perform their analysis (following the idea of aspect A).

---

[14] If you have tried out a dynamic dashboard, you will agree that moving a slider is a different experience to just entering figures. It has a haptic component.

2.4 Inverse Stress Test

The goal of an inverse stress test is to uncover unrecognized sources of danger that could endanger the existence of the company. To achieve this, inverse stress tests must identify events that could jeopardize the survival of the institutions.

The same idea as in the previous Sect. (2.3) can be used to perform an inverse stress test.[15] By simultaneously shifting different parameter sliders, the risk manager can analyze the impact of the parameter shifts. In the inverse stress test, the risk manager looks for combinations that put the existence of the company at risk.

For example: When a bank is below a BBB rating, the bank is not bankrupt, but the refinancing costs could be far above the refinancing costs of its peer group, meaning that the bank could no longer offer competitive prices. This state could be the result of a single event (e.g. default of the biggest client) or a combination of a number of events (e.g. default of the eighth and ninth biggest clients in combination with an interest rate shock of 100 BP).

Dynamic dashboards are an ideal tool to discover such "near death experiences" of an institute. Even though there are tools to discover all scenarios that jeopardize the existence of the company, in practical risk management it is easier to focus on a small number of scenarios to be communicated to senior management.

3 Use Cases for Dynamic Dashboards

3.1 Use Case—Client Interface: Portfolio Manager Dashboard

3.1.1 Purpose of the Portfolio Manager Dashboard

Asset managers (especially wealth managers in banks[16]) negotiate detailed investment strategies and boundaries to achieve the risk-return profile requested. A very common boundary is to set limits by asset class. An example of an actual portfolio composition is shown in Fig. 2.

---

[15] Inverse stress tests (or reverse stress tests) first became popular after the financial crisis in 2008/09 and have found their way into the standard risk management toolset (for details see Liermann and Klauck, Verbessertes Risk Management: Banken im Stresstest 2009; Grundke 2011).

[16] The use case can be extended to asset managers for banks and insurers.

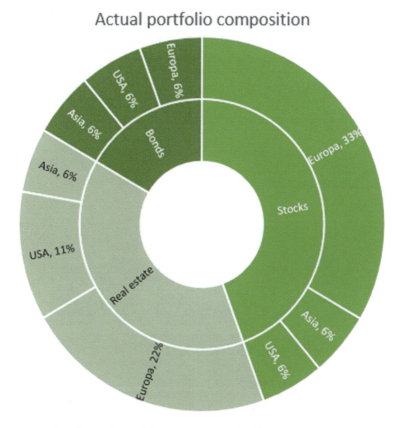

Fig. 2 Example of actual portfolio composition (© ifb SE)

Table 1 Example limit structure (© ifb SE)

		Max %	Max %
Real estate	Europa	33	50
	USA	33	
	Asia	33	
Stocks	Europa	33	50
	USA	33	
	Asia	33	
Bonds	Europa	10	30
	USA	10	
	Asia	10	

In order to keep the requested risk profile, limits (in the simplest form as volume limits) are set for the clusters of the asset universe (example in Table 1).

Table 2 Limit usage in t_0 (© ifb SE)

	Actual Value	Limit	
	portfolio portion in t_0 (%)	Asset class (%)	Limit usage (%)
Real estate	39	50	78
Stocks	44	50	89
Bonds	17	30	56

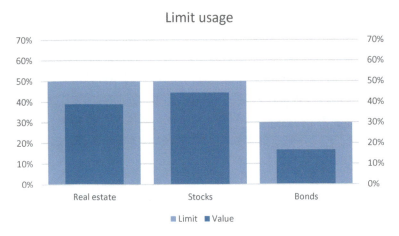

Fig. 3 Limit usage in t_0 (© ifb SE)

The actual structure can change due to changes in the portfolio value (driven by market deployments) and the portfolio compositions (driven by buying and selling assets). The asset manager client dashboard aims to anticipate the portfolio value structure for future periods driven by assumed value driver developments. The dashboard can simulate the development due to market impacts and the response by the asset manager (or the client) to stay within agreed boundaries.

Figure 3 and Table 2 show such a limit structure and the corresponding usage of the limits today (in t_0).

3.1.2 Goal and Aim of the Asset Manager Client Dashboard

The goal of the asset manager client dashboard is to anticipate the impact of market changes on the limit structure given by an investment guideline. This impact anticipation can help to transform the portfolio in an early stage and smoothen the regrouping process in order to meet the given investment guideline.

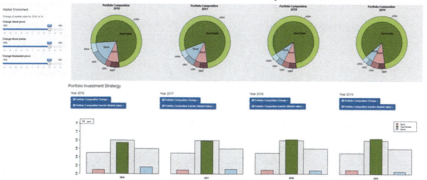

Fig. 4 Shiny dashboard: portfolio manager dashboard (© ifb SE)

The implemented sliders can use real-world observable figures (which directly affect the asset value, such as interest rates, credit spreads, FX rates or stock prices) as well as detected value drivers (see Valjanow et al. 2019; Liermann und Viets, Predictive Risk Management 2019) for a general overview of the concept of value-driver-driven planning and prediction).

3.1.3 Example Implementation in R Shiny Implementation in R Shiny

We provide a dashboard example implemented by using R Shiny. Both visualizations on the right-hand side illustrate the development of portfolio value and composition, where the portfolio limit is fixed as the shadow in the histogram. In the top left panel "Market Environment", various market driver scenarios can be selected by using sliders, and the driver changes are relative and yearly (Fig. 4).

The drop-down menus in the middle of dashboards allow users to correct or determine the financial investment strategy by selling, buying or transferring financial instruments, for a particular business year (Fig. 5).

3.1.4 Example Implementation in MicroStrategy

We implement the same dashboard by using MicroStrategy Dossier. Three sliders are set at the top, where the impact of market drivers is selected. The visualizations below show the portfolio value and decomposition development from 2016 to 2020, where the portfolio limit is marked as the red dotted line in the histogram. Note that we do not have an investment strategy menu here, since MicroStrategy Dossier does not provide such

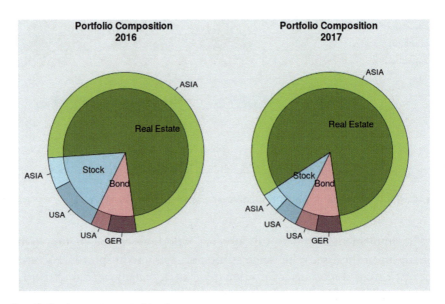

Fig. 5 Shiny dashboard: portfolio manager dashboard: drop-down menus (© ifb SE)

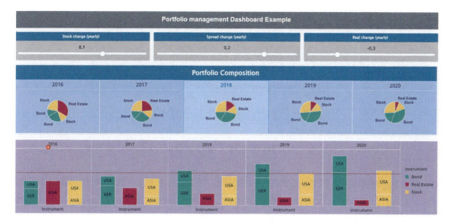

Fig. 6 MicroStrategy dashboard: portfolio manager dashboard (© ifb SE)

features, but we will discuss in the next section how MicroStrategy Dossier is developer-friendly and most of the customizing can be done by "dragging and dropping" (Fig. 6).

3.2 Use Case—Impairment Projection

One of the many examples of accounting and risk management becoming more dynamic and more future-oriented is the IFRS 9 impairment calculation update from 2014 (see IASB 2014). IFRS 9 Phase 2 introduces a calculation update, differentiating between three stages and two methods of calculating the expected loss of a financial asset.

Most of the financial assets are assigned to stage 1 and the impairment allowance is measured by the credit losses from default events expected over the next 12 months (in a present value view). The second stage contains assets with "significant increase in credit risk" (SICR) and are measured by a lifetime expected loss.[17] The third stage contains all defaulted assets. The calculation is analogous to the stage 2 assets.

This improvement in the impairment estimation brings a dynamic component in the providing of credit losses. As this is an important factor in the P&L, a simulation of this factor is an interesting task for bank management.[18]

---

[17] The lifetime expected loss is the (present) value of the potential credit loss over the full term of the asset.

[18] In the US Gaap with CECL (Current Expected Credit Losses) 2016 improvements, the P&L becomes even more dynamic, because (to simplify a bit) CELC is like IFRS 9 just without a stage 1 (the lifetime expected loss has to the calculated for all assets).

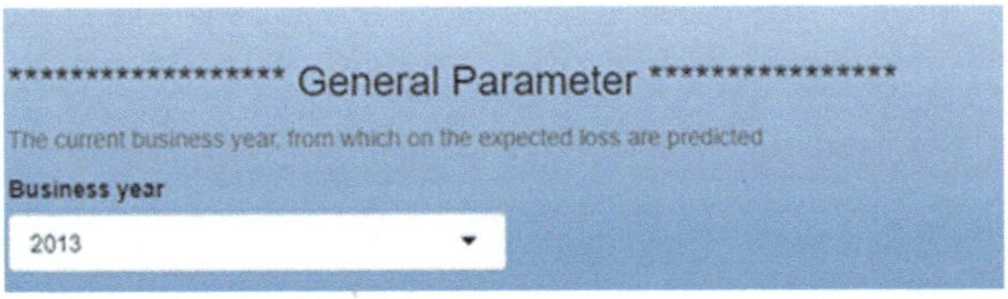

Fig. 7 Impairment projection dashboard: business year (© ifb SE)

3.2.1 Purpose of the Impairment Projection Dashboard

The development of the creditworthiness of clients is correlated with macroeconomic and sector-specific developments. As the 12-month and the lifetime expected loss are driven by the probability of default, there is a strong connection between macroeconomic and sector-specific developments and the impairment.

The impairment projection dashboard uses the statistically verifiable connection between the GDP[19] (as an expression of macroeconomic development) to simulate the impact on the impairment value changes. This includes the jumps from stage 1 to stage 2, which can have a significant impact in a mild recession.

3.2.2 Example Implementation in R Shiny

In the first block, the current business year needs to be chosen. The probability of default and expected loss will be predicted from this year on. In this example, the business year is set to 2013 (Fig. 7).

The dashboard consists of two analytical parts. In the first part, we model the relationship between PD (probability of default) and macroeconomic factors by using linear regression, where the macroeconomic factors themselves are treated as time series and modeled by using ARIMA models. Here, two macroeconomic factors, the growth of GDP and unemployment rate, are used. Since the current business year is set to 2013, the prediction is made for 2014, 2015 and 2016 and the predicted values are marked in red (Fig. 8).

Note that, in the left-hand box, we can manipulate the value of macroeconomic factors for years 2012 and 2013 (the blue squares). After the manipulation of historic values, the ARIMA and linear regression models are retrained, and predictions are recomputed. In the example below, we adjust the GDP growth to be closer to zero. Under this impact, the predicted probability of default grows (Fig. 9).

---

[19] GDP—Gross domestic product.

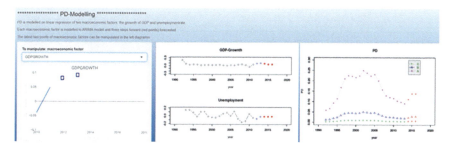

Fig. 8 Impairment projection dashboard: PD modeling (© ifb SE)

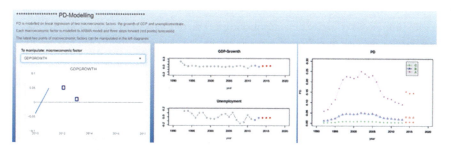

Fig. 9 Impairment projection dashboard: PD modeling under the GDP impact (© ifb SE)

In the second analytical part, the expected loss is forecast for the years 2014, 2015, and 2016 based on the predicted probability of default as above. It is possible to switch between different regulatory standards and choose the cute rate (re-default rate) between impairment levels. The portfolio holding structure and the loss given default can be set by turning the knob buttons in the sidebar (Fig. 10).

In the following example, we increase the loss given default to 0.77. Unsurprisingly, the predicted expected loss also increases since the expected loss is linearly dependent on the loss given default. Here, we assume that the loss given default is constant from year to year (Fig. 11).

In the last example, we increase the (absolute) weight of credits from rating class "A". Since the "good" credit component accounts for a larger portion, the predicted expected loss gets smaller (Fig. 12).

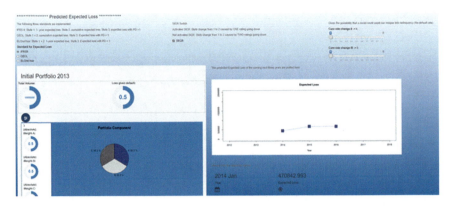

Fig. 10 Impairment projection dashboard: predicted expected loss (© ifb SE)

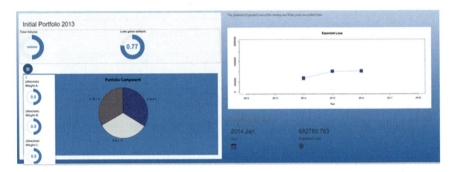

Fig. 11 Impairment projection dashboard: predicted expected loss under increased LGD (© ifb SE)

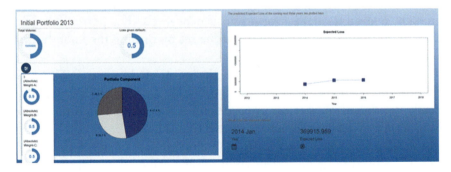

Fig. 12 Impairment projection dashboard: predicted expected loss under modified portfolio components (© ifb SE)

3.3 Use Case—Intraday Liquidity Stress Test

The use case for an intraday liquidity stress test is described in Sect. 2 of (Liermann et al., Intraday Liquidity—Forecast Using Pattern Recognition 2019). A lean description is offered in Sect. 4.1 of this chapter.

3.4 Use Case—Integrated Stress Test

The integrated stress test is a risk management method to simulate and aggregate the impact of significant changes in the surroundings of an institute. Usually, the stress scenario parameters are derived from a narrative regarding the sustainable changes in the market and client environment. The scenario parameters thus derived are then applied to the risk estimate (left side of Fig. 13) and to the value of the total assets that can be mobilized to cover potential losses (right side of Fig. 13). The risk can be expressed as an aggregated loss distribution for the institute. In standard risk management, the risk manager calculates the 99% quantile to express the risk facing the institution. The integrated stress test addresses the problem from the opposite direction. The integrated stress test calculates the (analytical) probability of

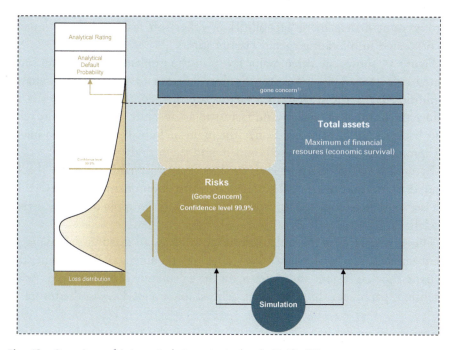

Fig. 13 Overview of integrated stress test—bank (© ifb SE)

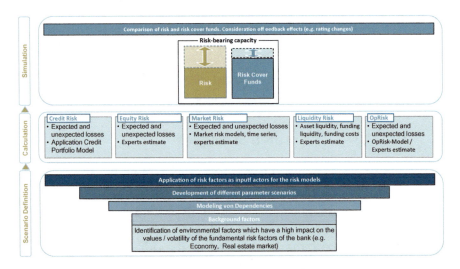

Fig. 14 Integrated stress tests—architecture layers (© ifb SE)

the institute's default by using the total asset value and the loss distribution (the probability is the area of the loss distribution above the value of the total assets).

The analytical default probability can be translated into an analytical rating in the case of the changing surroundings (analytical rating does not take into account management capabilities or other soft factors that are usually incorporated into a rating agency classification).

Figure 14 shows the three major layers in the implementation of an integrated stress test. Data processing is from bottom to top. In the Scenario Definition layer, the background factors are defined. The key aspect is to reduce the number of background factors to an absolute minimum. The relevant background factors could carry the main melody. If there are too many background factors, only noise is added, and the melody will fade.

By modeling the dependencies, the link is established between the background factors and the model parameters (third component of this layer). In the last step, these adjusted (or stressed) parameters are applied to the existing models.

The second layer is the Calculations layer. Here, all existing risk management models are recalculated with adjusted parameters. We assume the scenario shock is instant and the date for the calculation is not changed. As an extension, parameter shifts could be defined for several dates in the future.[20]

---

[20] The Financial Navigator (see Thiele 2021) is an example of this projection of the risk situation. More details of the idea of projecting the risk situation (in the context of financial risk) can be found in (Liermann and Viets, Predictive Risk Management 2019).

The simulation of the changes in the risk and the risk capital and their comparison are located in the third layer. These results can be acknowledged in a feedback loop back to the financial risks (e.g. a change in the bank's rating can impact the liquidity situation and thus the liquidity risk).

4 Tools for Dynamic Dashboards

In this section, we will introduce various developing tools, which are widely used for building and creating dashboards for business intelligence. Some of them are open source, some are not and require licenses. We are going to compare them according to the four aspects below. The Table 3 provides a summary of pros and cons. Further details will be discussed throughout this section.

4.1 Microsoft—Power BI

In 2011, Microsoft extended its reporting services by Power BI. This aims to provide interactive visualizations and business intelligence capabilities. In the vendor comparison reports, such as Gartner or Forrester, Microsoft's BI platform always ranks among the top.

Naturally, Power BI has all standard functionalities required for a classical dashboard. For entering the area of dynamic dashboards, Power BI can offer several methods. The first method is to develop a custom visual. These visuals are available in the visualization panel of both Power BI Desktop and Power BI service, and can be used for creating and editing Power BI content. A tutorial for developing a custom visual can be found in (Microsoft 2020).

Table 3 Pros and cons of tools (© ifb SE)

	Microsoft Power BI	SAP SAC	MicroStrategy	R Shiny
Developer-friendly	✓	✓	✓	✓
Customizing/designing	✓	✓	✓	o
Features and extensions	✓	✓	✓	o
Security and government	✓	✓	✓	✓

Fig. 15 Overview of visuals in Power BI (© ifb SE)

Power BI visuals can be developed in JavaScript or in typescript.[21] A path to quick results is to use D3.js library.[22]

As R and Python are popular for developing models (which is an important part of a dynamic dashboard), we would like to highlight another method to implement a dynamic dashboard in the Power BI platform. Power BI offers the opportunity to embed a "Visual R-script" element and/or "Python visual" element into the reporting canvas (Fig. 15).

In Fig. 16, the power BI Desktop is shown with the example of an intraday stress test dynamic dashboard.[23] On the left side we see a set of sliders:

- Reduction inflow—gives the percentage reduction of the inflows by client,
- Delay—delays the inflows and outflows by hours
- Delay inflow—delays the inflows by hours
- Delay outflow—delays the outflows by hours.

---

[21] TypeScript is a strict syntactical superset of JavaScript and is a proprietary programming language of Microsoft (see Microsoft 2020).

[22] D3.js can produce dynamic, interactive data visualizations in web browsers. It is written in JavaScript (for details see Bostock 2019).

[23] The business requirements of an intraday stress test can be found in Sect. 2 in (Liermann et al., Intraday Liquidity—Forecast Using Pattern Recognition 2019).

Dynamic Dashboards

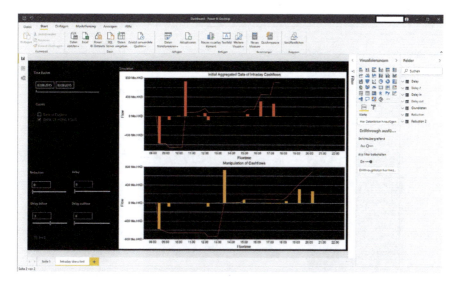

Fig. 16 Example of dynamic dashboard—Power BI (© ifb SE)

In the middle of Fig. 16, the cumulated flow of one day is displayed in the upper part and the impact of the sliders are shown in the lower part. This middle part is implemented by a "Visual R-script" element. The R-script inside the "Visual R-script" element is composed of three parts: (1) converting the data to easily apply the model, (2) applying the model (slider impact) and (3) drawing the graph. The raw data (before manipulation) and the slider value of the Power BI canvas are passed to R using the data.frame type. The possibilities to develop models (or slider impacts) are only restricted by the abilities of R and the available packages.

Figure 17 shows in the lower part an example R script implementing the dynamic dashboard in Power BI.

The same approach can be taken in Power BI for Python and the "Python visual" element.

4.2 SAP—SAC

SAP Analytics Cloud (SAC) is one of the most famous SAP BI solutions, which combines BI, planning, predictive and analytics capabilities into one simple cloud environment. It is powered by a connecting HANA database and provides real-time business analyses. SAC is pre-customized and can be developed easily by drag and drop. Open-source flexibility is particularly beneficial when integrating R visualizations, where the SAC needs to be configured to connect to an R environment. In advance, users may

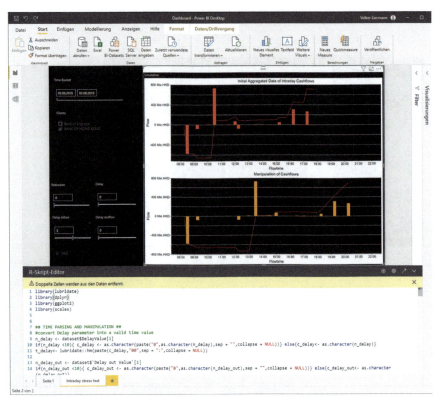

Fig. 17 Power BI including R Script Editor (© ifb SE)

assign roles, security and access permissions based on user types and product features, and this increases the flexibility of SAC to meet various business requirements (Fig. 18).

4.3 MicroStrategy

MicroStrategy Dossier is an interactive display which allows users to quickly and easily visualize various business data. It is pre-customized and formatted for the purpose of business reporting, so that the dashboard can be created easily by drag and drop. In Fig. 19, we provide a screenshot of the MicroStrategy Dossier desktop. The user can pick any dataset attributes from the far-left panel and drop them into the visualization panel in the center. Various visualizations are provided on the right panel and can be switched easily. On the other hand, the pre-formatting means that the features and visualizations are restricted to business reporting and cannot be customized as flexibly as open-source platforms.

Dynamic Dashboards 175

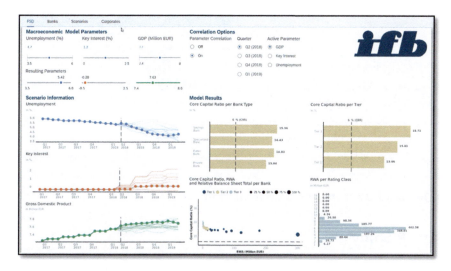

Fig. 18 Example of SAC dashboard (© ifb SE)

Fig. 19 MicroStrategy developing desktop (© ifb SE)

In addition, the dossier can be shared by email, be embedded in a web page or be shared in MicroStrategy Web. MicroStrategy provides data governance, the overall management and integrity of data across the enterprise, with certified dossiers. Documents, reports, datasets and cards can also be certified, so that you can ensure that these objects also comply with your company's data governance policies.

Fig. 20 Word cloud and interactive map (© ifb SE)

4.4 R Shiny

Shiny is an open-source R library that enables building interactive web applications in the R environment. It provides comprehensive features and extensions with high flexibility for designing and customizing visualization. In the following, we provide two examples of visualizations implemented by using the packages *word cloud* and *leaflet*, separately. Further examples are summarized in (R Shiny Extensions) (Fig. 20).

Shiny applications can be deployed to server or cloud. R provides RStudio Connect, which is a platform for publishing Shiny applications. It allows users to share dashboards, security policies and scheduled execution of reports for business purposes.

In addition, the library is constantly updated, improved and expanded as more people can work on its improvement. However, as with other open-source software, the development of Shiny applications is script-based and requires basic programming and debugging knowledge in R. In the following figure, we provide the code script for a simple Shiny dashboard with one slider for input and one histogram visualization (Fig. 21).

4.5 Python—Plotly and Dash

In Python, the most common way to implement a dashboard is by using plotly.py[24] and dash.[25] Plotly was originally developed in Python and

---

[24] plotly.py is an open-source library for Python and can be used in a browser (see Plotly, Inc. 2019).
[25] Dash is a Python framework designed for developing analytic web applications. There is an open-source option, which can be executed on a local computer (see Plotly, Inc. 2020). Plotly Inc. offers a fee-based server version.

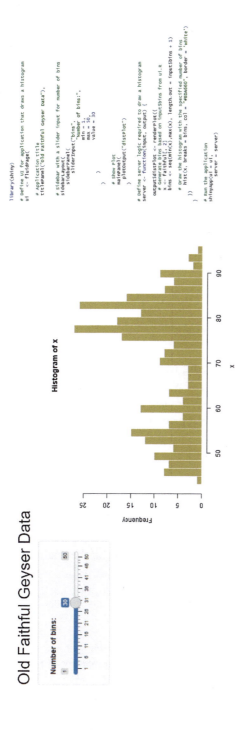

Fig. 21 R Shiny script example (© ifb SE)

Django,[26] and has open-source and commercial versions. The Plotly frontend is written in JavaScript and incorporates the library D3.js.[27]

Dash is an extension to Plotly.js, Flask[28] and React.[29] Dash offers some more interactive elements. Dash Open Source runs and is deployed locally, while Dash Enterprise (commercial license from Plotly) can run on server environments (including clouds like Microsoft Azure and Amazon's AWS).

There are multiple APIs for connecting Plotly to other languages like R, MATLAB, Node.js and Julia.

5 Summary

The world will constantly change, and decision-making is getting more and more complex. There is a demand for micro- and model-based decision support. This model-based decision support uses a model to project the KPI[30] or KRI[31] to get a clearer picture of the future (with all restrictions such a projecting of the future has).

5.1 Demands and Tools

The situation is ideal for going to the next step. There are multiple applications of a dynamic simulation with a convenient user interface (see Sects. 2 and 3). Section 4 illustrates quite convincingly that all major software vendors and many of the open-source providers offer solutions beyond the standard dashboarding.

5.2 Outlook

The upcoming growing availability of data and Big Data clears the way for more model-oriented decision-making. However, purely data-based decision-making is neither reasonable nor should this be the goal, due to the uncertain

---

[26] A free and open-source web framework, based on Python. It follows the model-template-views (MTV) paradigm (see Django Software Foundation 2020).

[27] For D3.js see Bostock (2019).

[28] Flask is a web framework written in Python by Armin Ronacher, see.

[29] React is a JavaScript software library providing a framework for user interface components (see Facebook Inc. 2020). React was developed by Facebook and is also used by Instagram. It is available under the MIT open-source license.

[30] KPI—Key Performance Indicator.

[31] KRI—Key Risk Indicator.

time consistency of the modeled relations. The growing amount of data can support in illustrating the impact of scenarios compared to the impact of stress narratives.

Literature

Bostock, Mike. 2019. *D3.js—Data-Driven Documents.* Accessed August 18, 2020. https://d3js.org/.
Bostock, M., V. Ogievetsky, and J. Heer. 2011. "D^3 Data-Driven Documents." *IEEE Transactions on Visualization and Computer Graphics* 17 (12): 2301–2309. https://doi.org/10.1109/TVCG.2011.185.
Box, George E. P., Gwilym M. Jenkins, Gregory C. Reinsel, and Greta M. Ljung. 2016. *Time Series Analysis: Forecasting and Control.* Hoboken, NJ: Wiley.
Django Software Foundation. 2020. *Django.* Accessed December 15, 2020. https://www.djangoproject.com/.
Facebook Inc. 2020. *React.* Accessed December 15, 2020. https://reactjs.org/.
Grundke, Peter. 2011. "Reverse Stress Tests with Bottom-Up Approaches." *Journal of Risk Model Validation*: 71–90.
IASB. 2014. "IFRS 9." *IFRS.* Accessed September 24, 2020. https://www.ifrs.org/issued-standards/list-of-standards/ifrs-9-financial-instruments/.
Kahneman, Daniel. 2011. *Thinking, Fast and Slow.* New York: Farrar, Straus and Giroux.
Liermann, Volker, and Kai-Oliver Klauck. 2009. "Verbessertes Risk Management: Banken im Stresstest." *Die Bank*: 52–55.
Liermann, Volker, and Nikolas Viets. 2019. "Predictive Risk Management." In *The Impact of Digital Transformation and Fintech on the Finance Professional*, edited by Volker Liermann and Claus Stegmann. New York: Palgrave Macmillan.
Liermann, Volker, Sangmeng Li, and Johannes Waizner. 2021. "Distributed Calculation Credit Portfolio Models." In *The Digital Journey of Banking and Insurance, Volume II—Digitalization and Machine Learning*, edited by Volker Liermann and Claus Stegmann. New York: Palgrave Macmillan.
Liermann, Volker, Sangmeng Li, and Norbert Schaudinnus. 2019. "Deep Learning—An Introduction." In *The Impact of Digital Transformation and Fintech on the Finance Professional*, edited by Volker Liermann and Claus Stegmann. New York: Palgrave Macmillan.
Liermann, Volker, Sangmeng Li, and Victoria Dobryashkina. 2019. "Intraday Liquidity—Forecast Using Pattern Recognition." In *The Impact of Digital Transformation and Fintech on the Finance Professional*, edited by Volker Liermann and Claus Stegmann. New York: Palgrave Macmillan.
Microsoft. 2020. "Home for Microsoft Documentation and Learning." *Tutorial: Develop a Power BI Circle Card Visual*, Febuary 9. Accessed October 15, 2020. https://docs.microsoft.com/en-us/power-bi/developer/visuals/develop-circle-card.

———. 2020. *TypeScript*. Accessed October 15, 2020. https://www.typescriptlang.org/.

Plotly, Inc. 2019. *plotly.py*. Accessed October 15, 2020. https://github.com/plotly/plotly.py.

———. 2020. *dash*. Accessed October 15, 2020. https://github.com/plotly/dash.

Shumway, Robert, and David Stoffer. 2017. "ARIMA Models." In *Time Series Analysis and Its Applications*, by Robert H. Stoffer and David S. Shumway, 75–163. Springer International Publishing.

Thiele, Markus. 2021. "Financial Navigator—A Modern Approach to Analytical Banking." In *The Digital Journey of Banking and Insurance, Volume I—Disruption and DNA*, edited by Volker Liermann and Claus Stegmann. New York: Palgrave Macmillan.

U.S. Army Heritage and Education Center. 2019. "Who First Originated the Term VUCA." *U.S. Army Heritage and Education Center—FAQ*, May 7. Accessed October 15, 2020. https://usawc.libanswers.com/faq/84869.

Valjanow, Simon, Philipp Enzinger, and Florian Dinges. 2019. "Value-Driver-Oriented Planning—Management-Oriented Design and Value Driver Identification." In *The Impact of Digital Transformation and Fintech on the Finance Professional*, edited by Volker Liermann and Claus Stegmann. New York: Palgrave Macmillan.

High-Performance Applications

Xenia Bogomolec

1 Introduction

The increasing performance of technologies always comes with a side effect: hacking tools become more efficient as well. There are several open-source tools publicly available, which benefit from parallel computing as well as efficient operations. We want to introduce you to one of them, the password recovery tool hashcat (https://hashcat.net/hashcat/).

2 Hash Functions

Password recovery is just a nice term for hacking hashed passwords. Since passwords need to be known to their owner only, it is a basic security requirement to only store hashes of passwords on the server side. Ideally, the application provider should not be able to recover a password. This is ensured by so-called hashing algorithms, which produce a pseudo random output (pseudo random generators). That means that the hash value is a random number (in hexadecimal representation) or random string of fixed length, regardless of the length of the input string. Unlike an encryption algorithm,

---

X. Bogomolec (✉)
Quant-X Security & Coding GmbH, Hanover, Germany
e-mail: xb@quant-x-sec.com

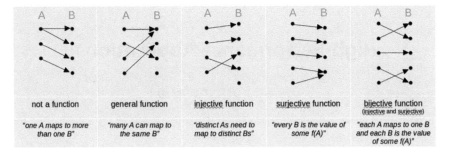

Fig. 1 Math functions (© Quant-X Security & Coding GmbH)

hashing algorithms cannot be inverted. In mathematical terms, hash functions are not even injective: there are an infinite number of inputs but only $2^{(\text{hash length in bits})}$ possible outputs. This basic condition makes a backward map from hash value to input string impossible. The incredible security of hash functions stems from the property of collision resistance: finding two inputs with the same hash must be impractical, i.e. taking far too much time to compute (Fig. 1).

The original password of a given password hash can only be recovered by testing all possible passwords (the password keyspace during an attack) until a match is found. The simplest approach to this is called brute force attack. For the hashing and encryption algorithms currently used, this can take up to billions of years, depending on available technologies and knowledge. Mask attacks take advantage of how people can remember passwords easily. In the worst case, such a password recovery only takes a few seconds.

3 Password Cracking

First, the attacker needs to gain access to the hash of a password. This can happen, for example, through a malicious insider with administrator rights or any kind of a data breach. Countless huge providers have been affected by such breaches; Equifax is just one big name among them. The so-called hashing "salt", a random string which is added to the password to be hashed, does not increase the security of the hashed password itself. It is naturally stored with the password hash. Otherwise, the stored hash cannot be compared to the hash of the password during a login process. Usually the salt gets lost in a data breach together with the related password. The true benefit of the salt is: even if a password is used via multiple platforms or by several users, its hash will look different in each provider's database or in a password hash list published by hackers.

Once the hash is known, the amount of possible password candidates can often be reduced considerably with additional information, such as the known maximum length and allowed characters of a password. Such information can easily be found on user registration pages. Password hash lists from data breaches usually contain the hashing algorithm, user name, the password hash and the salt.

3.1 Attack Mechanisms

There are two main hash cracking patterns: brute force attacks and mask attacks.

3.1.1 Brute Force Attack

A **brute force attack** consists of computing the hashes of all possible password candidates with the known salt and comparing them with the password hash—until a match is found. Traditionally, this attack starts with all possible 1-character strings, then all possible 2-character strings and so on. For our example, we chose SHA-2, a hashing algorithm which is still widely used for password hashing.

If the password length n is not known and any possible 8-bit byte is allowed as a character, the maximum number of iterations (hash function calls followed by comparisons of the password candidate hash against the original password hash) will be $2^8 + 2^{16} + 2^{24} + \ldots + 2^{8n}$ for a password with n characters. This is the maximum because only as many of the 2^{8n} password candidates in the last term will have to be tested until the right password candidate is found. Given the above situation, a brute force attack on a password with 12 characters consists of

$$\text{maximum } 2^8 + 2^{16} + 2^{24} + \cdots + 2^{96} = 79,538,861,190,790,864,407,636,279,552$$
$$\text{minimum } 2^8 + 2^{16} + 2^{24} + \cdots + 2^{88} = 310,698,676,526,526,814,092,329,312$$

iterations on password candidates. With a rate of 23,012 million hashes per second for SHA-2 on an 8x Nvidia GTX 1080 processor, the attack takes more than 109,601,979,097 years to complete in the worst case, and about 428,132,730 years in the ideal case. The ideal case would be to find the original password with the first of the 2^{96} 12-character iterations (Fig. 2).

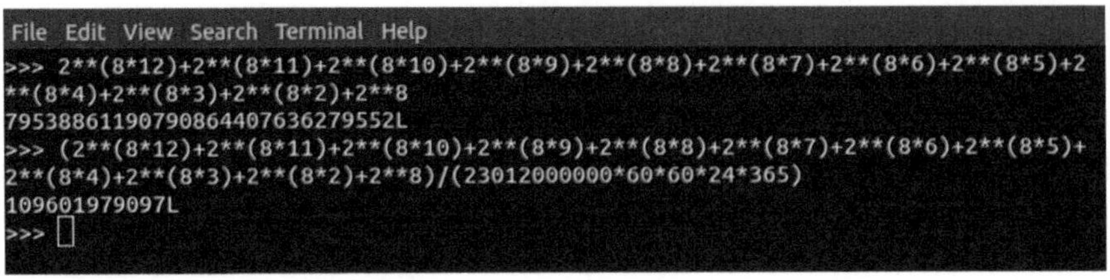

```
File Edit View Search Terminal Help
>>> 2**(8*12)+2**(8*11)+2**(8*10)+2**(8*9)+2**(8*8)+2**(8*7)+2**(8*6)+2**(8*5)+2
**(8*4)+2**(8*3)+2**(8*2)+2**8
7953886119079086440763627952L
>>> (2**(8*12)+2**(8*11)+2**(8*10)+2**(8*9)+2**(8*8)+2**(8*7)+2**(8*6)+2**(8*5)+
2**(8*4)+2**(8*3)+2**(8*2)+2**8)/(23012000000*60*60*24*365)
109601979097L
>>>
```

Fig. 2 Minimum iterations and required number of years (original screenshot) (© Quant-X Security & Coding GmbH)

Hashcat offers automated and configurable brute force attacks. For example, a restricted character set, minimum and maximum password candidate length can reduce the password candidate keyspace for an attack considerably.

3.1.2 Mask Attacks

Mask attacks are more sophisticated. Here, the password candidate keyspace is reduced considerably by applying a popular character pattern to all inputs. An example of such a pattern is a name and year. Thus, we fix the last 4 characters as digits {0,.., 9} and all previous characters as upper or lowercase letters {A, ..., Z, a, ..., z}. If the password length is 12, the necessary mask attack iterations reduce to a maximum of $52^8 + 10^4 = 53{,}459{,}728{,}541{,}456$ password candidates. With the same cracking rate of 23,012 million hashes per second, it takes less than 40 minutes to find the original password of the user (Fig. 3).

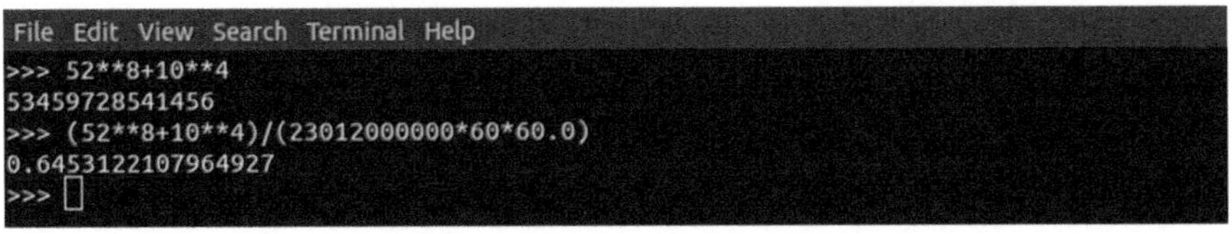

```
File Edit View Search Terminal Help
>>> 52**8+10**4
53459728541456
>>> (52**8+10**4)/(23012000000*60*60.0)
0.6453122107964927
>>>
```

Fig. 3 Maximum iterations and required number of years for mask attack (original screenshot) (© Quant-X Security & Coding GmbH)

3.2 Benefit of Slow Hash Functions

The length of SHA-2 hashes is 256 bits, so each comparison of SHA-2 hashes equals the comparison of 256 bits. If you look at hashcat password cracking speed lists on the internet (e.g. https://gist.github.com/epixoip/a83d38f412b4737e99bbef804a270c40), you will find that the cracking of SHA-2 hashes is only about three times slower than the cracking of SHA-1 hashes. This fact holds in spite of the 2^{128} times higher cryptographical complexity of SHA-2 over SHA-1 as functions. As a conclusion: SHA-2 hashed passwords are only about three times safer against brute force attacks with the tool hashcat than SHA-1 hashed passwords—a difference of no concern to a hacker.

The tool hashcat achieved such high performance by taking advantage of two facts:

1. Bit arrays, an array data structure that compactly stores bits. This structure is the basis for the bitmap tables, which are created specifically for each attack.
2. Parallel computing of hashes on available GPU (graphical devices) or CPU processing units.

Leveraging parallel computing depends on the algorithm. Some candidates do not offer this possibility, e.g. the winner of the Password Hashing Competition in July 2015, Argon2. Argon2 offers three configurable versions suitable for specific circumstances. One configuration parameter is the degree of parallelism. Argon 2 is designed by Alex Biryukov, Daniel Dinu and Dmitry Khovratovic from the University of Luxembourg.

The best protection against password cracking is to use slow hashing algorithms. The hash cracking speed for bcrypt on an 8x Nvidia GTX 1080 processor, for example, is 105,700 hashes per second. The above mask attack would take 16 years instead of 40 minutes if bcrypt was the chosen password hashing algorithm.

4 Summary

Anyone who knows how to use the password cracking tool hashcat can decrypt a poorly chosen password encrypted by a fast hashing algorithm, such as the ones from the SHA family, on their own personal computer in quite a short time. The price of an 8x Nvidia GTX 1080 processor on Amazon is currently around €300. Believing that you will never be affected by a data breach is not a safe attitude anymore. Neither can the complexity of the password requirements outpace the speed of evolving technologies. Slow hashing algorithms for password storage are the right answer to ever-growing cybercrime intelligence.

Quantum Computing

Quantum computing is one of the most disruptive computational technologies of our time. Quantum computers might be able to solve certain classes of computational problems (e.g., integer factorization[1]), being substantially quicker than classical binary computers. The major difference to a classical computer is that it does not operate based on the laws of classical physics but on the basis of quantum mechanical states.

This part gives an overview of quantum computing and quantum programming. The first chapter (Bogomolec und Gerhard "Post-quantum Secure Cryptographic Algorithms" 2021) gives an example of the disruptive power of quantum technology and the potential for quantum computers to break the industry standards for secure communication. The second chapter (Nonnenmann and Bogomolec "Quantum Technologies" 2021) offers a broad introduction to the different fields of quantum technologies, including quantum communication, quantum imaging, quantum sensing, quantum simulation and quantum computing. The subject of quantum computing is then broken down further into the following subjects: quantum annealing, gate-based quantum computing and topological quantum computing. The last chapter of the part (Nonnenmann "Quantum Computing, Categorical Quantum Theory" 2021) introduces the mathematical toolset of categorical theory to handle the complex matter of quantum programming.

---

[1] An important component of encryption technology like RSA.

Literature

Bogomolec, Xenia, and Jochen Gerhard. 2021. "Post-quantum Secure Cryptographic Algorithms." In *The Digital Journey of Banking and Insurance, Volume II—Digitalization and Machine Learning*, edited by Volker Liermann and Claus Stegmann. New York: Palgrave Macmillan.

Nonnenmann, Peter. 2021. "Quantum Computing, Categorical Quantum Theory." In *The Digital Journey of Banking and Insurance, Volume II—Digitalization and Machine Learning*, edited by Volker Liermann and Claus Stegmann. New York: Palgrave Macmillan.

Nonnenmann, Peter, and Xenia Bogomolec. 2021. "Quantum Technologies." In *The Digital Journey of Banking and Insurance, Volume II—Digitalization and Machine Learning*, edited by Volker Liermann and Claus Stegmann. New York: Palgrave Macmillan.

Post-quantum Secure Cryptographic Algorithms

Xenia Bogomolec and Jochen Gerhard

1 Introduction

The following article gives an overview of current developments in algorithmic solutions, and addresses the upcoming threats posed by quantum computers as well as unsolved problems in the classical IT landscape. It is an update of our 2018 publication in Computeralgebra-Rundbrief (Bogomolec und Gerhard 2018) and contains some new developments. However, the mathematics described are of course still the same. We thank the Fachgruppe Computeralgebra for their support.

The expected dawn of a new technological era certainly began when IBM offered its first commercially available 20-qubit quantum computers in November 2017. While, over the past year, it has still been discussed whether it is necessary to take quantum technology into account in the IT industry, the estimations about its capability evolution have become much more specific now.

X. Bogomolec (✉)
Quant-X Security & Coding GmbH, Hannover, Germany
e-mail: xb@quant-x-sec.com

J. Gerhard
Hofheim am Taunus, Germany
e-mail: jochen.gerhard@commerzbank.com

On the other hand, quantum algorithms, which are described in quantum theory and various mathematical areas such as complex linear algebra or category theory, offer more efficient solutions to known problems. In terms of cryptography, those alternative solutions to known mathematical problems, which are the basis for the security of cryptographical algorithms, are called quantum cryptanalyses.

Fortunately, scientific researchers have specialized in examining the various resulting challenges and questions since the beginning of this century. A series of conferences about post-quantum cryptography, the PQCrypto, started in 2006. They have taken place in a different city every year since 2010.

1.1 Quantum Technologies

Quantum–mechanical phenomena, such as superposition and entanglement, are used for communication, imaging, computing, simulation, sensing and metrology. While communication, sensing and simulation have been realized in publicly announced projects or products, universal quantum computing was only a matter of research until November 2017. The first quantum computing processors were introduced to the industry by (D-Wave Systems kein Datum) much earlier. They are so-called quantum annealers, devices which come close to the realization of the theory of adiabatic quantum computing and suitable for a restricted class of problems, such as optimization and machine learning.

With the advent of 65-qubit universal processors, quantum supremacy lies within reach, i.e. the potential of quantum computing devices to solve problems that classical computers practically cannot solve (Hsu kein Datum; Kelly 2018). IBM has announced that it is going to build a 1000-qubit prototype by 2023; Google is participating in the race with its record-breaking quantum processors Bristlecone (72 qb) and Sycamore (54 qb). A public overview of quantum processors and their architecture can be found on Wikipedia kein Datum.

1.2 Benefits

Quantum technologies offer and promise major benefits. So-called adiabatic quantum computers, e.g. the D-Wave 2000Q with 2048 qubits from D-Wave Systems in Canada, are able to solve optimization problems that would overburden a classical computer. Photon-based quantum key distribution devices from ID Quantique in Switzerland are used by the government in Geneva, DARPA and other institutions. China has built the 2000-km quantum communication channel QUESS between Beijing and Shanghai for banks, the Xinhua News Agency and the government, whose nodes receive keys from their quantum communication satellite. In 2017 they recorded feasible distances of up to 1200 km. In the future, quantum computers with enough stable qubits are expected to be able to help build complex materials as well as solve medical and environmental problems, among other things.

1.3 Threats

It has long been known that the security of the currently used cryptographic algorithms relying on the hardness of integer factorization and finding discrete logarithms (DLOG 1 systems) (Shor 1997) will expire with potent enough quantum computers. All public parameters like public keys from asymmetric key pairs can then be used to compute the corresponding private keys. With the knowledge of these private keys, encrypted data collected and assigned to the relevant key exchanges will no longer remain secret. For technologies like public distributed ledgers, where encrypted data is publicly available, this threat is even more serious.

2 Solutions

2.1 Quantum Key Distribution

QKD is an implemented cryptographic protocol for key distribution involving components of quantum mechanics. The security of encryption that uses quantum key distribution relies on the foundations of quantum mechanics. In this context, the process of measuring a quantum system in general disturbs the system itself. Therefore, any third party trying to gain knowledge of the key would be detected by the original communication parties.

Quantum key distribution networks have already been established in China (QUESS), Austria (SECQC), Japan (Tokyo QKD Network), Switzerland (SwissQuantum) and the USA (DARPA). The disadvantages for widespread practical usage are limited distances between communication partners and the need for expensive hardware. The fact that message source authentication does not come with QKD by default is rarely mentioned. Man in the middle attacks are also possible if the communication parties do not agree on an authentication protocol beforehand.

3 Post-Quantum Cryptography

The alternative to QKD are algorithms whose security relies on mathematical properties, like hardness of computing the inversion of a one-way function, even with a quantum computer. Hardness means that the computation takes an unrealistic amount of time, e.g. a billion years. There are four mathematical areas which offer solutions for post-quantum secure encryption, key exchanges and signatures. Some of them are still in the research process, others have been observed and challenged for decades. The advantages of post-quantum cryptography are that it can run effectively on devices currently used, such as smartphones, desktops and IoTs, and they can be established by pure software updates.

3.1 Code-Based

Syndrome decoding of linear error-correcting codes are NP-complete if they are considered as a decision problem with unbounded number of errors. This means that this problem cannot be efficiently solved by a deterministic computer (including all classical computers). On the other hand, some classes of linear codes have very fast decoding algorithms. The basic idea behind a code-based crypto system is to choose a linear code with a fast decoding algorithm and disguise it as a general linear code. Then the attacker has to use syndrome decoding to decrypt the message, while the message recipient, who also set up the system, can remove the disguise and use the fast decoding algorithm.

McEliece and the Niederreiter cryptosystems are two basic encryption schemes built on this setup. McEliece was the first scheme using randomization in the encryption process. Both systems consist of three algorithms:

1. Probabilistic key generation algorithm producing an asymmetric key pair
2. Probabilistic encryption algorithm
3. Deterministic decryption algorithm.

The private key is an $(n; k)$-linear error-correcting code represented by a generator matrix G, with a known efficient decoding algorithm. Originally, binary Goppa codes with the Patterson decoding algorithm were used. The public key is the generator matrix G perturbated by two randomly chosen invertible matrices S and P

$$G' = SGP$$

Equation 1: Generator matrix

where S, a ($k \times k$) matrix, functions as a scrambler and P is a ($n \times n$) permutation matrix. Parameters proposed by McEliece (1978) result in a public key of 2^{16} bytes size. The most effective attacks on McEliece use information-set decoding. To resist those in a quantum computing context, key sizes have to be increased by a factor of 4.

The Niederreiter scheme (Niederreiter 1986) applies the same idea to a parity check matrix H of a linear code. The encryption is about ten times faster than McEliece. McEliece was originally believed not to be usable for authentication or signature schemes because the encryption algorithm is not one-to-one and the total algorithm is truly asymmetric, meaning encryption and decryption do not commute. However, a one-time signature scheme based on McEliece and Niederreiter was proposed at the Asiacrypt in 2001 (Courtois et al. 2001):

1. Choose a hash function h and compute the hash value h(d) of the document d which has to be signed
2. Decrypt the hash value h(d) as if it were an instance of the ciphertext
3. Append the decrypted hash value to the document as a signature.

As the second step in the signature scheme almost always fails, the system additionally specifies a deterministic way of tweaking d until a hash value h(d) is found which can be decrypted. Verification then applies the public encryption function to the signature and compares it to the hash value of the document.

The most recently published code-based key exchange protocol is Ouroboros (Deneuveville et al. 2017). This uses quasi-cyclic codes in Hamming metric in the encryption algorithm; efficient decoding is achieved through bit flipping in the Random Oracle Model. Encryption and decryption are faster than RSA for comparative benchmarks (https://bench.cr.yp.to).

Ouroboros was proposed as a post-quantum secure cryptographic algorithm at the NIST, but removed from Round 2 in favor of the Classic McEliece scheme, which is one of the four Round 3 finalists for public-key encryption and key-establishment algorithms.

3.2 Hash-Based

This domain is limited to digital signature schemes which rely exclusively on the security of the underlying hash functions so far. The signatures themselves reveal a part of the signing key and can only be used for one message, the same as with one-time pads, such as visual cryptography shares.

Merkle tree signature schemes, introduced in 1979, combine a one-time signature scheme with a Merkle tree structure. The building blocks of the Merkle trees are one-time signature key pairs, with the node at the top being the global public key. This typically 256-bit large key can be verified with the path to another given public one-time key in the tree using a sequence of tree nodes, called the authentication path. The global private key is usually derived from a seed generated by a pseudo-random number generator and has the size of 256 bits as well. Therefore, the number of possibilities for such signatures is all possible combinations of the simple one-time signatures within the tree structure. This procedure considerably enhances the security of the scheme against brute force attacks.

The latest performance-improved hash-based signature scheme is Sphincs + (Rijneveld und Kölbl kein Datum), the advanced Sphincs (Bernstein et al. 2015) scheme presented at Eurocrypt 2015. Unlike its predecessors, XMSS and LMS, it is stateless, meaning that signing does not require an updating of the secret key. It is a so-called few-times scheme, where "few-times" means that after 264 signatures it is necessary to reinitiate the complete scheme. Its signature sizes range from 8 kb for NIST security level 1 to 30 kb for NIST security level 5. Sphincs + succeeded in passing Round 2 of the NIST standardization and is now proposed as an alternative candidate to the Round 3 finalists for digital signature algorithms: Crystals-Dilithium (algebraic lattice), Falcon (Fast Fourier lattice) and Rainbow (multivariate).

3.3 Lattice-Based

Lattice-based codes come with the challenge of finding the nearest lattice point or a shortest basis for a given lattice. Both problems and their approximations have been solved with NP-hard algorithms only. Given they are one of the longest known public key crypto systems, they can be fairly seen as the most promising post-quantum crypto approaches. Low memory requirements and high-speed computations let them run effectively on all currently and widely used devices. However, due to their significantly bigger key sizes they have not been as thoroughly researched and applied as RSA, EL Gamal (Hoffstein et al., An Introduction to Mathematical Cryptography 2008) or

DLOG systems. NTRU was the first successful lattice-based asymmetric cryptosystem. It was proposed and patented in 1996 (Hoffstein et al., NTRU: A Ring-Based Public Key Cryptosystem 1998). With the expiration of the patent in 2016, NTRU Prime (Bernstein et al. 2017), an improvement by eliminating worrisome algebraic structure, could be published. Their security relies on the interaction of a polynomial mixing system with the independence of reduction modulo to relatively prime integers p and q ($\gcd(p,q) = 1$). That means: at various stages of encryption and decryption the coefficients of the polynomials are reduced modulo q and/or modulo p. In particular, reduction modulo p and reduction modulo q do not commute with one another.

Another popular ingredient of lattice-based algorithms is the Learning with Errors (LWE) problem. This was used in BCNS (Bos et al. 2013), which phrased Peikert's key encapsulation algorithm as a key exchange protocol. BCNS was the first lattice-based algorithm integrated into the OpenSSL library.

With New Hope (Alkim et al. 2015), an improvement was achieved by choosing more efficient parameters and shifting from LWE to Ring Learning with Errors (RLWE). The New Hope protocol allows man in the middle attacks; message authentication must be implemented additionally. Google ran an experiment by using New Hope embedded in an ECC procedure for a certain number of connections between the Chrome browser and its own servers in 2016. Since 2017, Infineon has worked on the first generation of contactless post-quantum chips with Pöppelmann, one of the authors of the New Hope paper.

Dilithium (Ducas et al. 2017), a module-lattice-based signature scheme, was designed with the intention to be easy to implement against side-channel attacks, while offering efficiency comparable to previously developed lattice-based signature schemes. The key innovation is the replacement of Gaussian sampling by uniformly random sampling over a bounded domain. Furthermore, the public key sizes are reduced by more than a factor of 2.

All these algorithms except BCNS were submitted to the NIST post-quantum cryptography standardization process. The lattice-based Round 3 finalists are: NTRU and Crystals-Kyber (algebraic lattice) for public-key encryption and key-establishment algorithms, and Crystals-Dilithium (algebraic lattice), Falcon (Fast Fourier lattice) for digital signature algorithms.

3.4 Multivariate

The proven NP-hardness and NP-completeness of solving multivariate polynomial equations over a finite field F are the reasons why schemes with those asymmetric cryptographic primitives are considered good candidates for post-quantum security. Most of the published schemes use multivariate quadratics, namely polynomials of degree two.

The basic scheme consists of two affine transformations

$$S : F^n \to F^n$$

Equation 2: Affine transformation 1

$$T : F^m \to F^m$$

Equation 3: Affine transformation 2

and an easy-to-invert quadratic map

$$P' : F^m \to F^n$$

Equation 4: Quadratic map

The trapdoor $(S^{-1}, P'^{-1}, T^{-1})$ represents the private key, without which the public key $P = S \circ P' \circ T$ is assumed to be hard to invert. A first multivariate quadratic scheme, C^* (Matsumoto und Imai 1988), was presented at the Eurocrypt Conference 1988. After it was broken (Patarin, Cryptanalysis of the Matsumoto and Imai Public Key Scheme of Eurocrypt '88 1995), the general principle was used for stronger schemes, such as Hidden Field Equations (Patarin, Hidden Field Equations and Isomorphisms of Polynomials: Two New Families of Asymmetric Algorithms 1996) and Quad (Berbain et al. 2006).

Multivariate signature schemes provide the shortest signatures among post-quantum algorithms (GUI [Mohamed und Petzoldt 2015] 129 bit over GF(2) for a quantum security level of 80 bit). The signature x of a message m is created by hashing m into a vector $y \in F^n$ and computing $x = P^{-1}(y) = T^{-1}(P'(S^{-1}(y)))$. The receiver can simply compute the hash y and check if $P(x) = y$.

Medium Field Signature Schemes (Petzoldt et al. 2017) with fewer equations and variables in the public key offer a further reduction in key sizes, greater efficiency and scalable levels of security. It is the basis for the multivariate short signature system GEMSS (Casanova et al. kein Datum), which is an alternative candidate for the Round 3 finalists for NIST standardization.

The multivariate system Rainbow (Chen et al. kein Datum) has been chosen as one of three Round 3 finalists.

3.5 Isogeny-Based

One of the latest and most challenging post-quantum crypto ideas is the application of isogeny-based encryption schemes like Supersingular Isogeny Diffiehellmann (SIDH). With 2688-bit public keys at a 128-bit quantum security level, this scheme uses the smallest keys among post-quantum key exchanges. Additionally, it supports perfect forward secrecy, a property which preserves the confidentiality of old communication sessions even if long-term keys have been compromised.

Although not as thoroughly researched as the previously mentioned schemes, Microsoft published an experimental VPN library with a Supersingular Isogeny Key Encapsulation algorithm (SIKE) based on SIDH among an LWE key exchange and a signature algorithm using symmetric-key primitives and non-interactive zero-knowledge proofs (Microsoft Research Security and Cryptography Group kein Datum). SIKE has also been submitted to the NIST standardization process of post-quantum cryptography schemes. It has been chosen as one of five alternative public-key encryption and key-establishment algorithms for the final round.

In a YouTube video of a Microsoft research session where SIKE is presented to other researchers by Christophe Petit, he states at the end: "I wouldn't bet national security on it". On the other hand, SIDH was also described as "the hottest thing we have" in the keynote of the pqcrypto conference 2017.

4 Summary

Post-quantum cryptographic algorithm designers also work with other NP-hard problems from mathematical areas besides the ones we mentioned. We have, for example, Saber (Team SABER kein Datum), a secure key encapsulation mechanism (KEM) whose security relies on the hardness of the Module Learning with Rounding problem (MLWR) as NIST Round 3 finalist for public-key encryption and key-establishment algorithms.

In general, parameter choices are much more delicate for post-quantum cryptographic schemes than they are for classical ones. Furthermore, classical asymmetric schemes mostly rely on number theory, a topic studied in early university courses, whereas post-quantum algorithms tend to include mathematics from courses usually taught at later stages of study.

It will not only be a challenge to distinguish and weigh the complex influences on security of post-quantum encryption schemes; there will also be an increased need for cooperation between mathematicians, computer scientists and programmers to mitigate flaws in implementations, configurations and applications.

For someone who is not familiar with the concept of a mathematical conjecture, it is hard to understand the ground on which the security of cryptography is built and what time can do to it, with or without regard to emerging technologies. Who can say for sure that no one has been generating one RSA key pair after another for decades and storing them in a huge database, where they can simply assign a private key to its public key if it is in their collection? How many distinctive usable key pairs can even be expected within the range of a 4096-bit integer?

Literature

Alkim, E., L. Ducas, T. Pöppelmann, and P. Schwabe. 2015. "Post-Quantum Key Exchange—A New Hope." *IEEE Security and Privacy.*

Berbain, C., H. Gilbert, and J. Patarin. 2006. "A Practical Stream Cipher with Provable Security." *Springer Advances in Cryptology—Eurocrypt.*

Bernstein, D., C. Chuengsatiansup, T. Lange, and C. van Vredendaal. 2017. "NTRU Prime: Reducing Attack Surface at Low Cost." *Cryptology ePrint Archive.*

Bernstein, D. J., D. Hopwood, A. Hülsing, T. Lange, R. Niederhagen, L. Papachristodoulou, M. Schneider, P. Schwabe, and Z. Wilcox-O'Hearn. 2015. "SPHINCS: Practical Stateless Hash-Based Signatures." *Springer, Advances in Cryptology—EUROCRYPT.*

Bogomolec, X., and J. Gerhard. 2018. "Post-Quantum Secure Cryptographic Algorithms." *Computeralgebra-Rundbrief 63.*

Bos, J. W., C. Costello, M. Naehrig, and A. D. Stebila. 2013. "Post-Quantum Key Exchange for the TLS Protocol from the Ring Learning with Errors Problem." *Proceedings of the 45th Annual ACM Symposium on Theory of Computing.*

Casanova, A., J.-C. Faugere, G. Macario-Rat, J. Patarin, L. Perret, and J. Ryckeghem. n.d. "GeMSS: A Great Multivariate Short Signature." https://wwwpolsys.lip6.fr/Links/NIST/GeMSS_specification.pdf.

Chen, M.-S., J. Ding, M. Kannwischer, J. Patarin, A. Petzoldt, D. Schmidt, and B. Y. Yang. n.d. "Rainbow Signature." https://www.pqcrainbow.org/.

Courtois, N. T., M. Finiasz, and N. Sendrier. 2001. "How to Achieve a McEliece-Based Digital Signature Scheme." *Asiacrypt.*

Deneuveville, J. C., P. Gaborit, and G. Zémor. 2017. *A Simple, Secure and Efficient Key Exchange Protocol Based on Coding Theory.* https://ouroboros.rocks/docs/overview.

D-Wave Systems. n.d. *The First and Only Quantum Computer Built for Business.* https://www.dwavesys.com/.

Ducas, L., T. Lepoint, V. Lyubashevsky, P. Schwabe , G. Seiler, and D. Stehlé. 2017. "CRYSTALS—Dilithium: Digital Signatures from Module Lattices." *Cryptology ePrint Archive.*

Hoffstein, J., J. Pipher, and J. H. Silverman. 1998. "NTRU: A Ring-Based Public Key Cryptosystem." *SpringerLink International Number Theory Symposium.*

———. 2008. *An Introduction to Mathematical Cryptography.* Springer Science + Business Media.

Hsu, J. n.d. *Spectrum IEEE Tech Talk,* January 9, 2018. https://spectrum.ieee.org/techtalk/computing/hardware/intels-49qubit-chip-aims-for-quantum-supremacy.

Kelly, J. 2018. *Google AI Blog.* https://ai.googleblog.com/2018/03/a-preview-of-bristlecone-googles-new.html.

Matsumoto, T., and H. Imai. 1988. "Public Quadratic Polynomial-Tuples for Efficient Signature-Verification and Message-Encryption." *Springer Eurocrypt.*

McEliece, R. 1978. "A Public-Key Cryptosystem Based on Algebraic Coding Theory." *DSN Progress Report 42–44.*

Microsoft Research Security and Cryptography Group. n.d. *Microsoft PQCrypto VPN.* https://github.com/Microsoft/PQCrypto-VPN.

Mohamed, M. S. E., and A. Petzoldt. 2015. *The Shortest Signatures Ever.* TU Darmstadt (Germany), Kyushu University (Japan).

Niederreiter, H. 1986. "Knapsack-Type Cryptosystems and Algebraic Coding Theory." *Problems of Control and Information Theory.*

Patarin, J. 1995. "Cryptanalysis of the Matsumoto and Imai Public Key Scheme of Eurocrypt '88." *Springer CRYPTO .*

———. 1996. "Hidden Field Equations and Isomorphisms of Polynomials: Two New Families of Asymmetric Algorithms." *Eurocrypt.*

Petzoldt, A., M.-S. Chen, J. Ding, and B.-Y. Yang. 2017. *HMFEv—An Efficient Multivariate Signature Scheme.* Post-Quantum Cryptography: Springer.

Rijneveld, J., and S. Kölbl. n.d. *The SPHINCS+ Reference Code.* https://github.com/sphincs/sphincsplus.

Shor, P. W. 1997. "Polynomial Time Algorithms for Prime Factorization and Discrete Logarithms on a Quantum Computer." *SIAM Jouranl on Computing,* 26 ed.: 1484–1509.

Team SABER. n.d. "MLWR Based KEM." *SABER.* https://www.esat.kuleuven.be/cosic/pqcrypto/saber/.

Wikipedia. n.d. *List of Quantum Processors.* https://en.wikipedia.org/wiki/List_of_quantum_processors.

Quantum Technologies

Peter Nonnenmann and Xenia Bogomolec

1 Introduction

Quantum computing is the least evolved area of quantum technologies besides quantum communication, quantum sensing, quantum metrology, quantum simulation and quantum imaging. But it is the area with the highest potential impact on science, industry and society. In the following sections, we want to outline the potential, latest achievements and effects of the evolution of quantum technologies on other technologies, such as encryption algorithms on binary devices.

2 The Basis of Quantum Technologies

Quantum technologies are quantum physical principles applied to engineering. The creation of practical applications—such as quantum computing, quantum communication, quantum simulation, quantum sensors, quantum

P. Nonnenmann (✉)
DHBW Mannhein, Mannhein, Germany
e-mail: peter.nonnenmann@quant-x-sec.com

P. Nonnenmann · X. Bogomolec
Quant-X Security & Coding GmbH, Hannover, Germany
e-mail: xb@quant-x-sec.com

metrology and quantum imaging—is based on properties of quantum mechanics, in particular quantum entanglement, quantum superpositionand quantum tunneling. The only language that can describe quantum technologies accurately is mathematics. Any other explanation or metaphorical explanation will never fully capture the facts of a quantum mechanical process. Besides quantum theory, functional analysis and category theory are suitable tools to model quantum mechanical processes.

3 (Evolved) Quantum Technologies

3.1 Quantum Communication

The transport of data via quantum technologies is covered by the area of quantum communication. The data itself is still binary, typically represented by photons in optical cables. The difference between this and classical networks is the protection of the data by quantum encryption, which uses known symmetric encryption algorithms combined with quantum key distribution (QKD). Quantum key distribution replaces the asymmetric key encryption of a hybrid encryption algorithm in a classical setting.

The security of encryption using quantum key distribution relies on the foundations of quantum mechanics. In this context, the process of measuring a quantum system in general disturbs the system itself. Therefore, any third party trying to gain knowledge of the key would be detected by the original communication parties. This setting still requires the authentication of legitimate communication parties to avoid man-in-the-middle attackers (see Aziz and Hamilton 2009).

DARPA[1] established the first QKD network in 2002, and several organizations followed its example, such as SECOQC[2] in Vienna (2008), SwissQuantum in Geneva (2009) and the international quantum communication channel between China and the Institute for Quantum Opticsand Quantum Informationin Vienna (2016) launched by the QUESS[3] space mission. The latter covered a ground distance of 7500 km (4700 mi), enabling the first intercontinental secure quantum video call. Encryption keys are distributed via satellites. The challenge posed by the instability of qubits

---

[1] Defense Advanced Research Projects Agency is an agency of the United States Department of Defense that conducts research projects for the armed forces of the United States.
[2] Secure Communication based on Quantum Cryptography is a European Union project that aims to develop quantum cryptography.
[3] Quantum Experiments at Space Scale is a research project by the Chinese Academy of Science in the field of quantum physics.

is solved by network nodes and quantum repeaters. A 2000 km fiber line was operational by 2017, in particular for governmental and financial industry communication between Beijing and Shanghai.

Considering that China has severe encryption restriction laws in general, the significant investment in quantum secure communication for government and finance indicates the criticality of the risk they see posed by evolving quantum technologies. Many other countries, organizations and consortia have been established or are currently setting up QKD networks. The coronavirus crisis has raised global awareness of the criticality of secure communication and triggered another push to invest in quantum communication structures.

The laws of quantum mechanics do not allow making an exact copy of a quantum state, e.g., in a qubit stream, which is the content of the **no-cloning theorem**, and they forbid the deletion of one of two copies of a general quantum state (qubit), according to the **no-deleting theorem**. This latter theorem is obtained from the former by **dualization**, or time-reversal in physics terms. Dualization is an exact notion of category theory, thus the two theorems together make a strong case for the categorical formulation of quantum theory (see Nonnenmann 2021 on **Categorical Quantum Theory**, especially the notion of **Tensor Category**). Note also that the no-deleting theorem establishes a certain stability of qubits which in other respects are very unstable (see the notion of decoherence below).

But a man in the middle could still measure the original qubit stream and reinitiate a new one for the message recipient originally intended.

When the state of a generic qubit is being transmitted from one point in space to another, we call this phenomenon **teleportation**, where those points could be separated by light-years.

Teleportation is based on the phenomenon of entanglement, which Einstein called "spooky action at a distance" ("geisterhafte Fernwirkung," see Einstein et al. 1972) and led to his formulation of the Einstein-Podolsky-Rosen (EPR) paradox. This is not a paradox but rather an emergent phenomenon of quantum mechanics that lies at the heart of the theory and technologically is in turn the basis of an important QKD protocol, namely the EPR protocol (see Sect. 6 in Lomonaco 1998).

Teleportation has already been realized in the laboratory (see the QUESS space mission above for one example). We shall consider entanglement in some greater detail in the subsection on quantum algorithms below.

3.2 Quantum Imaging

This new field of quantum optics utilizes quantum correlations such as quantum entanglement in order to image objects with higher resolution and other tomography criteria than classical optics can realize. It might be useful for storing patterns of data in quantum computers and transmitting large amounts of highly secure encrypted information. An example of quantum imaging is quantum sensing, mentioned in the next section together with quantum metrology.

3.3 Quantum Sensing and Metrology

A quantum sensor is a device that exploits quantum correlations, in particular quantum entanglement, to achieve a sensitivity or resolution that is better than can be achieved using classical sensor systems. These sensors rely on the often-enigmatic behavior of subatomic particles, where the classical conditions of Newtonian physics do not exist.

Quantum sensing is used to precisely measure magnetic fields. Among other applications, quantum gravity sensors are being used and evolved in order to make the underground visible. For the financial industry, quantum sensors are mostly interesting in the context of QKD networks.

Together with quantum hypothesis, quantum metrology forms the theoretical model of measurement at the basis of quantum sensing. It is the study of high-resolution and exceedingly sensitive measurements of physical parameters, by using quantum theory to describe the involved physical systems. Quantum metrology exploits the phenomena of quantum entanglement and quantum squeezing in particular. This field promises measurement techniques with considerably higher precision than measurements performed in classical measuring frameworks.

3.4 Quantum Simulation

Quantum simulators are quantum devices designed to provide insight about particular physical problems related to quantum systems which cannot be modeled by a supercomputer and are difficult to study in a quantum laboratory. In contrast to a programmable "digital" quantum computer, a quantum simulator cannot solve the same class of quantum problems. These are special quantum systems designed to simulate a chosen system.

A Universal Quantum Simulator was a hypothesis introduced by Yuri Manin (1980) and Richard Feynman (1982) in the 1980s. In contrast to a classical Turing machine, it would not experience an exponential slowdown when simulating quantum phenomena. Quantum processors currently built, such as Google's Sycamore (54 qubits) and IBM's Hummingbird (65 qubits) are realizations of a Universal Quantum Simulator.

3.5 Quantum Computing

There are two basic quantum computing approaches: gate-based quantum computing and quantum annealing. Gate-based quantum computing is built on the quantum circuit model which operates quantum logic gates, the quantum equivalent of classical logic gates for conventional digital circuits. Quantum annealing is based on the adiabatic quantum computing model.

4 Quantum Annealing

The computation model adiabatic quantum computing uses quantum mechanical processes operating under so-called adiabatic conditions. Other than gate-based quantum computing, it relies on the continuous-time evolution of a quantum state from a well-defined initial value to a final value.

Quantum annealing captures the model of adiabatic quantum computing with physical systems operating in open environments at finite temperatures. It is a metaheuristic for identifying the global minimum of an objective function or a given set of candidate solutions.

D-Wave Systems, founded in 1999, was the world's first company to sell quantum annealers. Its early customers included Google and NASA, and its investors are Goldman Sachs and Bezos Expeditions, among others. D-Wave's 5000-qubit system, which uses its Pegasus chip with 15 connections per qubit, has been available since this year (2020).

A quantum annealer is no universal quantum machine, but it can solve optimization, machine learning and material scientific problems which would overstrain any binary computer. Volkswagen uses D-Wave systems to solve complex logistical problems. Mathematically spoken, a quantum annealer can solve Quadratic Unconstrained Binary Optimization (QUBO), Discrete Quadratic Model (DQM) and Binary Quadratic Optimization (BQM).

5 Gate-Based Quantum Computing

In contrast to quantum annealers, gate-based quantum computers are Universal Quantum Turing Machines, a concept equivalent to the above-mentioned Universal Quantum Simulators. This means that every arbitrary quantum algorithm can be executed on such machines, by constructing and composing the quantum gates necessary to execute that algorithm. As we shall see below, all quantum gates can be represented by unitary matrices, which are always invertible matrices. These are called, in quantum computing, **reversible** gates. In the 1960s and 1970s, Rolf Landauer and Charles H. Bennett showed that writing information is a reversible operation, and that it is deleting information that is an **irreversible**, energy-consuming process. Since quantum computers use only unitary, invertible gates they do not dissipate energy, nor do they generate heat.

5.1 Foundations—Gate-Based Quantum Computing

We focus on quantum computing (QC), and here we shall need only finite-dimensional complex vector spaces V, and the prototype is, where we denote vectors in row-notation:

$$C^n := \{(z_0, ..., z_{n-1}) : z_i \in \mathbb{C}\}$$

Equation 1: Vector of complex numbers

$\mathbb{C}$ the field of complex numbers, n a natural number.

Here we follow the treatment in Chapter 5 in Yanofsky and Mannucci (2013).

Consider a classical, that is non-quantum mechanical, system with only two states. We shall represent the two possible states of such a system, also called a **classical bit** and written as $|0\rangle$ and $|1\rangle$ by the canonical basis vectors in the vector space $\mathbb{C}^2$.

$$|0\rangle := (1, 0), \quad |1\rangle := (0, 1)$$

Equation 2: Canonical basis

The symbol $|.\rangle$, which is called the Dirac ket symbol, is very useful in quantum mechanical calculations, but the reader can regard it here just as a formal notation.

Definition: A **quantum bit** or **qubit** is a unit vector in $\mathbb{C}^2$.

We shall represent a qubit $|\psi\rangle$ as an arbitrary unit vector in $\mathbb{C}^2$, which is also called a **state**:

$$|\psi\rangle = (z_0, z_1) = z_0|0\rangle + z_1|1\rangle$$

Equation 3: Representation of a qubit

where $|z_0|^2 + |z_1|^2 = 1$.

In QC, such a linear combination (Eq. 3) in the vector space is called a **superposition**.

We note that a classical bit is a special type of qubit. The **Born rule** of quantum theory states that $|z_0|^2$ is the probability that after measuring the qubit, it will be found in the state $|0\rangle$. And $|z_1|^2$ is the probability that after measuring the qubit, it will be found in the state $|1\rangle$.

Therefore, a quantum computer is a **quantum probabilistic machine**, because the laws of quantum mechanics only tell us the probability with which the result of a measurement is $|0\rangle$ or $|1\rangle$. Note that this is different from classical probability theory: classical probabilities are real numbers between 0 and 1 whereas quantum probabilities come from complex numbers. Due to their vector nature, complex numbers can add up with the result having a larger or smaller length, a phenomenon called **interference** in physics.

Practically useful quantum computers should have more than only one qubit. **n-qubit quantum computers** are described mathematically by the important notion of tensor product of vector spaces.

Given any two vector spaces V and W, we shall form the **tensor product** of V and W, and denote it by $V \otimes W$, which is defined as the linear hull of the set of "tensors" of all vectors:

$$V \otimes W := Lin\{v \otimes w : v \in V, w \in W\}$$

Equation 4: Definition tensor product

Note for the mathematically inclined reader: this vague notion of "formal product" can be made rigorous by defining the tensor product via a universal property which can be viewed as a category-theoretic definition (see the section on Categorical Quantum Theory).

In QC, two or more qubits are assembled using this tensor product, namely given two qubits $|\psi\rangle$ and $|\varphi\rangle$ we can build a special state of a **two-qubit system** as

$$|\psi\rangle \otimes |\varphi\rangle = z_{00}|00\rangle + z_{01}|01\rangle + z_{10}|10\rangle + z_{11}|11\rangle$$

Equation 5: Two-qubit system

where $\{|00\rangle, |01\rangle, |10\rangle, |11\rangle\}$ are the canonical basis vectors in the two-qubit state space $\mathbb{C}^4 \simeq (\mathbb{C}^2 \otimes \mathbb{C}^2)$ where $\simeq$ means isomorphic.

The **n-qubit state space** is

$$(\mathbb{C}^2)^{(\otimes n)} \simeq \mathbb{C}^{(2^n)}$$

Equation 6: n-qubit state space

A crucial point in the whole of QC, especially in quantum cryptography, is that the tensor product in Eq. 5 is only a special type of a general state in a two-qubit system. A state like the one in Eq. 5 that can be written as a tensor product of two single qubits is called **separable** or **decomposable**, whereas a vector that cannot be written as the tensor product of two qubits shall be called **entangled**.

The quantum processing of qubits is implemented in QC by **quantum gates**.

A **quantum gate** is a linear, unitary operator that acts on qubits.

In the finite-dimensional case considered here, a linear, unitary operator is a complex, unitary matrix A that acts on $\mathbb{C}^{(2^n)}$:

$$A : \mathbb{C}^{(2^n)} \to \mathbb{C}^{(2^n)}$$

Equation 7: Quantum gate

The group of unitary matrices is a subgroup of the group of invertible matrices, implying that all quantum gate operations, except the measurements, are invertible, in the QC jargon also called **reversible**.

Examples of quantum gates with $n = 1$, that is one-qubit gates, where i is the imaginary unit, include (matrices are always written row-wise):

$$Id = \sigma_0 = [1\ 0\ 0\ 1], \quad NOT = \sigma_1 = [0\ 1\ 1\ 0],$$
$$\sigma_2 = [0\ -i\ i\ 0], \quad \sigma_3 = [1\ 0\ 0\ -1]$$

Equation 8: Examples of quantum gates (Pauli matrices)

where the σ_i are the **Pauli spin matrices**.

These and other matrices (gates) are multiplied iteratively with the starting vectors (qubits), to yield the quantum processing of the qubits.

An important special class of quantum gates is the **Clifford gates**, which are defined as the elements of the **Clifford group**. We define:

The Unitary group:

$$U(n) := \left\{ A \in GL(n) | A^{-1} = A^* \right\}$$

Equation 9: Unitary group

where A^* is the conjugate transpose of A.
The Pauli group:

$$P(n) := \left\{ e^{\frac{i\theta\pi}{2}} \sigma_{j_1} \otimes \ldots \otimes \sigma_{j_n} | \theta = 0, 1, 2, 3 j_k = 0, 1, 2, 3 \right\}$$

Equation 10: Pauli group

The Clifford group:

$$Cl(n) := \left\{ A \in U(2^n) | A P(n) A^* = P(n) \right\}$$

Equation 11: Clifford group

which is the normalizer of the Pauli group.

However, the **Gottesman-Knill Theorem** states that if a QC uses only gates from the Clifford group, then it can be efficiently simulated by a classical device which is the reason that many quantum implementations also use additional gates not in the Clifford group.

5.2 Algorithms—For Gate-Based Quantum Computing

In the following sections we briefly describe some **quantum algorithms**, that is algorithms that are executable on quantum computers.

5.3 Entanglement Quantum Circuit

IBM installed a QC platform (IBM 2020), that is, one can compose quantum circuits there, and then execute them on a real quantum computer. More precisely, there are several backends operational, e.g., in Valencia and Melbourne. We composed a quantum circuit to entangle two qubits, the results were as follows:

Figure 1 shows the quantum circuit: from top-down, one sees the 5 qubits, ($q1, q2, q3, q4, q5$), from left to right represents time, i.e., the successive application of the quantum gates. We used only qubits $q3$ and $q4$, this means

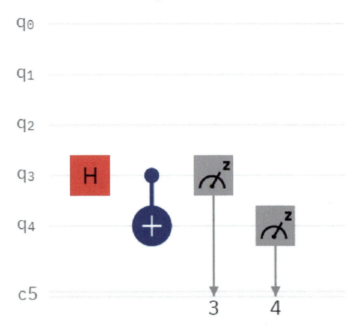

Fig. 1 Entangle circuit (original image) (© Quant-X Security & Coding GmbH)

a generic state is a vector in $\mathbb{C}^4$ written

$$(z_1, z_2, z_3, z_4) = z_1|00\rangle + z_2|01\rangle + z_3|10\rangle + z_4|11\rangle$$

Equation 12: Generic state as a vector

where $\{|00\rangle, |01\rangle, |10\rangle, |11\rangle\}$ is the computational basis.

The Hadamard (H) gate and the CNOT map are defined as follows:

$$H = \frac{1}{\sqrt{2}}\begin{bmatrix} 1 & 1 & 1 & -1 \end{bmatrix}$$

Equation 13: Hadamard (H) gate

$$CNOT := \begin{bmatrix} 1000 & 0100 & 0001 & 0010 \end{bmatrix}$$

Equation 14: Controlled NOT gate

We initialized $q3 \otimes q4 = |0\rangle \otimes |0\rangle = |00\rangle$, then applied a Hadamard gate to $q3$, then a CNOT gate to both qubits. Finally, we measured $q3$ and $q4$.

In detail:

$$CNOT \cdot [H \cdot |0\rangle \otimes |0\rangle] = \frac{1}{\sqrt{2}}|00\rangle + 0|01\rangle + 0|10\rangle + \frac{1}{\sqrt{2}}|11\rangle$$

Equation 15: Application Hadamard gate and CNOT to $q3$

where the dot · represents matrix multiplication, and the state on the right-hand side of Eq. 15 is indeed an entangled vector, that is qubits $q3$ and $q4$ are entangled.

Measuring this last state, one gets the bits $|00\rangle$ with probability ½, and the bits $|11\rangle$ with probability ½, the other basic states with probability 0.

The corresponding probability distribution is depicted in Fig. 2:

The actual result after 1024 experiments was not this idealized distribution, which IBM came up with later; the real distribution was:

$$P(|00\rangle) = 0.44, \quad P(|01\rangle) = 0.13, \quad P(|10\rangle) = 0.06, \quad P(|11\rangle) = 0.35$$

Equation 16: Actual distribution

, but one can see that the expected bits were indeed predominantly $|00\rangle$ and $|11\rangle$.

The last printout shows the results in terms of a generalization of the so-called **Bloch sphere** (Fig. 3).

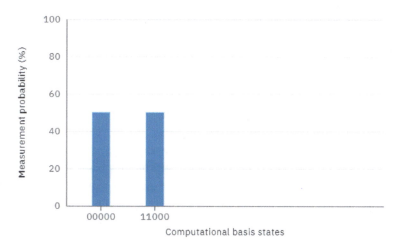

Fig. 2 Entangle probability (original image) (© Quant-X Security & Coding GmbH)

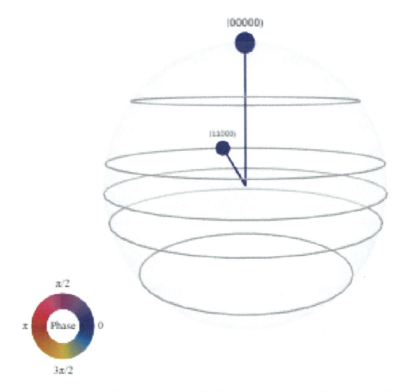

Fig. 3 Entangle sphere (original image) (© Quant-X Security & Coding GmbH)

The Bloch sphere itself is just the two-dimensional sphere in $\mathbb{R}^3$ with radius 1, but this can only be used to describe one qubit, the two entangled qubits here can only be described by a higher-dimensional analog of the Bloch sphere, called the **Bloch body**.

5.4 Deutsch's Quantum Algorithm

In this introduction to QC, we can only describe in some detail this simplest quantum algorithm, which solves a problem specifically designed for quantum computing, but whose methods are being used in the more involved algorithms, culminating in Shor's factoring algorithm, which can factor numbers in polynomial time. When potent enough quantum computers are operational, then the standard asymmetric cryptosystems which rely on the hardness of integer factorization can be broken, implying that global data security is at stake.

Deutsch's algorithm solves the following problem: Given is a function $h : \{0, 1\} :\to \{0, 1\}$. The task now is to find out whether the given function is constant $h(0) = h(1)$ or balanced/equilibrium $h(0) \neq h(1)$.

There are four functions $\{0, 1\} \to \{0, 1\}$, defined with the assignments:

$$f(0) = f(1) = 0,$$
$$g(0) = g(1) = 1,$$
$$\alpha(0) = 0, \ \alpha(1) = 1,$$
$$\beta(0) = 1, \ \beta(1) = 0$$

Equation 17: Deutsch's algorithm functions

Call such a function h **constant** if $h(0) = h(1)$, and **balanced or invertible** if $h(0) \neq h(1)$.

The first two functions above are constant, the last two balanced.

Given one of the four functions, the Deutsch algorithm determines if the function is constant or balanced. To solve this problem with a classical algorithm, we must evaluate the function **twice**, whereas Deutsch's algorithm only needs **one** function evaluation to determine if the function is constant or balanced. This is possible by putting two qubits in superposition of **two** states, and this superposition encodes the necessary information, as follows:

We have

$f \ is \ constant \Leftrightarrow (by \ definition) f(0) = f(1) \Leftrightarrow f(0) \oplus f(1) = 0$

Equation 18: Equivalence 1

The second equivalence, like all following calculations, can be proven by case distinction (Fallunterscheidung), because all calculations are performed mod 2, that is in the binary field

$F_2 := \{0, 1\}$ with addition $\oplus$ and multiplication $\cdot$ are to be taken mod 2.

Equation 19: Equivalence 2

As an example, consider the second equivalence above, where ■ denotes the end of a (short) proof.

1st case: $f(0) = f(1) = 0 \Leftrightarrow 0 \oplus 0 = 0$ ■

2nd case: $f(0) = f(1) = 1 \Leftrightarrow 1 \oplus 1 = 0$ ■

As all operations in a QC must be unitary, we encode the function to be tested f in the unitary quantum gate U_f, depicted in Fig. 4.

The matrix U_f is defined as follows (Eq. 21). We use the following standard notation in the QC literature:

For the two qubits $|x\rangle$, $|y\rangle$ we write

$$|xy\rangle = |x\rangle|y\rangle := |x\rangle \otimes |y\rangle$$

Equation 20: Tensor product of qubits

for their tensor product. Then we define

$$U_f(|x\rangle|y\rangle) := |x\rangle|y \oplus f(x)\rangle$$

Equation 21: Definition of U_f

that is, the input x to $f(x)$ is left unchanged (upper qubit), so we store it in this way, and can always tell what the input x was, which is the definition of an injective function.

Now Deutsch's algorithm is being implemented by the following quantum circuit.

The following calculations show the quantum processing and prove that the algorithm is correct (as mentioned above, they can be easily proven by case distinction).

As depicted in Fig. 5, we initialize the qubits as qubits $|0\rangle$, $|1\rangle$, then apply a Hadamard gate to both (Fig. 6):

by matrix multiplication, and the definition of the tensor product. Then we apply the quantum gate U_f to the last state (omitting the tensor symbol $\otimes$).

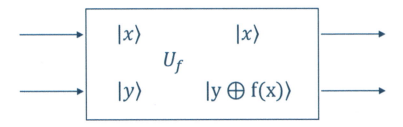

Fig. 4 Quantum gate U_f (© ifb SE)

Fig. 5 Deutsch algorithm—quantum circuit (© ifb SE)

$$(H \otimes H) \cdot (|0\rangle \otimes |1\rangle) = \frac{1}{2}(|0\rangle + |1\rangle) \otimes (|0\rangle - |1\rangle) =: |\varphi\rangle$$

Fig. 6 Deutsch algorithm—applying the Hadamard gate (© ifb SE)

$$U_f \cdot |\varphi\rangle = \frac{1}{2}(|0\rangle(|f(0) \oplus 0\rangle - |f(0) \oplus 1\rangle) + |1\rangle(|f(1) \oplus 0\rangle - |f(1) \oplus 1\rangle))$$
$$= (-1)^{f(0)} \frac{1}{2} \left(\left(|0\rangle + (-1)^{f(0) \oplus f(1)} |1\rangle \right) (|0\rangle - |1\rangle) \right)$$

Equation 22: Deutsch algorithm—applying U_f

by the definition of U_f. We measure only the left (top) qubit and do not need the second factor for the proof, so we omit it and consider only the top qubit.

$$|\omega\rangle = \frac{1}{\sqrt{2}} \left(|0\rangle + (-1)^{f(0) \oplus f(1)} |1\rangle \right)$$

Equation 23: Top qubit

and apply a Hadamard gate to it again by matrix multiplication.

$$H \cdot |\omega\rangle = \frac{1}{2} \left(\left(1 + (-1)^{f(0) \oplus f(1)} \right) |0\rangle + \left(1 - (-1)^{f(0) \oplus f(1)} \right) |1\rangle \right) = |\Psi\rangle$$

Equation 24: Applying a Hadamard gate to the top qubit

$|\Psi\rangle$ is the final state.

Now, we measure $|\Psi\rangle$, and

$$|\Psi\rangle = 0 \Leftrightarrow f(0) \oplus f(1) = 0 \Leftrightarrow f \text{ is constant}$$

Equation 25: Final state measure—f is constant

(see Eq. 18) and

$$|\Psi\rangle = 1 \Leftrightarrow f(0) \oplus f(1) = 1 \Leftrightarrow f \text{ is balanced}$$

Equation 26: Final state measure—f is balanced

To summarize, we have evaluated f only once, that is we have applied U_f only once and have determined if f is constant or balanced.

5.5 Grover's Search Algorithm

Grover's search algorithm (Grover 1996) finds a particular element in a set of n elements in just $\sqrt{n}$ steps, with high probability. Mathematically, we are given a function $f:\{0, 1\}^n: \rightarrow \{0, 1\}$ and the quantum algorithm finds the unique input x_0 such that $f(x_0) = 1$, with $\sqrt{n}$ function evaluations. Although this is only a quadratic speed-up, for large n this can be significant, and because it is a general search algorithm, it could be important for the fast solution of NP-hard search problems where the search space is typical of the order 2^n or $n!$, like the traveling salesman problem, the knapsack problem or one of the many NP-hard graph problems (see Bogomolec et al. 2019).

5.6 Shor's Factoring Algorithm

This quantum algorithm was discovered in 1994 by P. Shor (1997) and solves integer factorization. More formally, given an integer N, it finds the prime factor decomposition of N. This is considered a breakthrough in quantum computing because it has polynomial complexity, in contrast to classical devices that have at best sub-exponential complexity.

The problem of factoring integers is very important. Much of the World Wide Web's security is based on the fact that it is "hard" to factor large integers on classical binary devices. Peter Shor's amazing algorithm (Shor 1997) factors integers in polynomial time and really brought quantum computing into the limelight.

Shor's algorithm is based on the following fact: the factoring problem can be reduced to finding the period of a certain function, which is solved using Simon's periodicity algorithm, which is in turn a generalization and modification of Deutsch's algorithm (see above).

It is to be stressed that although Shor's algorithm solves the factoring problem, factoring is not believed to be an NP-complete problem. The factoring problem, as a decision problem, is an NP-problem, but is not known to be NP-complete. In terms of quantum computers, this means that even if there were a large-scale quantum computer, we would not be able to use Shor's algorithm to solve all known NP-complete problems, in contrast to Grover's algorithm (see the discussion above).

5.7 The HHL Algorithm

This is a 2009 quantum algorithm for solving linear equation systems, designed by Harrow et al. (2009).

Unitary operations, U here, are quantum-analogs of roots of unity, that is, for an (n, n) system, we calculate the quantum-analogs of the n-th complex roots of unity.

Moreover, a quantum calculation of eigenvalues by Quantum Fourier Transform and further gates is implemented.

6 Topological Quantum Computing

A major obstacle to solving the problem of technological realization of quantum computation is the quantum mechanical phenomenon of **decoherence**.

When a quantum system interacts with its environment (Nonnenmann et al. 2008), it can no longer be described by a well-defined state (**pure state**), but only by a probabilistic mixture of pure states (**mixed state**), mathematically treated by density matrices, describing a collection of random variables. Furthermore, the calculation and the information contained are destroyed during the interaction of the quantum system with the environment. "Topological quantum computation with anyons" could potentially come to the rescue. When fermions such as electrons are confined to a thin surface, that is they behave like two-dimensional particles and are interchanged, they can acquire "any" phase, hence their name. The exchange of two such anyons can be expressed via representations of the so-called **braid group** and, hence, it permits one to encode information in topological features of a system composed of many anyons. Kitaev suggested the possibility that such topological excitations would be stable, and could thus be used for robust quantum computation. For the mathematics of anyons, see the buzzwords braids, topology and modular tensor categories (see also Nonnenmann 2021).

Decoherence is the loss of purity of the state of a quantum system as the result of interaction with the environment (Nonnenmann et al. 2008). In physics jargon, a well-defined state is known as a pure state, whereas a probabilistic mix of pure states is called a mixed state, mathematically treated by density matrices. When a quantum computer interacts with its environment, the calculation and the information contained is destroyed. "Topological quantum computation with anyons" could potentially come to the rescue. When fermions such as electrons are confined to a thin surface, that is they behave like two-dimensional particles and are interchanged, they can acquire "any" phase, hence their name. The exchange of two such anyons can be expressed via representations of the so-called braid group and, hence, it permits one to encode information in topological features of a system composed of many anyons. Kitaev suggested the possibility that such topological excitations would be stable and could thus be used for robust quantum computation.

7 Summary

As we have seen in this short introduction to quantum computing, there are already a steadily growing number of potent quantum algorithms today as well as relatively small prototypes of physically realized quantum computers, but again with a steadily increasing number of stable qubits. The n-qubit state space being $\mathbb{C}^{2^n}$, the dimension of the state space of a quantum computer with only $n = 500$ qubits equals $2^{500} \approx 10^{150}$. This compares to 10^{80}, which is the estimated number of atoms in the universe. Therefore, the number of qubits really needed is not very large. The number of scientific articles on the realization of QC with more and more qubits is also steadily increasing, one of the latest being (Hanks et al. 2020). This paper is reviewed in this article (Swayne 2020).

Literature

Aziz, Benjamin, and Geoff Hamilton. 2009. *Detecting Man-in-the-Middle Attacks by Precise Timing*. Athens: Third International Conference on Emerging Security Information, Systems and Technologies.

Bogomolec, Xenia, John Gregory Underhil, and Stiepan Aurélien Kovac. 2019. *Towards Post-Quantum Secure Symmetric Cryptography: A Mathematical Perspective*.

Einstein, Albert, Hedwig Born, and Max Born. 1972. *Briefwechsel 1916–1955*. Reinbek bei Hamburg: Rowohlt.

Feynman, Richard. 1982. "Simulating Physics with Computers." *International Journal of Theoretical Physics* 21: 467–488. https://doi.org/10.1007/BF02650179.

Grover, L. K. 1996. "A Fast Quantum Mechanical Algorithm for Data Base Search." *Protocol of the 28th Annual ACM Symposium on Theory of Computing*, 212–219.

Hanks, Michael, Marta P. Estarellas, William J. Munro, and Kae Nemoto. 2020. *Effective Compression of Quantum Braided Circuits Aided by ZX-Calculus.* Japan.

Harrow, A. W., A. Hassidim, and S. Lloyd. 2009. "Quantum Algorithm for Linear Systems of Equations." *Physical Review Letters* 103 ed.: 1–15.

IBM. 2020. *IBM Quantum Experience.* Accessed October 15, 2020. https://quantum-computing.ibm.com.

Lomonaco, Samuel J., Jr. 1998. *A Quick Glance at Quantum Cryptography.* Baltimore: University of Maryland Baltimore County.

Manin, Yu. 1980. *Computable and Uncomputable (in Russian).* Moscow: Sovetskoye Radio.

Nonnenmann, P., D. Schuch, and R. Berger. 2008. "Effective Description of Environmental Effects with Possible Applications to Extended Systems and Fundamental Questions." Poster presentation at the 44th Symposium on Theoretical Chemistry.

Nonnenmann, Peter. 2021. "Quantum Computing, Category Theory." In *The Digital Journey of Banking and Insurance, Volume II—Digitalization and Machine Learning,* edited by Volker Liermann and Claus Stegmann. New York: Palgrave Macmillan.

Shor, P. W. 1997. "Polynomial Time Algorithms for Prime Factorization and Discrete Logarithms on a Quantum Computer." *SIAM Journal on Computing* 26 ed.: 1484–1509.

Swayne, Matt. 2020. "New Circuit Compression Approach Could Deliver Real-World Quantum Computers Years Ahead of Schedule." *The Quantum Daily.* Accessed December 15, 2020. https://thequantumdaily.com/2020/11/16/new-circuit-compression-approach-could-deliver-real-world-quantum-computers-years-ahead-of-schedule/.

Yanofsky, Noson S., and Mirco A. Mannucci. 2013. *Quantum Computing for Computer Scientists.* New York: Cambridge University Press.

Categorical Quantum Theory

Peter Nonnenmann

1 Introduction

Although we present the basic definitions of category theory, it may appear prohibitively abstract to some readers. But it is precisely this abstract use of, for example, diagrams that renders category theory so broadly applicable.

As mentioned previously in Sect. 1.1 of (Nonnenmann und Bogomolec 2021), quantum technologies can only be described precisely in the language of mathematics, more precisely the theory of Hilbert Spaces and Unitary Operatorson Hilbert Spaces, also called Functional Analysis, which we described previously. Very recently, roughly from 2008 onward, another approach has emerged, namely through category theory, where so-called string diagrams and graphical calculi have become a lingua franca, which turned out to be a very natural and thus appropriate setting for quantum computing and quantum information. Moreover, for so-called topological quantum computing with anyons (not to be confused with the negatively charged anions), tensor categories are the correct frame, as in them the variety of low-dimensional topological objects, like tangles (entanglement!), knots, links, braids and ribbons, can be accurately formulated and manipulated.

P. Nonnenmann (✉)
DHBW Mannheim, Mannheim, Germany
e-mail: peter.nonnenman@quant-x-sec.com

Quant-X Security & Coding GmbH, Hannover, Germany

The mathematical formulation of quantum mechanics was created by Heisenberg, Schrödinger and Dirac, and von Neumann gave it a mathematically rigorous form, completed roughly by the end of the 1920s.

Very recently, from around 2008 onward, a rather different treatment emerged, based on category theory. This was first mainly due to Abramsky and Coecke, but it is now an active and very productive field of research pushed by many mathematicians, physicists and computer scientists, but also (Neural, Bayesian) network and control theorists, game theorists, linguists and cognition and AI researchers.

2 Basic Definitions

2.1 Definition Category

We shall now provide a few basic definitions of category theory.

Definition: A **category** C consists of the data of

1. a class $Ob(C)$ whose elements are called **objects**
2. a class $Hom(C)$ whose elements are called **morphisms** or **arrows**
3. maps

identity

$$id : Ob(C) \to Hom(C)$$

Equation 1: Category identity

source

$$s : Hom(C) \to Ob(C)$$

Equation 2: Category source

target

$$t : Hom(C) \to Ob(C)$$

Equation 3: Category target

composition

$$\circ : Hom(C) \times_{Ob(C)} Hom(C) \to Hom(C)$$

Equation 4: Category composition

such that

(a) for any object $V \in Ob(C)$ and its identity morphism $id_V \in Hom(C)$ we have

$$s(id_V) = t(id_V) = V$$

Equation 5: Source and target of the identity

(b) for any morphism $f \in Hom(C)$ we have

$$id_{t(f)} \circ f = f \circ id_{s(f)} = f$$

Equation 6: Left / Right identity

(c) for any morphisms f, g, h satisfying $t(f) = s(g)$ and $t(g) = s(h)$ we have

$$(h \circ g) \circ f = h \circ (g \circ f)$$

Equation 7: Associativity

Here, $Hom(C) \times_{Ob(C)} Hom(C)$ denotes the class of pairs (f, g) of **composable** morphisms in the category, i.e., such that

$$t(f) = s(g)$$

Equation 8: Source and target

The conventional notation for the composition of f and g is $g \circ f$ or gf. The object $s(f)$ is called the **source** of f, and $t(f)$ its **target**. For the **identity morphism** of V we write id_V. We denote by $Hom_C(V, W)$ the class of morphisms in C, whose source is V, and whose target is W.

If $f \in Hom_C(V, W)$, we write

$$f : V \to W$$

A morphism $f : V \to W$ is an **isomorphism** if there exists a morphism $g : W \to V$ such that $g \circ f = id_V$ and $f \circ g = id_W$.

V and W are then called **isomorphic**, written $V \simeq W$.

The most common categories are the category Set of sets and set functions, the category Gr of groups and group homomorphisms and the category $Vect(k)$ of vector spaces over a field k and k-linear maps between them.

In all of these examples, the composition is the composition of (structured) maps, but there are more general categories where the composition is something more sophisticated.

2.2 Definition Functor

Definition: A **functor** $F : C \to D$ from the category C to the category D consists of a map
  $F : Ob(C) \to Ob(D)$ and of a map (which we denote also by F) $F : Hom(C) \to Hom(D)$ such that

(a) for any object $V \in Ob(C)$ we have

$$F(id_V) = id_{F(V)}$$

Equation 9: Functor identity

(b) for any morphism $f \in Hom(C)$ we have

$$s(F(f)) = F(s(f)) \text{ and } t(F(f)) = F(t(f))$$

Equation 10: Functor — Source/target commutativity

(c) if f, g are composable morphisms in C, we have

$$F(g \circ f) = F(g) \circ F(f)$$

Equation 11: Functor is a category morphism

Categories and functors have only really been defined in order to define natural transformations.

2.3 Definition Natural Transformation

Definition: Let F, G be functors both from the category C to the category D. A **natural transformation** η from F to G written $\eta : F \Rightarrow G$ is a family of morphisms in D:

$$\eta(V) : F(V) \to G(V)$$

Equation 12: Natural transformation

indexed by the objects in C, such that for any morphism $f : V \to W$ in C, the following square commutes in D (Fig. 1):

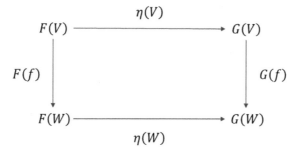

Fig. 1 Natural transformation (© ifb SE)

I.e., we have

$$G(f) \circ \eta(V) = \eta(W) \circ F(f)$$

Equation 13: Commutativity

This starting definition shows a glimpse of the use of various kinds of **diagrams** in category theory, which carry over to various kinds of applications.

These include **circuit diagrams** like quantum circuits or neural network architectures, or **string diagrams** that are being used in topological quantum field theory and topological quantum computing.

2.4 Definition Quantum Category

We now axiomatize the properties of the tensor product in the category of k-vector spaces in the following definition.

Definition: A **tensor category** or **quantum category** C is a category, armed with a **bifunctor** $\otimes$, also called the **tensor product**,

$$\otimes : C \times C \to C$$

Equation 14: Tensor product

This means that

(a) we have an object $V \otimes W$ associated to any pair (V, W) in $Ob(C)$

(b) we have a morphism $f \otimes g$ associated to any pair (f, g) in $Hom(C)$, such that

$$s(f \otimes g) = s(f) \otimes s(g) \text{ and } t(f \otimes g) = t(f) \otimes t(g)$$

Equation 15: Source / Target of tensor product

(c) if u and v are morphisms such that $s(u) = t(f)$ and $s(v) = t(g)$ then

$$(u \otimes v) \circ (f \otimes g) = (u \circ f) \otimes (v \circ g)$$

Equation 16: Middle four exchange

(d) and

$$id_{V \otimes W} = id_V \otimes id_W$$

Equation 17: Identity of tensor product

(e) a tensor category must also satisfy the **Pentagon Axiom** and the **Triangle Axiom**, which we do not cover in this introduction.[1]

3 Applications to Quantum Computing and Neural Networks

There are many applications of this categorical framework; here we briefly describe a very recent implementation of tensor categories, which are also called monoidal categories, in a Python environment, see (de Felice et al. 2020). For a thorough introduction to categorical quantum theory and the calculus of (string) diagrams, see the textbook (Coecke und Kissinger 2017).

Quote from (de Felice et al. 2020) "Quantum circuits are a standard model for quantum computation. They form the arrows of a **PROP**[2] i.e. a symmetric monoidal category generated by one object, called a **qubit**.

We define $Circ$ as the free PROP generated by n-qubit gates

$$g : n \to n$$

Equation 18: n - gubit gates

---

[1] These two terms can be found in any introduction to the monoidal category.
[2] Product and Permutation category is a symmetric strict monoidal category.

scalars

$$\{s : 0 \to 0\}_{s \in \mathbb{C}}$$
Equation 19: Scalars

post-selection

$$\{bra_i : 1 \to 0\}_{i \in \{0,1\}}$$
Equation 20: Post - selection

and preparation

$$\{ket_i : 0 \to 1 | i = 0, 1\}$$
Equation 21: Preparation

of ancilla qubits in the computational basis
Circuit evaluation is defined as a monoidal functor

$$eval : Circ \to Tensor(\mathbb{C})$$
Equation 22: Circuit evaluation

which sends each gate $g : n \to n$ to its unitary matrix",

$$eval(g) : 2^n \to 2^n$$
Equation 23: eval

where $\mathbb{C}$ is the complex numbers and where $Tensor(\mathbb{C})$ is the complex tensor category, which we also do not define here in this introduction, as well as other specific notions, see (de Felice et al. 2020), and references therein.

"Given the circuit for an n-qubit state $c : 0 \to n$, measurement results are a tensor $measure(c) : 1 \to 2^n$ of positive reals in $Tensor(\mathbb{R}^+)$, computed using the Born rule."

In the language of tensor categories, one can formulate the so-called snake equation, and the snake equation implies the correctness of the teleportation protocol, which we considered in Sect. 3.1 in (Nonnenmann und Bogomolec 2021).

3.1 Natural Language Processing

In (de Felice et al. 2020), quantum algorithms for natural language processing (NLP) were constructed and implemented on quantum hardware. These were defined as functors $NLP : G \to Circ$ from a pregroup grammar category to the category of circuits $Circ$.

A proof of concept was implemented using the Python environment (de Felice et al. 2020).

But the frame of tensor categories is much broader and includes, among many other applications, the formulation of neural network architectures and their algorithms, Quote from (de Felice et al. 2020)

"Let NN be the Lawvere theory generated by

sum

$$+ : 2 \to 1$$

Equation 24: NN - Sum

activation

$$a : 1 \to 1$$

Equation 25: NN − Activation

finite set of weights $\{w_i : 1 \to 1 | i \in W\}$ and biases $\{b_i : 0 \to 1 | i \in B\}$."

The morphisms of NN are the diagrams of neural network graphs, and, for example, the backpropagation algorithm is part of a functor $BACKPROP : NN \to Learn$, where $Learn$ is a Cartesian category of supervised learning algorithms, see the references in (de Felice et al. 2020).

4 Summary

For the mathematical treatment of topological quantum computing with anyons, categorical quantum theory is the adequate frame. The initial physical realization of the two-dimensional anyons is made possible by recent advancements in solid state physics, which won the 2016 Nobel Prize in Physics (see [American Physical Society 2016]).

An even more recent advancement in this field was announced in 2019 by NIST, The National Institute of Standards and Technology (see [NIST 2019]).

They found a possible "topological superconductor," which could overcome the industry's problem of quantum coherence. Should this or other progress in this technology become scalable and yield a quantum computer with "many" qubits, then the quantum industry would make a vast leap forward, and the solution to important, complex problems in cybersecurity, finance, health and environmental science would be within reach.

Literature

American Physical Society. 2016. "2016 Nobel Prize in Physics." *American Physical Society*. Accessed December 8, 2020. https://www.aps.org/publications/apsnews/201611/nobel.cfm#:~:text=Michael%20Kosterlitz%20won%20this%20year's,%2C%20superconductors%2C%20and%20other%20materials.

Coecke, Bob, and Aleks Kissinger. 2017. *Picturing Quantum Processes: A First Course in Quantum Theory*. Cambridge: Cambridge University Press.

de Felice, Giovanni, Alexis Toumi, and Bob Coecke. 2020. "DisCoPy: Monoidal Categories in Python."

NIST. 2019. "Newfound Superconductor Material Could Be the 'Silicon of Quantum Computers'." *National Institute of Standards and Technology (NIST)*. August 15. Accessed December 8, 2020. https://www.nist.gov/news-events/news/2019/08/newfound-superconductor-material-could-be-silicon-qua.

Nonnenmann, Peter, and Xenia Bogomolec. 2021. "Quantum Technologies." In *The Digital Journey of Banking and Insurance, Volume II—Digitalization and Machine Learning*, edited by Volker Liermann and Claus Stegmann. New York: Palgrave Macmillan.

Process and Process Optimization

Processes are an important topic in digital transformation, which is why the fourth part is dedicated to this subject only. The subtitle of the first volume of this book series is *Disruption and DNA* highlighting that certain subjects are changing disruptively, while some subjects remain unchanged (the DNA of a bank or insurance company). Only a few of the business processes are about to change, but the way processes are carried out will change significantly driven by digital transformation. The processes following certain traceable and comprehensible patterns can be automated and can even include components of automated decision-making.

Digitalization or the electronic processing of data or information leaves marks that can be used to analyze[1] and optimize the process via so-called process mining. A combination of performing automated repetitive steps (using RPA[2]) with machine-learning-based decision-making is defined as hyperautomation. Hyperautomation is the next level of RPA.

This part starts with a chapter exploring the origin and purpose of RPA and process mining (Czwalina et al. 2021). Within the chapter, the question of why the tasks of RPA and process mining are not performed by a business process engine is raised and answered. The next chapter (Rautenburger and Liebl 2021) gives a comprehensive overview of the technology of process mining. Process mining has the potential to bring full transparency to business processes but demands specific skills to set up and implement a

---

[1] Following the real process with the help of digital marks, rather than assuming that the ARIS process documentation is anywhere near the reality of the lived process.
[2] Robotic Process Automation.

process mining project. This includes roles, responsibilities and other organizational aspects. The part closes with two chapters with practical applications of use cases in process optimization. The third chapter (Liermann et al. "Hyperautomation [Automated Decision-Making as Part of RPA]" 2021) discusses a use case implementing hyperautomation by combining RPA with machine-learning-based automated decision-making. The fourth and last chapter explores and documents the requirement for an SPPI classification. It shows a possible path from a rule-based word searching and matching process up to a natural language processing of bond and credit documents.

Literature

Czwalina, Marie Kristin, Chiara Jakobs, Christopher Schmidt, Matthias Jacoby, and Sebastian Geisel. 2021. "Processes in a Digital Environment." In *The Digital Journey of Banking and Insurance, Volume II—Digitalization and Machine Learning*, edited by Volker Liermann and Claus Stegmann. New York: Palgrave Macmillan.

Liermann, Volker, Sangmeng Li, and Johannes Waizner. 2021. "Hyperautomation (Automated Decision-Making as Part of RPA)." In *The Digital Journey of Banking and Insurance, Volume II—Digitalization and Machine Learning*, edited by Volker Liermann and Claus Stegmann. New York: Palgrave Macmillan.

Rautenburger, Lars, and Alexander Liebl. 2021. "Process Mining." In *The Digital Journey of Banking and Insurance, Volume II—Digitalization and Machine Learning*, edited by Volker Liermann and Claus Stegmann. New York: Palgrave Macmillan.

Processes in a Digital Environment

Marie Kristin Czwalina, Chiara Jakobs, Christopher Schmidt, Matthias Jacoby, and Sebastian Geisel

1 Introduction

In the last few decades, competitive pressures have continuously risen due to the effects of globalization, shortened product life cycles, and advanced technologies, which forced companies to objectively and critically review their business processes. As a result, alternative, innovative ideas must be developed, introduced and the respective technologies implemented in order to successfully cope with competitive pressures in the future. In fact, advances in technology drive digital innovations on a continuous basis, where technology

---

M. K. Czwalina (✉) · C. Jakobs · C. Schmidt · S. Geisel
ifb SE, Grünwald, Germany
e-mail: Marie-Kristin.Czwalina@ifb-group.com

C. Jakobs
e-mail: Chiara.Jakobs@ifb-group.com

C. Schmidt
e-mail: Christopher.Schmidt@ifb-group.com

S. Geisel
e-mail: Sebastian.Geisel@ifb-group.com

M. Jacoby
ifb International AG, Zürich, Switzerland
e-mail: Matthias.Jacoby@ifb-group.com

that used to be rather evolutionary has become revolutionary. Technological developments in Blockchain, artificial intelligence, and advanced robotics, in particular, are no longer a trend but offer great potential for firms to improve their performance. Starting this trend, Process Engines were introduced and Process Mining as well as Robotic Process Automation (RPA) gained attention in the context of process automation within the past few years. In fact, they are perceived as three main components in a digital environment, by driving effective transformation of companies, especially within the banking and insurance sector (Fig. 1).

More specifically, business benefits such as improved process transparency, process quality, reduction of lead time, and consequently significant cost reduction can be realized with the introduction of these automation technologies. However, even though synergies between the three can be achieved when used in combination, no standard and leading Process Engine has been developed by vendors that incorporates all three components.

This gives rise to the following question: *Why was the vision of an all-embracing Process Engine not fulfilled in the last two decades?*

In order to provide a reasonable answer to this question, this article first provides an overview of processes in general, before introducing the concept of process optimization, which is an essential prerequisite when aiming for process automation. In a second step, three main process components in a digital environment, namely Process Engines, Process Mining, and RPA, are introduced. After having discussed the associated business benefits as well as challenges, a classification into heavyweight and lightweight IT is performed,

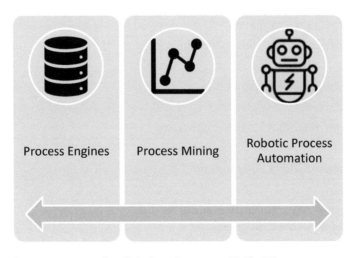

Fig. 1 Main components of a digital environment (© ifb SE)

in order to emphasize crucial handling differences. Consequently, connections and interactions between the three are described in order to finally provide a conclusion to the above-mentioned research question. In the last step, an estimate of how the process components presented might evolve in the future is provided, before the article is summarized.

2 Process Optimization

The terms process and business process are part of standard business vocabulary nowadays. When searching these on the internet, there are numerous different definitions. However, some universal statements can be filtered out of the various approaches.

A process is a targeted creation of a service or product through a sequence of logically related activities that are carried out within a period of time according to certain rules (Vahs 2007).

A business process can be seen as a collection of connected tasks that create value in terms of the delivery of a product or a service to a client. It can also be defined as a set of tasks and activities that contribute to an organizational goal, once completed. The prerequisite is that the process involves clearly defined inputs—that are made up of all factors that contribute (either directly or indirectly) to the added value of a service or product—and a single output (Appian 2020). External factors, such as regulations or management decisions, have a permanent effect on the process. Furthermore, processes depend on different kinds of resources. This is referred to as the value chain, as illustrated in Fig. 2.

Business processes are usually recorded in a process map. Like a traditional map, such process maps can be helpful to give an orientation with regards to the structure of a process on a larger scale. Moreover, it provides an overview of the essential processes of a company, as well as their interrelationships. The graphical representation ensures transparency, manageability, and the possibility to identify optimization potential. Furthermore, the process map gives an understanding on how a company is organized.

In the course of time, due to the increasing complexity of companies' structures and processes, different categories of processes have been established in order to visually separate certain areas within a company: management processes, core processes, and supporting processes, as shown in Fig. 3. Following that, processes of the process map are usually categorized into

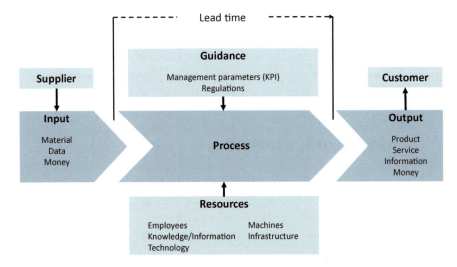

Fig. 2 The value chain (© ifb SE)

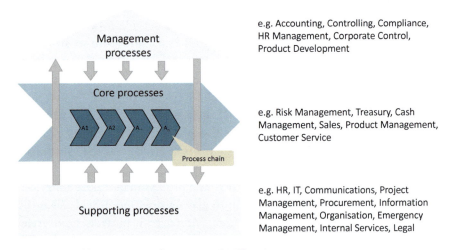

Fig. 3 The different types of processes (© ifb SE)

those. Moreover, as can be seen in Fig. 3, core processes can either run independently or based on each other. In the latter case, they build the process chain.

Management processes are used to plan, diagnose and control core and supporting processes. They have an instructive or decisive character. Decisions are mainly made by management and consequently these processes describe the operational regulation of the company from their point of view.

Core processes are the fundamental processes of the company. They directly contribute to value creation and profit generation.

Supporting processes ensure that core processes run smoothly. They are necessary for a business process but are not directly related to the business purpose. Customers are usually not willing to pay extra for them.

One example is the financial processes of a company. They are most likely part of the management or supporting processes as they do not directly create value or generate profit for the company. Still, they build the beating heart of the entire corporation as their output gives an insight into the actual and future financial status. Financial processes are divided into internal accounting, also known as controlling, and external accounting. Various forms of financial processes run in different cycles of time:

- Daily (e.g. billing, payments);
- From one closing period to the other (e.g. monthly closing, annual closing, consolidation);
- Regularly on request (e.g. finance report, Key Performance Indicator (KPI) report);
- Unique (e.g. Mergers & Acquisitions (M&A), where a trigger is needed).

Financial processes have a high potential for automation. Daily processes, such as billing or payment of invoices, offer particular automation potential, as they usually follow the same principle and all necessary information is available. Before processes can be automated, however, standardizing and/or optimizing them is recommended. But what is process optimization?

Process optimization can be described as the planned effort to improve the effectiveness and efficiency of certain processes. For this purpose, different approaches—such as a one-off method or methods applied continuously—can be used. The one-off method is typically triggered by an individual event, like a problem or cost pressure, which is usually initiated by management. Based on the analysis of the current situation and the future direction, optimization potential can be identified. Thanks to one-off process optimization, quick wins can be generated as unnecessary process steps are simply eliminated. Continuous optimization of processes is an ongoing pursuit of perfection. There are a variety of methods, such as Six Sigma or Kaizen

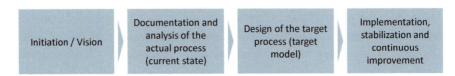

Fig. 4 Four phases of process optimization (© ifb SE)

(Hofmann 2020), that can help to improve every process by focusing on optimizing those activities that will generate the most value for customers, while eliminating as many unnecessary intermediate steps as possible. Improvements can mainly be achieved by reducing costs and processing times while increasing quality. At this point it is important to mention that process optimization is an ongoing process where predefined goals will be met, but optimization will never be fully completed (Dogan 2020).

As can be seen from the explanations given, process optimization is a complex task that requires a structured approach. In many projects focusing on sustainable process optimization, a procedure in four phases individually tailored to the respective framework conditions of the company and the specific process has proven useful. These phases are shown in Fig. 4 and will be explained in more detail in the following paragraphs.

The phase Initiation/Vision includes activities such as determination of a vision, derivation of goals from this vision, definition of project scope, definition of project objectives, and identification of affected persons or departments including the allocation of specific resources. Furthermore, a project plan will be set up and a kick-off meeting will take place to clarify the customer's expectations.

The next phase usually starts with the identification and recording of the actual processes before they are analyzed and mapped. Additionally, quick wins as well as improvement potential can be identified and evaluated. It is necessary to check for dependencies to other projects, activities, or cross-functional processes to ensure that all affected stakeholders get involved in the analysis.

In the Design of the target process phase the implementation plan is developed. Target processes are defined, while taking into account process and interface dependencies as well as restrictions and redundancies of the affected processes. Also, system support must be checked and ensured. An important part of this phase is to prioritize areas for improvement by, for example, centralization and standardization of processes. From a management point of view, it is also necessary to coordinate with other projects, establish training and ensure knowledge and communication management.

Processes in a Digital Environment

The Implementation phase contains the implementation of the new process and the appointment of a process owner. Beforehand, testing of the systems is mandatory. The whole optimization process will be finalized with the handover to the process owner.

The objective of process optimization is usually to increase quality while reducing costs and improving throughput times. Figure 5 shows the relations between these three attributes and the resulting influence on effectivity, productivity, and capacity.

But these are only three of numerous possible improvements. In this context, digitalization and automation of certain processes also have an impact on companies. Due to the increasing importance of digitalization and automation and the related requirements and possibilities, they influence the optimization of processes and should therefore be considered. Nevertheless, it is very important to keep in mind that there is a strict order when it comes to optimization, digitalization, or automation of processes. Processes always need to be standardized and optimized first, as automation and digitalization are just instruments that complete these goals. Otherwise, the chaos that might already exist would be automated, which would be very ineffective and increase the risk of the entire automation or digitalization effort having to be repeated. Thus, after processes are optimized and standardized as explained above, they can be automated with the tools described in the next section.

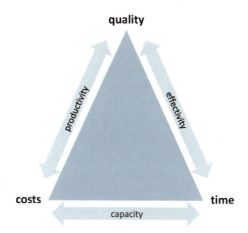

Fig. 5 The magic triangle (© ifb SE)

3 Three Core Components of Automation

3.1 Business Process Engine

In order to enable process participants to design, execute, visualize and monitor processes, cohesive systems termed "Process Engines" were developed. Nowadays there are different terms for Process Engines, such as Business Process Management Suite(BPMS). According to Gartner, BPMSs "support the entire process improvement lifecycle—from process discovery, definition and design to implementation, monitoring and analysis, and through ongoing optimization" (Gartner Inc. 2020a). Considering this definition, BPE is a system offering process participants a graphical user interface for the design of process models to increase process transparency and quality, a workflow engine for the semi-automated or automated execution of processes to reduce lead times and to monitor capabilities to continuously optimize the process outcome (Krallmann et al. 2013, 365).

For the execution of a process, the Process Engine requires a workflow model. In principle, a workflow model is a modeled process enriched with technical details such as resource requirements, distinction of cases, and work instructions. The model itself needs to be designed in the modeling language of the Process Engine by a process participant in order to represent the real-world process. Commonly, Process Engines currently on the market use the business process modeling notation 2.0 (BPMN 2.0) (International Organization of Standardization (ISO) 2013). The level of detail of a modeled workflow enables the Process Engine to semi-automatically or automatically execute and coordinate the functions represented by the model (Gadatsch 2020, 11ff.). After a workflow model is deployed on the Process Engine, the engine—triggered by an event—creates a new workflow instance for each workflow execution, which runs independently from other instances (Weske 2012, 87). In order to coordinate the workflow instances among each other, the Process Engine gathers data related to the execution of an instance, such as the status information, to trigger a workflow after the execution of the preceding workflow is completed. The forwarding, initialization, and other control instructions executed by the Process Engines are designed and configured in the workflow model (Luczak and Becker 2003, 33).

As can be seen in Fig. 6, Process Engines are categorized as either standalone or embedded Process Engines. Standalone Process Engines are independent software products and facilitate the development and operation of processes as an autonomous application. Embedded Process Enginesare

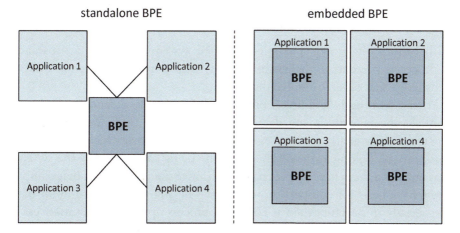

Fig. 6 Standalone vs. embedded BPE (© ifb SE)

integrated as a component into another application and enable a process-oriented configuration of an application (Luczak and Becker 2003, 44). Either engine type enables the integration of frontend applications, middleware software, backend applications, or external applications and services. For the integration, Process Engines utilize interface technologies such as web services to gather or exchange data or information (Krallmann et al. 2013, 366). The key difference between standalone and embedded Process Engines is the potential use. A standalone Process Engine is applied to orchestrate processes that are not part of the use case of an application and to manage the process landscape at large. Therefore, the standalone Process Engine relies on the functionality of other applications or services during the execution of a workflow instance. Embedded Process Engines allow the user of the application in which the Process Engine is embedded to configure and enhance this application using a process-oriented approach.

The business benefits of process transparency, process quality, reduction of lead time, and cost reduction by automation materialize only if the processes executed by the Process Engine are well defined, require minimal need for change, and show a high frequency of execution (Krallmann et al. 2013, 361). For example, one process suitable for Process Engine execution is the "Know Your Customer" (KYC) check. This process requests customer data from different internal systems or external services such as credit rating agencies to validate the identity of a new customer. In order to align this process between business units, e.g., savings and credit, the Process Engine triggers the KYC process for all business activities regardless of the business unit.

3.2 Process Mining

With historically grown and self-developed systems, creating transparency in processes presents a challenge. Process Mining is a new and innovative technology that aims to resolve this issue.

Process Mining is building a bridge between the classic and model-based manual process analysis and data-centric approaches (van der Aalst 2016). The technology analyzes actual event data in IT systems, which provides the possibility of looking at processes as they are being carried out by the system. This enables a fact-check of process models once documented so that companies have a basis for comparison to reality. The analysis of actual event data is especially important when it comes to process optimization initiatives: it provides the security that the process being optimized is fully understood and looked at. Once documented, process models do have the tendency to fall behind in their representation when a process is updated. Additionally, Process Mining offers the possibility to compare the process performance before and after optimization. This enables organizations to check the effectiveness of their process optimization initiatives objectively and based on data on a continuous basis.

In order for Process Mining to provide value, the process needs to be executed with the support of some digital system. Otherwise, there are no traces in the systems to be analyzed by the technology. The bare minimum of information Process Mining needs consists of three parts:

- Case ID
- Time stamp
- Event activity

With case ID, time stamp and event activity extracted from the system, the process can be visually represented with every single variant within the timeframe the data is being analyzed from, down to the level of a single activity—based on actual process data.

From a business perspective, the technology brings various benefits. One example is checking the conformance of the process execution with the guidelines associated with it, such as compliance with the dual control principle. Another example is the possibility to identify exactly where a process is lacking performance as well as which process steps are carried out often enough and which steps are most time consuming in order for the process to be evaluated as a candidate for automation (Rautenburger and Liebl 2021).

3.3 Robotic Process Automation

In addition to Process Engines and Process Mining, RPA is another tool frequently used and stimulates the automation of firm processes, where machines are able to match or even outperform humans in a variety of activities (Manyika et al. 2017). More specifically, RPA can be defined as follows:

> *Robotic Process Automation (RPA) is a productivity tool that allows a user to configure one or more scripts (which some vendors refer to as "bots") to activate specific keystrokes in an automated fashion. The result is that the bots can be used to mimic or emulate selected tasks (transaction steps) within an overall business or IT process. These may include manipulating data, passing data to and from different applications, triggering responses, or executing transactions. RPA uses a combination of user interface interaction and descriptor technologies. The scripts can overlay on one or more software applications.* (Gartner, Inc. 2020b)

In order to provide a better overview on how RPA is placed in the context of automation solutions, a distinction between Attended Process Automation, Unattended Process Automation, and Intelligent Process Automationcan be made, as depicted in Fig. 7.

Consequently, RPA can be described as a deterministic approach, which enables full automation of processes where structured and semi-structured

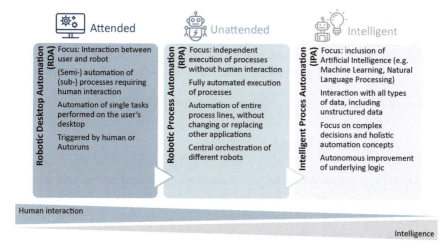

Fig. 7 Overview of process automation solutions (© ifb SE)

data can be treated. In contrast to more advanced technologies, such as artificial intelligence, robots designed for RPA are neither able to learn nor do they possess context awareness.

For RPA to be successful, however, an assessment of suitable processes is essential in order to identify the processes where RPA can make the biggest difference. Thus, processes should ideally be highly manual, rule-based, and routine tasks with high volumes, by accessing several applications and handling different transactions like a human would do. Moreover, processes with high volumes are especially suitable for robots as robots can operate 24 hours a day, 7 days per week, and 365 days each year (Ostdick 2016).

From a technical viewpoint, RPA is often referred to as "lightweight IT," where the robot works on the presentation layer only, meaning that there is only an interaction with existing software, but no changes and adaptations to the programming code of the underlying software are performed (Lacity and Willcocks 2015). As human employees usually interact on the presentation layer of a software program only, robots simply mimic this approach. This key component of RPA allows a business unit to ensure technological independency (Forrester Research 2011), reduces implementation efforts and complexity, and at the same time increases speed and ease of technological deployment (Lacity and Willcocks 2015; Willcocks and Lacity 2016).

Besides these technical advantages, there are several benefits associated with the implementation of RPA from a business perspective. These include, for example, enhanced speed and quality, as the robot can work constantly without making any mistakes, resulting in expanded service availability as well as increased regulatory compliance (Lacity and Willcocks 2016). Case studies conducted in this field found a return on investment varied between 30 and 200 percent during the first year (Lhuer 2016) as well as cost reductions between 25 and 40 percent (Lamberton 2016; Soybir and Schmidt 2021).

4 Why They Exist

In Sect. 3, three components for the visualization, optimization, and automation of processes were introduced. Despite the different technologies used by these components, the question arises "Why do three different components exist to visualize, optimize and automate processes? And does one of these components offer the full range needed to effectively manage process automation within an organization?".

In order to answer these questions, this section summarizes the advantages and challenges of process automation in the context of Business Process Engines (BPE), Process Mining, and RPA. Furthermore, the three components are classified into heavyweight and lightweight IT to emphasize the discrepancies in handling them. Finally, the section concludes with an approach describing the interactions between the components to cover the whole spectrum of process visualization, optimization, and automation.

4.1 Business Process Engines—Advantages and Challenges

For standalone BPEs to organize end-to-end processes or embedded BPEs as process tools within an enterprise application, a process model is required in order to automate a process. The methodology for the design and implementation of a process model is dictated by the chosen BPE and requires a specialized skill set (Penttinen et al. 2018, 3). The design of a process in a process model involves the process designer as a specialist in the modeling methodology and the process participants as process experts in order to avoid deviations between the model and the process. A lack of interaction between the process designer and the process experts during the process design phase, however, might result in multiple iterations to reach the desired outcome (van der Aalst et al., Robotic Process Automation 2018, 271).

The completeness of the process model depends on deviations modeled in the process model, termed process variants. The decision as to whether a process variant should be automated and modeled depends on its frequency of occurrence as well as on whether the associated modeling and implementation costs reflect the corresponding cost savings. In order to avoid exponential costs, the process designer and process experts must decide when the process model is mature enough to be automated. For the decision-making process, the process designer and experts rely on their experience, empirical values of prior executions or estimates regarding manual activities or execution time of involved enterprise applications (Johannesson and Perjons 2011, 166ff.).

For automation, the BPE depends on interfaces to internal or external enterprise applications providing execution capacities for the modeled process activities. The interfaces either supply data to or receive data from the BPE, which is received by following or provided by prior process activities (Gadatsch 2020, 49). However, BPEs often do not include the required interfaces or data transfer requirements are not met. Therefore, a separate business requirements analysis as well as additional interface programming or adaptation by IT specialists to support the process automation is needed (Waldorf et al. 2009, 12).

Processes are subject to change based on market or internal requirements, therefore requiring business experts, or rather business process owners, to monitor process executions, identify optimization potential, and address changes to the technical experts via a ticket system (van der Aalst et al., Robotic Process Automation 2018, 271). Based on the requirements formulated in the ticket, the process within the BPE is adapted by internal or external technical process experts. Afterward, the process owner evaluates the outcome of the process and might make another change request if the desired outcome is not achieved.

In summary, the automation of processes with a BPE applies to end-to-end processes or processes within distinct applications, depending on the type of Process Engine. Moreover, a cross-departmental team for the design and implementation of the processes and the required interfaces is necessary. Consequently, due to the involvement of different departments and external experts, automation projects including BPEs tend to be lengthy and costly projects. Furthermore, the maintenance of the end-to-end processes involves roles which are solely established for this purpose and therefore need to be set up within the existing organization.

The above-mentioned challenges as well as BPE advantages listed in Sect. 3.1 are summarized below (Fig. 8).

Even though standalone and embedded BPEs face similar challenges, the reasons why there is no distinct market leader for both types of BPE differ. In general terms, BPEs are one option to realize the integration of enterprise applications along the value chain of an organization in heterogenous environments. The so-called enterprise application integration (EAI) can be realized by integrating enterprise applications on data, application, or process

Advantages	Challenges
Process transparency	Dependency on cross-departmental teams for design/implementation of processes interfaces
Enhanced process quality	Time and cost intensive projects
Cost reduction	BPE maintenance requires set-up of roles solely established for this purpose

Fig. 8 Overview—advantages and challenges of BPEs (© ifb SE)

level. Organizations that decide to integrate enterprise applications on data level implementing an enterprise bus or application level by relying on a message broker are not inclined to implement a BPE for process automation, because this would mean a complete change within the IT architecture (Lublinsky 2001, 27; McKeen and Smith 2002, 456–457). In order to realize process automation and monitor the alignment of the execution with the value chain, these organizations would rather use other process automation techniques such as process design tools in combination with Process Mining.

Embedded BPEs are limited to the boundaries of the enterprise application, which results in offering process automation functionalities solely to process activities within this enterprise application and not to process activities outside of this enterprise application (Luczak and Becker 2003, 44).

4.2 Process Mining—Advantages and Challenges

Process Mining deals with the challenges of process design and process maintenance by creating process models based on the technical execution trace of a process recorded in the log files of the involved enterprise applications (van der Aalst and Dustdar 2012, 82).

In order to obtain a process model that represents the process instances in relation to the quantity of process variants executed on an average business day, the selected logs should include a time span representing normal business volumes and not merely exception cases, which might have resulted from weather phenomenon, seasonal occurrences or global events (van der Aalst and Dustdar 2012, 84f.). Enterprise application logs capture every execution step with additional information in order to assist IT experts in analyzing errors occurring within an application. This information density is perceived as a disruptive factor in creating a structured process model by Process Mining tools. Before mining the logs of enterprise applications, they must be analyzed and reduced to pivotal information required for the execution of the Process Mining tool (Jagadeesh Chandra Bose and van der Aalst 2009, 175).

Process Mining tools analyze the traces of the recorded process instances in the log files and develop a process model with a main branch and process variants. Despite the visualization of the succession of process activities, some activities carry technical terms and might not be legible without the insight of the process expert. Furthermore, manual activities involved in the execution of a process instance are not logged from the enterprise application and therefore not recognized by the Process Mining tool. The analysis for process optimization potential demands the involvement of process experts in order to complete the process model or to define multi-dimensional performance

Fig. 9 Overview—advantages and challenges of process mining (© ifb SE)

indicators to assess the performance of each process instance. When analyzing a mined process, one should take into account that configuration changes in the enterprise applications might result in improvements of the execution parameters such as throughput, but changes to the business activities executed by the enterprise application have a greater impact on the business results of the process (van der Aalst et al. 2007, 730).

For the automation and optimization of processes, Process Mining assists process participants in understanding the actual process flow of process instances including involved enterprise applications. In combination with process metrics, process optimization tasks can be defined. These tasks are either assigned to the responsible departments in order to change manual process activities or to the IT department to adapt the IT configuration. Similar to BPEs, the effects of the implemented changes are visible to the process participants only after another execution of the Process Mining tool. Subsequently, further optimization potential can be defined. The execution of a processing activity influences the execution of the following process execution. For the prioritization and decision on process optimizations, an organizational unit should be included with an understanding of the overall process.

The main advantages and challenges associated with Process Mining are depicted in Fig. 9.

4.3 Robotic Process Automation—Advantages and Challenges

RPA serves to automate graphical user interface interactions to reduce the tedious, monotonous, and repetitive tasks of human workers (van der Aalst et al., Robotic Process Automation 2018, 270). Automation with RPA focuses on the independent execution of (sub-) processes without the need for human interaction. In order to avoid a productivity loss due to not streamlining the robotic automation of activities or (sub-) processes with the end-to-end process (Osmundsen et al. 2019, 6925), the business departments applying RPA should clarify the requirements of a process for being eligible for automation as well as the responsibilities for maintaining the robots (Medling et al. 2018, 5). Similar to BPEs, the automation with RPA should ideally cover activities or (sub-) processes with high business volumes to free human workers from administrative tasks, resulting in enhanced productivity (van der Aalst et al., Robotic Process Automation 2018, 270). Therefore, business departments should analyze the activities and (sub-) processes and define their eligibility for automation and the related optimization potential before initializing the automation. More specifically, while automating activities or (sub-) processes without a holistic view of the end-to-end process might result in faster execution times for the individual activity or (sub-) process as well as productivity gains in one department, envisaged productivity gains or customer benefits might fail to materialize due to shortages in other activities of the overall process (Medling et al. 2018, 4; Penttinen et al. 2018, 4).

In general, robots implemented with RPA can mimic human interactions with enterprise applications to perform a certain activity. A typical example would be to extract data from one file, such as an Excel spreadsheet or an e-mail, and insert it into another file or system, such as CRM, for further processing. For more mature processing activities such as handling a credit application in the SAP banking modules, a solution architect and RPA developer are needed. More specifically, they are able to create a maintainable solution including codified human interactions and decision rules and identify reusable components, which can be added and contribute to other RPA projects (Osmundsen et al. 2019, 6922). Despite the need for a specialized skill set for complex RPA, RPA projects are usually driven and maintained by the respective business units with no or limited involvement of the IT department. Consequently, business departments can act in a flexible and agile manner without affecting the IT system architecture. In fact, robots utilize the graphical user interfaces and available features of existing enterprise applications, thereby eliminating the need for interface creation and therefore IT involvement (Penttinen et al. 2018, 3f.). This practice enables the business department to drive automation autonomously. Nevertheless, organizations applying RPA should consider IT involvement or the establishment of a center of excellence for the maintenance of the implemented RPA robots to utilize the productivity gains for the long term (Osmundsen et al. 2019, 6925).

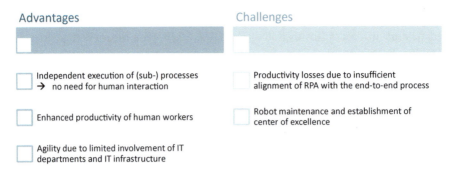

Fig. 10 Overview—advantages and challenges of RPA (© ifb SE)

The above-mentioned advantages and challenges are summarized below (Fig. 10).

In sum, RPA provides business departments with an agile solution to create productivity gains by working with enterprise applications without the involvement of IT experts. In order to realize productivity gains with a long-term perspective, business departments need to establish responsibilities to maintain and refine existing robots.

4.4 Component Classification

The previous sections illustrated the advantages as well as challenges of working with and establishing BPEs, Process Mining, and RPA within an organization and emphasized the focus of the different process automation technologies. The next section clarifies why one individual solution incorporating all features of the named process automation technologies does not exist. Therefore, a distinction between heavyweight and lightweight IT is necessary, as outlined in the following.

Heavyweight IT is a knowledge paradigm, where enterprise applications should guarantee stability and efficiency by following established governance processes. Typical examples of heavyweight IT include backend systems, which are implemented and maintained by the IT department of an organization using software engineering methodologies. Adaptations to the systems emerging from changes in the requirements of the respective business process require a written specification and the involvement of the IT department to realize the adjustment (Bygstad 2017, 181f.). Consequently, the IT department is expected to interfere with the underlying logic of an enterprise application or system, such as the data or system architecture (Penttinen et al. 2018, 2).

Due to the digital transformation of organizations, the IT department is depicted as a central role for transformation. This trend resulted in IT departments being confronted with consistent operation of enterprise systems on the one hand, as well as innovation enabling on the other hand (Horlach et al. 2016, 1418). The increased demand for innovation and therefore the increased burden on IT departments reduces the speed of innovation within an organization as the IT department must prioritize projects to be realized with available resources.

Lightweight IT as a knowledge paradigm focuses on the rapid development and deployment of customer-facing and business-oriented technology to reduce the time-to-market cycle and provide business users simple and immediate solutions for their needs. Due to the focus of lightweight IT on the demand of the business departments, technology specified as lightweight IT is managed by the business departments themselves. Thus, lightweight IT is characterized as inexpensive and easy-to-use technologies to satisfy business needs (Bygstad 2017, 181f.). In fact, technologies categorized as lightweight IT act on the presentation layer, such as a graphical user interface of an enterprise solution and therefore do not require any adaptations to the underlying IT system architecture and consequently no IT involvement (Penttinen et al. 2018, 2).

Nevertheless, lightweight IT depends on functions provided by heavyweight IT, such as data repositories or data processing. Some lightweight IT technologies such as mobile applications require preparational activities in order to interact with heavyweight IT (Horlach et al. 2016, 1422).

Based on the different principles, such as stability and efficiency fulfilled by heavyweight IT or agility and reduced time-to-market by lightweight IT, both paradigms exist in parallel and interact with each other to satisfy business, governance, and organizational requirements (Horlach et al. 2016, 1421). However, interaction does not comply with integration. Through the integration of lightweight IT into heavyweight IT, the technical and organizational complexity increases and the development and deployment of lightweight IT in this highly integrated context would require experts to understand the dependencies that have arisen. In order to keep the characteristics of these two paradigms, the technologies should be embedded in the company as loosely coupled modules, both technically and organizationally. (Bygstad 2017, 190). Loosely coupled is a technical term and describes the interaction of software components with few or no knowledge of the underlying systems they are interacting with. Regarding the organizational integration of the paradigm lightweight IT, literature recommends the establishment of a separate center of excellence and a culture of dual speed to benefit from both paradigms (Horlach et al. 2016, 1423). Despite its own organizational structure, the center of excellence for lightweight IT interacts with the IT department (center of excellence for heavyweight IT) to ensure the governance, security, architecture, and infrastructure needed for the justified establishment of lightweight IT technologies (Willcocks et al. 2015, 22, 28). Table 1 summarizes the characteristics of heavyweight and lightweight IT to enable categorization of the process automation technologies.

In order to emphasize the discrepancies in handling the process automation technologies BPE, Process Mining, and RPA, the technologies are categorized as heavyweight or lightweight IT.

Firstly, Table 2 visualizes the classification of BPEs as a heavyweight IT technology, due to the focus on the stable and efficient execution of end-to-end processes or application-internal processes organized by the BPE. Due to the need for specialized technical skills to deploy and maintain processes within a BPE and the required adaptation of the IT architecture to facilitate change, the governance for the BPE is located in the IT department of an organization. Secondly, the technology Process Mining cannot be clearly categorized. Even though business departments are provided with an understanding of how the business process is executed by the involved enterprise systems as well as an overview on key performance indicators to define adjustments to the process, the IT department is essential to set up the Process Mining tool. Moreover, process optimizations affect the IT architecture and simultaneously impact human activities within the business units. Thirdly, RPA can be classified as lightweight IT, due to its agile and business-oriented

Table 1 Characteristics of heavyweight and lightweight IT (© ifb SE)

Characteristics	Heavyweight IT	Lightweight IT
Focus	Stability and efficiency	Business oriented and time-to-market
Governance	IT department	Business department
Adaptability	Changes to IT architecture	Changes to presentation layer

Table 2 Categorization of process automation technologies (© ifb SE)

Characteristics	Business process engine	Process mining	Robotics process automation
Focus	Heavyweight IT	Lightweight IT	Lightweight IT
Governance	Heavyweight IT	Heavyweight IT	Lightweight IT
Adaptability	Heavyweight IT	Heavyweight IT/Lightweight IT	Lightweight IT

character as well as its governance within a business-driven center of excellence (Osmundsen et al. 2019, 6918). In consequence, the right combination of these components enables an organization to benefit from the dual speed of innovation, as outlined in the following section.

4.5 Component Combination

In order to provide an understanding of how the above-mentioned technologies can be combined to create benefits for the digital transformation of an organization, the next section illustrates some examples of interactions between BPEs, Process Mining, and RPA.

BPEs predefine the process flow including various enterprise applications. Process Mining discovers a process flow and the deviations (process variants) by analyzing the log files of enterprise applications. Deploying a Process Mining tool on top of the BPE would result in the discovery of an already modeled process flow and process variants, which would not result in in-depth new insights (van der Aalst et al. 2010, 88). Instead of deploying Process Mining on top of the BPE, Process Mining should be used to visualize the process flow and variants of the involved enterprise applications, which is often not modeled in detail. Comparing these insights to the estimates made in the process model of the BPE enables the business department in cooperation with the IT department or the application specialist to identify optimization potential for the process in the enterprise applications and the activities conducted by human workers by visualizing the actual activities processed to accomplish a task and resource allocation in relation to the time perspective (van der Aalst et al. 2007, 714f.).

The interaction of BPEs and RPA highlights the different process views of the two technologies. More specifically, BPE focuses on the execution of the end-to-end process and RPA on the added value of automating processes for the business department and the customer. This manifests the beneficial interactions between BPE and RPA. The functions of RPA are utilized to automate (sub-) processes of the end-to-end process, which were classified as too costly to automate with BPE. These optimizations of (sub-) processes or activities achieved with RPA consequently result in enhanced process metrics for the end-to-end process and ultimately in higher quality of the business outcome (Penttinen et al. 2018, 4). While the development of interfaces for the processes in BPEs is a great cost factor, the functions of RPA should be considered to enable the interactions between legacy systems and BPEs (Willcocks et al. 2015, 17). In organizations with an established process center of excellence or similar units, RPA development efforts can benefit from the knowledge established for the process analysis, design, and optimization in these units before configuring robots to carry out processes (Willcocks et al. 2015, 31).

Similar to the interaction between BPEs and Process Mining, the efforts invested in process analysis, design and development result in benefits for RPA. More specifically, it provides the opportunity to detect potential activities for automation by visualizing the throughput, the potential cases, and resource shortfalls. These and other performance indicators enable the RPA project participants to prioritize (sub-) processes and activities for automation and standardization prior to robot development (Geyer-Klingenberg et al. 2018, 2). The visualization performed by Process Mining tools differs from the sole robot monitoring view of RPA tools and Process Mining compares the process execution of several instances (Geyer-Klingenberg et al. 2018, 4). The Process Mining technology allows business and IT departments to create an overall roadmap for process automation with BPEs and RPA.

Overall, the preceding sections investigated the questions of "Why do three different components exist to visualize, optimize and automate processes? And does one of these components offer the full range needed to effectively manage process automation within an organization?", thereby covering the overall research question of this article of why the vision of an all-embracing Process Engine was not fulfilled in the last two decades. In summary, all three components cover a different aspect of process automation and can—in a loose combination—benefit from each other to solve the challenges of process automation.

5   Summary and Outlook

Considering the fast pace at which technology advances, a question arises: Will the three technologies described continue to co-exist and complement each other or will there be a type of BPE that combines their capabilities and therefore eliminates the need for them?

As indicated in Sect. 4.1, an embedded form of a Business Process Engine is limited to the application it is embedded in. Therefore, it is capable of automating processes that are executed within that application, but unable to break the boundaries of its embedding. Since a lot of business processes span multiple applications, the functionality of an embedded BPE cannot be considered sufficient for RPA and Process Mining to be replaced.

Also, looking at the situation in the financial market as of today, the functionality of a standalone BPE will not be sufficient to eliminate the need for

RPA and Process Mining—with the exception of those companies that have only one ERM solution covering all their business needs in place.

A standalone BPE, although capable of executing processes across different applications of an enterprise, requires some sort of interface to the applications it is supposed to interact with in order to execute processes. In the financial industry, the application landscape tends to be outdated and therefore lacks standardization and the required connectivity capabilities (McKinsey & Company 2019). In consequence, for a standalone BPE to eliminate the need for RPA, either interfaces between the BPE and the target applications would have to be built or the applications would need to be replaced. Either way, such undertakings are usually cost- and time-intensive, especially when it comes to legacy systems offering core business capabilities which are vital for businesses' operations. The same logic applies to a standalone BPE replacing Process Mining. Additionally, the depth of standalone BPEs' analytics capabilities currently does not match that of Process Mining. In the future, BPEs might be able to catch up in this regard and provide further in-depth knowledge concerning the processes they execute. Still, the connectivity problem is likely to remain for a long time. At the point where it is solved, companies will still face the challenge of complexity. As described throughout Sect. 4, Business Process Engines are classified as heavyweight IT. Therefore, they increase complexity and take away a certain amount of agility by introducing the permanent need for expert knowledge prior to making any changes to business processes' functionality. In consequence, the desirability of integrating lightweight IT, such as RPA and Process Mining, into heavyweight IT is to be questioned.

However, there are providers offering systems called intelligent business process management suites (iBPMS), which—compared to BPEs—add more capabilities for greater intelligence within business processes (Gartner, Inc. 2020c). These capabilities include integration with social media, real-time decision-making, and streaming analytics. Additionally, some providers also offer RPA capabilities within their products. Along with the already established BPE capabilities such as process validation, simulation, and process intelligence, iBPMSs present a strong case for being able to combine all three forms of technology—RPA, BPE, and Process Mining. With their low code offering, in particular, iBPMSs resemble a promising solution for companies to make their processes more agile through fast and scalable development. Still, business processes must be modeled initially in order to be implemented into the Business Process Engine—whether it is an intelligent system or not. In this regard, Process Mining offers a valuable functionality, namely process discovery, where a process is executed in the current environment prior to implementation. Afterward, the monitoring of processes can be done within the Business Process Engine as such. Yet, organizations have to determine individually whether or not the implementation of an iBMPS is suitable for them, as not every company may be in need of the entire spectrum of functionality, which might lead to the system being too expensive or complex for the company's actual goals.

In conclusion, a BPE alone will most likely not be able to entirely replace RPA and Process Mining. Even though intelligent business process suites are capable of combining the three technologies to a certain degree, they still exist with their individual functionalities. Therefore, the three components of automation are likely to remain in the future, even if they are conflated under the umbrella of a single product.

Literature

Appian. 2020. "www.appian.com." *Business Process Definition. What Is a Business Process?* Accessed September 14, 2020. https://www.appian.com/bpm/definition-of-a-business-process/.

Bygstad, Bendik. 2017. "Generative Innovation: A Comparison of Lightweight and Heavyweight IT." *Journal of Information Technology, Jg* 32: 180–193.

Dogan, Erkan. 2020. "Industrial-Engineering-Vision.de." *Prozessoptimierung.* Accessed September 14, 2020. https://industrial-engineering-vision.de/prozessoptimierung/.

Forrester Research. 2011. *The Role of IT in Business-Driven Process Automation.* Cambridge: Forrester Consulting.

Gadatsch, Andreas. 2020. *Grundkurs Geschäftsprozess-Management.* Wiesbaden: Springer Vieweg.

Gartner, Inc. 2020a. "Gartner Glossary." *Business Process Management Suites (BPMSs).* Accessed October 6, 2020. https://www.gartner.com/en/information-technology/glossary/bpms-business-process-management-suite.

Gartner, Inc. 2020b. *Gartner.com.* https://www.gartner.com/en/information-technology/glossary/robotic-process-automation-rpa.

Gartner, Inc. 2020c. *Gartner.com.* Accessed October 2, 2020. https://www.gartner.com/reviews/market/intelligent-business-process-management-suites.

Geyer-Klingenberg, Baldauf, F. J., J. Nakladat, and F. Viet. 2018. "Process Mining and Robotic Process Automation: A Perfect Match." *16th International Conference on Business Process Management (BPM).* Sydney, Australia.

Hofmann, M. 2020. "Methoden der Prozessoptimierung." In *Prozessoptimierung als ganzheitlicher Ansatz,* edited by M. Hofmann, 35–70. Wiesbaden: Springer Gabler.

Horlach, Bettina, Paul Drews, and Ingrid Schirmer. 2016. "Bimodal IT: Business-IT Alignment in the Age of Digital Transformation." *Proceedings of Multikonferenz Wirtschaftsinformatik* 3: 1417–1428.

International Organization of Standardization (ISO). 2013. "ISO/IEC 19510:2013: Information Technology—Object Management Group Business Process Model and Notation." 07.

Jagadeesh Chandra Bose, R. P., and W. M. P. van der Aalst. 2009. "Abstractions in Process Mining: A Taxonomy of Patterns." In *Business Process Management. BPM 2009. Lecture Notes in Computer Science, Vol. 5701*, edited by U. Dayal, J. Eder, J. Koehler and H. A. Reijers, 159–175. Berlin, Heidelberg: Springer.

Johannesson, Paul, and Erik Perjons. 2011. "Design Principles for Process Modelling in Enterprise Application Integration." *Information Systems, Jg* 26: 165–184.

Krallmann, Hermann, Annette Bobrik, and Olga Levina. 2013. *Systemanalyse im Unternehmen - Prozessorientierte Methoden der Wirtschaftsinformatik*. Berlin: De Gruyter.

Lacity, M. C., and L. P. Willcocks. 2015. "hbr.org." *What Knowledge Workers Stand to Gain from Automation*. June 19. Accessed 2020. https://hbr.org/2015/06/what-knowledge-workers-stand-to-gain-from-automation.

Lacity, M. C., and L. P. Willcocks. 2016. "A New Approach to Automating Services." *Management Review* 58(1): 41–49.

Lamberton, C. 2016. *Get Ready for Robots. Why Planning Makes the Difference Between Success and Disappointment*. Accessed June 11, 2018.

Lhuer, X. 2016. "McKinsey.com." *The Next Acronym You Need To Know About: RPA (Robotic Process Automation)*. Accessed June 11, 2018. https://www.mckinsey.com/businessfunctions/digital-mckinsey/our-insights/the-next-acronymyou-need-to-know-about-rpa.

Lublinsky, Boris. 2001. "Achieving the Ultimate EAI Implementation." *eai Journal* 2: 26–31.

Luczak, Holger, and Jörg Becker. 2003. *Workflowmanagement in der Produktionsplanung und -steuerung*. Berlin Heidelberg: Springer Verlag.

Manyika, J., M. Chui, M. Miremadi, J. Bughin, K. George, P. Willmott, and M. Dewhurst. 2017. *A Future That Works: Automation, Employment, and Productivity*. McKinsey Global Institute.

McKeen, James D., and Heather A. Smith. 2002. "New Developments in Practice II: Enterprise Application Integration." *Communications of the Association for Information Systems* 8: 451–466.

McKinsey & Company. 2019. "www.McKinsey.com." www.McKinsey.com. 4 11. Accessed September 21, 2020. https://www.mckinsey.com/industries/financial-services/our-insights/it-modernization-in-insurance-three-paths-to-transformation.

Medling, Jan, Gero Decker, Richard Hull, Hajo A. Reijers, and Ingo Weber. 2018. "How Do Machine Learning, Robotic Process Automation, and Blockchain Affect the Human Factor in Business Process Management?" *Communications of the Association for Information Systems* 43: 1–23.

Osmundsen, Karen, Jon Iden, and Bendik Bygstad. 2019. "Organizing Robotic Process Automation: Balancing Loose and Tight." *Proceedings of the 52nd Hawaii International Conference on System Sciences* 6918–6926.

Ostdick, Nick. 2016. "UiPath.com." *5 Factors in Choosing Which Processes to Automate.* September 29. Accessed 2020. https://www.uipath.com/blog/5-factors-in-choosing-which-processes-to-automate.

Penttinen, E., H. Kassalon, and A. Asatiani. 2018. "How to Choose Between Robotic Process Automation and Back-End System Automation?" *Paper presented at European Conference on Information Systems.*

Rautenburger, Lars, and Alexander Liebl. 2021. "Process Mining." In *The Digital Journey of Banking and Insurance, Volume II—Digitalization and Machine Learning*, edited by Volker Liermann and Claus Stegmann. New York: Palgrave Macmillan.

Soybir, Sefa, and Christopher Schmidt. 2021. "Project Management and RPA." In *The Digital Journey of Banking and Insurance, Volume I—Disruption and DNA*, edited by Volker Liermann and Claus Stegmann. New York: Palgrave Macmillan.

Vahs, Dietmar. 2007. In *Organisation: Einführung in die Organisationstheorie und -praxis*, 222. Stuttgart: Schäffer-Poeschel.

van der Aalst, W. M. P. 2016. *Process Mining: Data Science in Action.* Heidelberg: Springer.

van der Aalst, W. M. P., and S. Dustdar. 2012. "Process Mining Put into Context." *IEEE Internet Computing* 16: 82–86.

van der Aalst, W. M. P., H. A. Reijers, A. J. M. M. Weijters, B. F. van Dongen, A. K. Alves de Medeiros, M. Song, and H. M. W. Verbeek. 2007. "Business Process Mining: An Industrial Application." *Information Systems* 32: 713–732.

van der Aalst, W. M. P., M. Bichler, and A. Heinzl. 2018. "Robotic Process Automation." *Business & Information Systems Engineering* 60: 269–272.

van der Aalst, W. M. P., V. Rubin, H. M. W. Verbeek, B. F. van Dongen, E. Kindler, and C. W. Günther. 2010. "Process Mining: A Two-Step Approach to Balance Between Underfitting and Overfitting." *Software System Model* 9: 87–111.

Waldorf, Jerry A., Yanbing Lu, and Alex Demetriades. 2009. Web Browser as Web Service Server in Interaction with Business Process Engine. United States of America Patent US 7,506,072 B2. March 17.

Weske, Mathias. 2012. *Business Process Modelling Foundation.* Switzerland: Springer Nature.

Willcocks, L. P., and M. C. Lacity. 2016. *Service Automation: Robots and the Future of Work.* Steve Brookes Publishing.

Willcocks, Leslie P., Mary Lacity, and Andrew Craig. 2015. "The IT Function and Robotic Process Automation." *LSE Research Online Documents on Economics*, 1–39.

Process Mining

Lars Rautenburger and Alexander Liebl

1 Introduction

Process miningtechnology creates real transparency about the different variants within a process by reconstructing process models on a real-data basis and then offers a wide range of analysis options. This enables real process knowledge to be gained in a way that is case-specific and demand-oriented. Based on this knowledge, correlations can be detected, well-founded starting points for process improvements and automation can be identified and their effect can be measured directly through renewed process mining.

For this reason, process mining is also called "up-front technology" in the context of process improvement projects and serves as the basic technology for modern transformation projects, which strive for the goal of hyperautomation.

L. Rautenburger (✉) · A. Liebl
ifb SE, Grünwald, Germany
e-mail: Lars.Rautenburger@ifb-group.com

A. Liebl
e-mail: Alexander.Liebl@ifb-group.com

1.1 Process Mining Brings Full Transparency to Business Processes

By reconstructing and visualizing a process based on the data in the IT systems ("digital footprints"), process mining technology represents the process as it really is. The result is a process picture that realistically reflects the actual process flows—with all branches and down to the work step level. It therefore provides an overview of all process variants occurring in practice and automatically displays the most frequently occurring process variant. Various perspectives, filters and in-depth analyzes support the identification of improvement potential in process execution. Inefficiencies (e.g. process loops) and their causes, avoidable idle times, compliance violations, and unused automation potential become visible. This visibility allows a derivation of concrete and comprehensible optimization measures, which will reduce the complexity and increase the process quality when implemented.

1.2 How to Set Up Process Mining to Reach Full Transparency and Transform it Into Valuable Optimizations

In order to really generate the possible insights and to be able to really add value, it is crucial to set up process mining properly as it functions as basic technology and forms the foundation for all subsequent analyzes and possible optimizations. As this is a Big Data use case, it is especially important to know what should be analyzed and for which purpose, and which data is relevant for finding results (IEEE Task Force on Process Mining 2012). Even with process mining and all its associated possibilities, the solution space is only as large and promising as the underlying database.

The necessary steps for the successful installation of process mining as a starting point to achieve complete process transparency and the successful approach to process evaluation and the derivation, implementation, and performance measurement of optimizations are described in detail in this chapter.

1.3 Structure of the Chapter

In the following sections, we describe all aspects necessary to set up successful process mining and how to best utilize the findings to optimize the process. In Sect. 2 we begin with a brief introduction to process mining technology and its functionality. Section 3 covers all process mining project steps from the beginning to the end, which also includes the initiation and measurement of optimization efforts. This is followed by Sect. 4 where we will cover related organizational aspects as the required roles to drive such transformations and stakeholder and change management. Section 5 recaps the crucial success factors, provides an overview of the application and acceptance in the market and gives an outlook.

2 The Process Mining Technology—Definition, Functionality, and Requirements

The previous chapter "Processes in a Digital Environment" already introduced process mining as a technology used for creating transparency in an organization's processes (Czwalina et al. 2021). The following paragraph is a short recap of the technology's functionality and the requirements to be met for process mining to work and provide business value.

Process mining is a technique designed to discover, monitor, and improve real processes (i.e. not assumed processes) by extracting readily available knowledge from the event logs of IT systems (Gartner 2020).

This provides the possibility of analyzing processes based on how they are really carried out instead of having to rely on often outdated process documentation. This is especially important when it comes to initiatives that aim to change the processes in any way, since utilizing the process mining technology ensures that the process has been captured to its full extent and understood prior to making changes.

In today's world, most processes involve IT systems. Whenever a process step is performed with the help of an IT system, pieces of data are stored in that system. Process mining connects to the IT systems involved in a process, collects the data traces, and uses them to reconstruct the process as it actually happened according to the collected data. The minimum requirement for process mining is three pieces of information to be extracted from the supporting IT system (Burattin 2015):

- A unique case ID
- The activity performed
- The timestamp at which the activity took place.

The three pieces together form the so-called "minimal event log."

Fig. 1 Minimal event log analyzed by process mining (simplified illustration) (© ifb SE)

Once the data is extracted from the source system, the process mining technology can analyze the event log and reconstruct the process as sketched in Fig. 1. Additionally, the restructured process can be analyzed according to custom performance indicators. So, with process mining, root causes for inefficiencies and compliance violations can be identified on a solid fact base. This deep process knowledge enables the derivation and initialization of optimization measures that improve the process performance in the long term and accelerate the business.

3 The Steps of a Process Mining Project

In this section, every necessary step in a process mining project is described in detail, from the setting of objectives to the measurement of process improvements. All steps are illustrated in Fig. 2.

3.1 Setting the Objectives

The first step in setting up process mining is to focus on the goals of the entire initiative. However, a well-founded objective does not necessarily end with the selection of the target process. Instead, the following additional aspects must be understood and covered in order to take the right direction and meet expectations.

3.1.1 Define the Goals and Fields of Action

What is the analysis focus and the objective? Should costs be saved or waiting time for customers reduced? Of course, both questions can be answered within the framework of process mining. However, it is always important to know with which intention you approach process mining and with which view analyzes are currently being carried out. Even in the phases of analysis

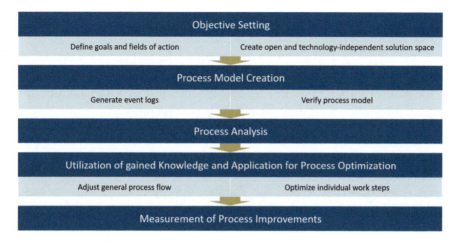

Fig. 2 Steps during a process mining project (© ifb SE)

and optimization, the constant focus on objectives helps not to lose focus. Without a clear picture of the objectives, the wide range of analysis options tempts you to dive into analyzes and optimizations that add value but do not fulfill the actual objectives. Depending on the focus of the analysis, it can also make sense to add relevant data to the pure process data in order to draw an even clearer picture.

3.1.2 Create an Open and Technology-Independent Solution Space

In any case, a project environment that is as solution-open as possible should be created at the beginning of the project. The larger the possible solution space, the better the findings from process mining can be processed. Therefore, avoid the common mistake of limiting the objective at the beginning and do not reduce it from "We want to save costs" to "How can we automate?", or even worse, "Where can we place a certain technology?". The more detailed and technology-driven the solution space is restricted, the more potential is wasted, since so many recommendations for action are already excluded without having reviewed a single analysis.

3.2 Set Up an Evaluable Process Model

After the successful and aligned target setting, the preparatory work for the actual process mining begins. Since process mining reconstructs the process on the basis of the data traces in the systems, the next step is to identify these traces and combine them into an evaluable process model.

3.2.1 Generate Event Logs

The second step is to create the database for process mining, on which the process reconstruction and the subsequent analyzes are based. For this purpose, so-called event logs are generated. They are essential for process mining and a critical success factor because they are the fundamental information carrier and the starting point for every process mining project. The quality of the output and the results of the analysis depend significantly on the existing input (van der Aalst 2016).

As described in the previous section, the objective and the associated expectations are relevant for the final evaluation of the process mining result. From the defined objectives, the requirements for the data necessary for the event logs must be derived. Only if sufficient data in evaluable quality is available for the respective process mining objectives and if the data can be linked together in a meaningful way and assigned to a respective process run will the use of process mining really add value.

Process mining is based on one or more linked event logs. An event log is composed of individual event data, which brings together the different process executions and, depending on the enrichment, further additional evaluable information. The digital traces left in the IT systems during process execution serve as event data. These can be, for example, database tables in ERP systems, event logs of CRM systems, transaction logs of messaging systems or logs of classic BPM workflow systems. Figure 3 shows the tree structure of an event log.

These data sources can either be imported and assigned to the process mining tool or directly queried, extracted, and defined via a direct connection of the process mining tool with the respective database. The direct connection is recommended because this way the update times can be defined and the latest data status is automatically reflected in the process model. If desired, an update can also be carried out with every change, thus providing live tracking of the process and all currently running executions.

In the context of data import/data extraction and the creation of event logs, the data model and relationships must also be defined and configured.

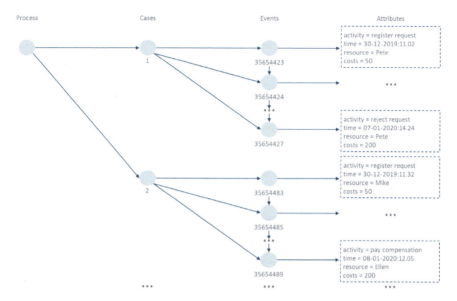

Fig. 3 Structure of event logs (example), own representation acc. to (van der Aalst 2016)

This defines which values and attributes (e.g. activities, status messages) are related to each other and how.

3.2.2 Verify Process Model

After all data has been prepared and the data model has been built, the reconstruction of the process model must be initiated and the result checked. At this point it is very important to involve a real process expert with the necessary expertise in order to identify anomalies or possible transformation errors during the event log generation.

Small test evaluations for the verification of the existing process model should be carried out without fail. If anomalies or deviations are identified, they should be inspected in detail. There are two possible reasons for this. An error may have occurred in the preliminary work (event log generation). In this case, it must be identified and repaired and the reconstruction of the process model must be started again. This must be repeated until the process model fits. The second possibility is that it is already an unexpected finding in the form of an unexpected deviation as illustrated in Fig. 4.

In any case, it is important to ensure that the process model is correct and reflects the data, regardless of whether it looks like what was expected or

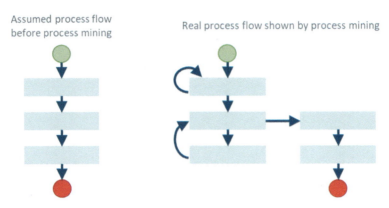

Fig. 4 Processes in theory and practice (© ifb SE)

not. As soon as the process model is "correct" and validated (i.e. represents a correct image of the data) the detailed evaluation can begin.

3.3 Analyze the Process and Gain Deep Process Knowledge

Once the process model has been created and validated, the real analysis of the process begins. Here, most process mining tools provide a large number of predefined analysis options and dashboards. Initial findings can therefore be identified very quickly. These need to be further deepened according to the objectives. Of course, the predefined analyzes can also be supplemented by own analyzes.

The objectives defined at the beginning ensure that the focus is not lost, as the newly gained process transparency over the entire process variations, including the individual work step execution, can easily seem overwhelming.

With regard to the optimization measures resulting from process mining, it is advisable to focus the analysis on the three to five most frequent process variants, since adjustments are most effective here. In addition, it should be analyzed why there are a large number of variants with a low throughput. These are either deviations from the defined process model or the fulfillment of special cases. In the latter, limiting the complexity should be considered, in order to simplify the process and thus exclude possible sources of error. Perhaps not every business requirement within the process really needs a single process variation and there are possibilities to combine and limit these via commonalities.

Concerning rule and compliance violations, the entire process with all its variants should always be analyzed in order to identify the root causes of these violations and to be able to eliminate them holistically. Even a single breach of compliance can result in high penalties.

In order to obtain the best possible analysis results, it is important to have a deep understanding of the structure of analysis dashboards and the functioning of process mining and its evaluations, as well as well-founded expert process know-how for the correct classification of the findings and drawing of the appropriate conclusions.

3.4 Utilize the Process Knowledge Gained and Optimize the Process

After the process analysis, action must follow the findings in order to realize the identified potential depending on the objectives, e.g., save costs, increase the process quality or shorten the lead time.

In process optimization, two types of optimization can be distinguished. Optimizations can be divided into the categories "Adaptation of the general process flow" and "Optimization of individual work steps."

The first is an optimization by adapting the general process flow, while the second focuses on the optimization of a single work step (e.g. through automation) within the general process flow.

Regardless of the optimization category, the potential with the greatest added value at reasonable effort should always be addressed first. For both categories, it is advisable to prioritize the identified added value potential before implementation, to coordinate it and then to implement it step by step. In this way, added value is gradually generated in a coordinated manner, and any—even previously unrecognizable—effects on the following measure can be taken into account before the implementation is started.

In the overall view, it is always advisable to start optimizing individual work steps only after the entire process flow has been optimized. This prevents individual work steps from being optimized without knowing the detailed requirements for their role in the new overall process. This should also be considered in the prioritization and execution sequence to save avoidable extra work.

The application and step-by-step processing of the added values of both optimization categories in the sequence described was successfully tested in practice.

Now, a detailed differentiation of the optimization categories, their respective triggers and problem definitions, as well as the representation of solution approaches for added value realization follows.

3.4.1 Adjustment of the General Process Flow

When adapting the process flow, the process flow will be adjusted to meet the new requirements. This can be triggered by the fact that the current process sequence does not meet the business requirements (either because the execution does not take place as planned or new business requirements have not successfully found their way into the process execution) or that certain audit standards (e.g. dual control principle) are not always adhered to. Figure 5 illustrates how the process can be affected through the adjustment of the general process flow.

3.4.2 Optimization of Individual Work Steps

After the overall process flow has been reorganized, the execution of individual process steps can be analyzed in more detail. If there are no compliance violations in the execution of a process step, the main focus lies on increasing efficiency. In the first step, this is usually approached with automation technologies of lower complexity in order to automate manually executed routine activities. The implementation possibilities are extensive, depending on the infrastructure in the company and the tools used. One technology used particularly frequently in these cases is Robotic Process Automation (RPA).

One of the two main reasons for the rapid spread of RPA is the technical independence of the involved infrastructure and systems that are affected by the process execution. This is achieved by using RPA technology to program bots that imitate human interaction with the systems to be operated during process execution. In this way, the bot executes routine tasks instead of human interaction. The second reason for the high popularity of RPA technology is that programming and deployment of the bots are quick and easy.

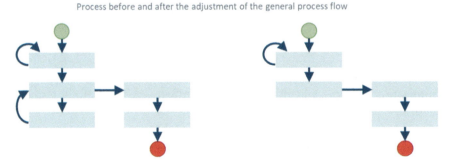

Fig. 5 Example of the effect of a general process adjustment (© ifb SE)

These are so-called "low code applications," which also allow less technically experienced users to configure a bot with manageable effort. The result of RPA is a reduction in the error rate in process execution and a reduced idle time, while at the same time relieving the burden on the employee, who can thus devote his or her attention to more value-creating activities.

Of course, this form of automation also has its limits, e.g., if the variation of the work execution of the individual step is too complex or not fully predictable. In this case, it is advisable to also use machine learning and artificial intelligence or a combination of such technologies that enables the automation of more complex working steps. Figure 6 describes some typical tasks RPA bots can perform easily.

Even if the single RPA application sounds simple, it often leads to problems in practice. But the problem is not the implementation of the robot but wrong assumptions and insufficient knowledge about the process step to be automated. The use of RPA only makes sense if it can be ensured that the process step is really a recurring activity with the same execution pattern

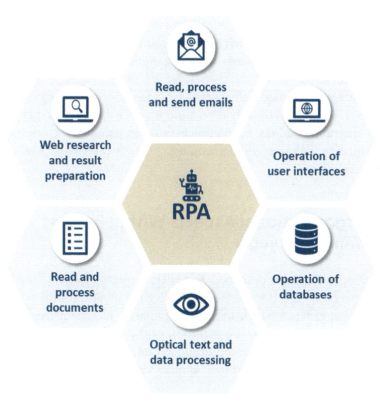

Fig. 6 Typical tasks performed by RPA bots (© ifb SE)

each time. This is the point where it becomes clear why process mining is also called up-front technology for RPA. Since process mining provides full transparency of all execution variants within a process and individual work steps, it is possible to identify with certainty which work step is suitable for automation with RPA and which exact execution variants the bot must cover.

3.5 Measure the Effectiveness of the Optimizations Performed with Process Mining

A further advantage of process mining and the resulting optimizations is that the effects are directly measurable as soon as the optimizations are applied in practice. Just as the original process execution left traces in the systems for evaluation, the optimized process execution leaves corresponding traces in the systems as well.

Since the data connection already exists due to the initial evaluation, the new traces can also be imported directly and evaluated using process mining without much effort. Even if the data is not fed into the tool via a direct database connection, it is only necessary to re-import the most current data. Where the data is located, which query is required and what to pay attention to when importing data is already known from the initial setup of the process model.

This fast and fact-based before/after comparison only involves little effort and makes it possible to directly determine whether the changes met expectations or the optimizations were implemented as planned. In case of lower performance or incorrect implementation, the direct feedback allows for quick corrections.

4 Organizational Aspects Within Process Mining Projects

In addition to the steps described and their respective pitfalls in a process mining project, this section focuses on the related organizational aspects.

The section explains which roles are required to successfully pass through all steps. This is followed by a description of the topic of change and stakeholder management in the context of process mining projects, which can lead to restrictions if not considered or if applied too late.

4.1 Roles and Responsibilities

In order to perform the steps of process mining successfully, the following roles are required as a minimum.

Business owner/process owner: The business owner or process owner defines the goals and the business focus of the process mining project. The necessary data is derived from these goals and defines the possible solution space for the analyzes.

IT expert/database expert: The IT or database expert derives the relevant data pools and possible input sources for the event log from the defined goals and analysis priorities.

Process mining expert(s): The process mining expert and his main tasks can be divided into two roles as sketched in Fig. 7. In the role of the data engineer he takes care of the technical setup, data configuration, and providing the master process model. If the process mining expert takes over the analyst role, he takes care of the whole evaluation of the reconstructed process in line with the defined objectives.

Due to the different focus of tasks, there is often a dedicated person for each role.

We shall now describe how the key players introduced interact in the project progress and in which situation it makes sense to involve additional roles to support them.

The business owners set the goals, so that the IT expert can then identify the corresponding data repositories. The IT expert checks the quality of the data and its suitability for process mining with the data engineer. If necessary, they transform the raw data into a structure that meets the requirements of an event log. To complete the setup of the initial evaluable process model, the data engineer configures the event logs and their relationship in the process mining tool. After the acceptance of the process model by the process owner, the data analyst builds the dashboard and analyzes to identify optimization potential in line with the target. If the data analyst does not have the required

Data Engineer builds the process model

Analyst analyzes the process and identifies optimization potential

Fig. 7 Main tasks of a process mining expert (© ifb SE)

domain knowledge with regard to the analyzed process, he should analyze the process with a domain expert to be sure that all analyzes support the aligned goals and their findings have been properly interpreted.

At this point, it is important to identify how to make the most out of the findings, which means discussing how the potential should be realized and what effects the different approaches have. External consultants who bring domain know-how and a good understanding of technology and its impact on the organization can offer a lot of value during this process and should be used as a sparring partner to the business/process owners and analysts. After the measures have been decided, they should be implemented. Depending on the preferred solution and technology used, it may be useful to carry out implementation in cooperation with specific experts.

4.2 Change and Stakeholder Management

An often-underestimated aspect within the context of process mining projects, which usually aim to transform findings into improved process performance, is insufficient change and stakeholder management. The transparency and incontestable truth of the process mining results are phenomenal, but also hold potential for conflict and can lead to discrepancies.

This leads to the situation that process mining initiatives have to cope with start-up difficulties or the planned measures lead to inconsistencies and uncertainty among the workforce across all levels. Therefore, it is of enormous importance to involve not only top management and the relevant managers right from the start, but also to inform and involve all levels down to the individual employees about the motivation and the goals pursued at an early stage. It must be communicated that this project is not about identifying culprits but about working together on the big picture.

Those employees whose everyday work is directly affected by the process adjustments should be actively involved in the change especially. This also means dealing with the rumor and justified fear that process optimization and the use of Robotic Process Automation will lead directly to staff reductions. In practice, this is rarely the case and not the primary goal pursued. On the contrary, RPA is not intended to replace employees, but to support them in routine activities and relieve them of repetitive, non-creative work. The aim is not to reduce staff, but to regain process transparency, simplify and accelerate process execution and increase process quality. All transformations ultimately mean change and change must be actively managed to be successful for all parties involved.

What the challenges in a complete RPA project look like in detail and how they should be managed in terms of active change management is described in the chapter "Project Management and RPA" in the section "Challenges" (Soybir and Schmidt 2021).

5 Summary

In summary, it can be said that process mining technology—which reconstructs processes based on traces in IT systems—takes on the role of a basic technology and paves the way for achieving hyperautomation. Based on data, it shows where there is potential for optimization within a process and where the use of further technologies can make sense. Particularly in combination with Robotic Process Automation technology, the first automation potential can be quickly realized without much effort. These are the first steps on the way to hyperautomation, while the use and integration of advanced and more complex technologies such as machine learning and artificial intelligence continue to increase. Figure 8 illustrates the frequently used technologies to reach hyperautomation and the following chapter "Hyperautomation (Automated Decision-Making as Part of RPA)" explains the ideas behind hyperautomation by discussing a specific example (Liermann et al. 2021).

The large financial service providers and companies are clearly the pioneers here, but the medium-sized companies are also catching up. For small companies, the use of these Big Data and automation technologies often does not

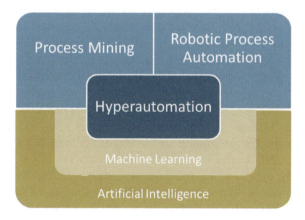

Fig. 8 Technologies used to reach hyperautomation (© ifb SE)

(yet) exceed the cost–benefit ratio. However, the overriding goal of hyperautomation has not yet been achieved even by the big pioneers. In particular, the meaningful and comprehensive application of machine learning and artificial intelligence is still in a strong development phase. Here, the authors expect a strong gain in knowledge in the coming years, which will reward the research and innovation enthusiasm of the first movers with a competitive advantage.

In order to successfully master the first step on this long and partly unknown journey with process mining, it is important to pay enough attention to the following core aspects already at the beginning of the project or possibly even in the pre-study phase. The analysis goal must be clearly defined and it must be ensured that the necessary data is available and integrated in good quality. Furthermore, it is important to involve all participants and "affected persons" from the very beginning and to actively take them on the journey. This is the only way to transform the identified potential into real added value that is seen and supported by the entire organization. If there is the necessary clarity and commitment of all participants, the chances are high that process mining will be successful and the findings can be transformed into meaningful actions and powerful follow-up projects.

Literature

Burattin, Andrea. 2015. *Process Mining Techniques in Business Environments.* Springer.

Czwalina, Marie Kristin, Chiara Jakobs, Christopher Schmidt, Matthias Jacoby, and Sebastian Geisel. 2021. "Processes in a Digital Environment." In *The Digital Journey of Banking and Insurance, Volume II—Digitalization and Machine Learning*, edited by Volker Liermann and Claus Stegmann. New York: Palgrave Macmillan.

Gartner. 2020. *Gartner Information Technology Glossary.* Accessed September 21, 2020. https://www.gartner.com/en/information-technology/glossary/process-mining#:~:text=Process%20mining%20is%20a%20technique,models%20from%20an%20event%20log.

IEEE Task Force on Process Mining. 2012. "Process Mining Manifesto." Accessed September 9, 2020. https://www.tf-pm.org/resources/manifesto.

Liermann, Volker, Sangmeng Li, and Johannes Waizner. 2021. "Hyperautomation (Automated Decision-Making as Part of RPA)." In *The Digital Journey of Banking and Insurance, Volume II—Digitalization and Machine Learning*, edited by Volker Liermann and Claus Stegmann. New York: Palgrave Macmillan.

Soybir, Sefa, and Christopher Schmidt. 2021. "Project Management and RPA." In *The Digital Journey of Banking and Insurance, Volume I—Disruption and DNA*, edited by Volker Liermann and Claus Stegmann. New York: Palgrave Macmillan.

van der Aalst, Wil. 2016. *Process Mining*. Berlin Heidelberg: Springer.

Hyperautomation (Automated Decision-Making as Part of RPA)

Volker Liermann, Sangmeng Li, and Johannes Waizner

1 Introduction

1.1 Initial Situation

Robotic Process Automation (RPA) is part of every digitalization strategy in banks and insurance companies. RPA has in recent years launched a fundamental new paradigm on how to automate and optimize processes.

RPA has been particularly successful in automating processes across systems (avoiding system discontinuities) and processes with clear "clicking" patterns. The automation potential reaches a limit when a manual decision (by a human) is still needed in the process.

In Fig. 1, the difference between classic and modern RPA is shown. Modern RPA widens classic RPA by the aspect of automated decision-making (some sources call this "hyperautomation" see Gartner, Gartner Top 10 Strategic

---

V. Liermann (✉) · S. Li · J. Waizner
ifb SE, Grünwald, Germany
e-mail: Volker.Liermann@ifb-group.com

S. Li
e-mail: Sangmeng.Li@ifb-group.com

J. Waizner
e-mail: Johannes.Waizner@ifb-group.com

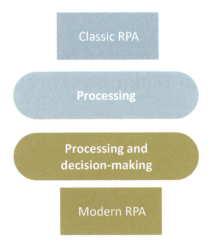

Fig. 1 Modern RPA (© ifb SE)

Technology Trends for 2020 (2019) and Gartner, Gartner Top Strategic Technology Trends for 2021 (2020)).

The adding of (automated) decision-making is not a one-step process. The recent projects have shown that a step-by-step approach delivers the best results and the highest acceptance. In Sect. 2, the idea of how to address this challenge is illustrated in more detail.

1.2 Structure of the Article

Section 2 introduces the general idea and the step-by-step approach to higher levels of automation. RPA and the software tool UiPath are very briefly introduced in Sect. 3. Section 4 discovers the machine learning aspects needed in the context of this use case. The following Sect. 5 gives insights into a practical application, i.e., how to integrate machine learning (Python-based model) into RPA (UiPath). Section 6 summarizes the key findings.

2 General Idea

In Sect. 1.1, we highlighted that a step-by-step automation of the processes works best. In this section, we will discuss different structures for taking these steps.

In Fig. 2, the five-step decision automation model is shown. The different levels show how to move step by step from manual decisions to autonomous

Hyperautomation (Automated Decision-Making as Part of RPA)

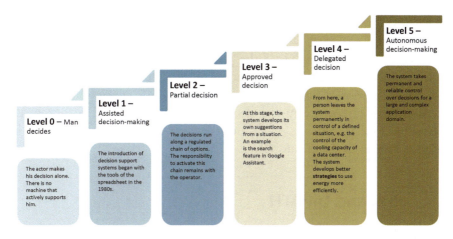

Fig. 2 Five-step decision automation model (© ifb SE)

decision-making. The five-step decision automation model is dealt with in detail (Bitcom 2017).

The automation of a process beyond classic RPA is challenging and needs to be approached step by step. While Fig. 2 gives a detailed structural view, the main blocks are described in Fig. 3.

The foundation for any model to work is formed in level A "learning." The relevant data is collected for a model calibration. The labels are especially hard to find in a structured form. Classic RPA can help with this task because RPA can seamlessly collect and save decisions made by a human in a user-friendly way. In traditional processes, this decision-driving information is—in most

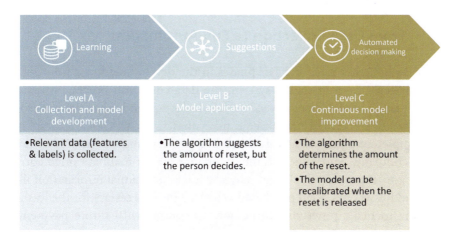

Fig. 3 Blocks for a step-by-step implementation (© ifb SE)

cases—lost after the process management has used it to select the further steps.

To ensure the correctness of the proposed decisions and to ensure the person involved has a good understanding of the status of the process automation level, the model proposes a decision in level B "suggestions," but the human can overrule the model decision. When the model has proposed reasonable decisions for a long time, then the last step (level C) can be entered. The process can run fully automated.

3 RPA and UiPATH

UiPath is one of several tools that can implement RPA procedures. It draws its strength from a graphic user interface that not only lets you string together abstract commands but even simply record mouse clicks that encompass and bring together the control of many different programs by a plethora of third parties. It is therefore easy to create a classic RPA robot that contains, for example, steps going through OfficeSuite products, web browsers, and SAP distributions all at once.

Regarding modern RPA as outlined in Fig. 1, UiPath offers, for example, the integration of external programming languages like Python that can assist the human user in the decision-making process by providing appropriate, custom algorithms. More details are given in the next section.

4 Machine Learning/Data Analysis

4.1 From Data Collection to Full Automation

Figure 3 highlights three steps or phases in the development of a fully automated system. Even in such a system, the data collection process, which is the key part of level A, does not stop. Data collection and usage can therefore themselves be structured into three similar phases. Let us take a use case of, for example, announcements of future invoices arriving at a motor vehicle leasing company. Said announcements present an approximate price corresponding to a specific vehicle and maybe contain additional information like billing addresses, etc., for a purchased vehicle. This is necessary for the leasing company to make provisions to be able to comply with future payments. However, the announced price may be merely a preliminary value and even faulty at times. The receiver of the announcement, henceforth called the user, will have to decide the actual amount of provisions that the company needs to make. This can range from simply approving the announced amount or double checking it against a list price and selecting the correct one, through to remembering and analyzing previous purchases.

As good and informed decisions are based on sufficient amounts of adequate data, the first step is the pure collection of such data.

Phase one will therefore be a period in which relevant data will be collected, manually processed, and evaluated until one achieves a dataset of input values, e.g., announced invoiced amounts, and validated output data. The latter here are the amounts that are validated, approved, and eventually paid. While the collection of the input data can be automated at this point, the generation of the output data is still a fully manual process.

Once the first phase is completed to a satisfactory degree, one can start to incorporate more automation into the process. In step one, not only was the decision-making excluded from automation, the at times cumbersome research of plausible pricing and comparison to empirical values was a manual process as well. The next phase tackles the latter issue.

Phase two uses the data collected in phase one to aid the user in his or her decision-making process by predicting and proposing a monetary amount for provisioning.

This is the point where hyperautomation enters the playing field. Simply collecting data, pushing it through a static process and ultimately pasting it into a sought-after format is the traditional or standard form of automation. In hyperautomation, a combination of different tools comes into play (Maddox 2019). Here, we combine RPA with a machine learning model, which analyzes the previously collected and prepared empirical data. Triggering the use of that model automatically within the traditional RPA framework brings us to a hyperautomated process. The final result of phase two is a semiautomatic procedure, where the user is predominantly just left with the decision-making process itself. That is whether to confirm the amount suggested by the model for the actual provisions, or to choose the amount extracted from the email invoice announcement. Exceptions might be vastly unintuitive values for both the proposed and extracted values. In that case, the user could opt for a third option, which is to do some manual research after all and set the actual amount him or herself. Note that during phase two the data gathering process of phase one continues, albeit in a more automated fashion. The training of the model should then also be updated in regular intervals incorporating the new data.

Phase three aims at further and ideally full automation. The goal is to eradicate a user as an ongoing decision-maker, instead letting the robot work its "magic" to the fullest.

A natural piece of information that is gathered in phase two is how often the user chooses to follow the model prediction and how many times he or she does not. This is a measurement of how well the model works. This, of course, is also influenced by the amount of data the model is based on, which keeps on increasing over the course of time. Assuming there are no fundamental mistakes in the implemented model, we can assume that the rate for choosing the predicted value increases, too. Not only this way, but also through the user's experience, we gain intuition and measurements regarding the quality of the model. This goes somewhat in the direction of cross-validation, i.e., testing the model on new data. Once it reaches a satisfactory degree, one can switch to always accepting the predicted value as the actual value that is reserved for provisions. At this point, only regular backtesting is required to make sure that the predictions and propositions of the model remain accurate.

4.2 Natural Language Processing for Data Extraction

Natural language processing, or NLP, is a field focused on the interaction between computers and human languages (Wikipedia 2020). A brief introduction to the models can be found in Section 4 in Liermann et al., Deep learning—an introduction (2019). Other applications of NLP can be found in Liermann and Schaudinnus, Real estate risk—appraisal capture (2019) and Schröder and Tieben (2021).

In our particular case, NLP can be a valuable asset—maybe even indispensable in practice. The key area for its application would here be the collection of data extracted from incoming emails that announce upcoming invoices. There are ways to force a certain format of the emails, for example by generating said format after submitting a form on a website, but those ways could be cumbersome, less user-friendly, or even redundant and resulting in more work and time for upkeep. Ideally, the sender sends the email in any way he or she likes, and the receiving computer is able to extract the sought-after information automatically. This is where NLP becomes necessary for automation.

NPL is not only a good idea in the final stages of implementation, nor should it be seen as the cherry on a cake. It could make a tremendous impact on automation at the earliest stage already, i.e., the collection of the initial data.

4.3 Features Engineering and Model Training

The dataset presented in this chapter is mockup data but reflects the structure of the real data. We simulate 13,730 datasets and an overview of the first nine samples is provided in Table 1.

The example data shown in Table 1 will be generated by an RPA tool (UiPath in our case). The RPA extracts the relevant data from incoming emails. The data collection process is covered for the user by the automated process. The extraction can be implemented rule-based (see Sect. 4.1) or can use more "error"-tolerant tools like NLP (see Sect. 4.2).

The column "Value" contains the value of invoice announcements. We aim to predict this column (label) based on the other columns (features). In this section, we are going to analyze the label and features and develop a machine learning method at the end. The following analysis is implemented by using R with ggplot2[1] and h2o library (H2O.ai 2019).

4.3.1 Label

The following analysis shows that the column "Value" contains only 12 categories among 13,730 data samples, see Fig. 4. It suggests that we consider it to be categorical (discrete) instead of numerical (continuous), which implies that we need to discover a classification model instead of regression. In the general case, we should extend a label to be continuous.

4.3.2 Features—Correlation

Feature selection is the process of reducing the number of input variables when developing a predictive model, to reduce the computational cost and improve the model performance. Although we do not have many features and samples, we still proceed with the feature selection to introduce a statistical-based approach by using a correlation matrix. Figure 5 illustrates the correlation matrix between all columns given in the dataset, where the correlation values are displayed by using different colors. Correlation-matrix-based feature selection is widely used to develop machine learning models, especially in case of Big Data. Clustering can be performed based on a correlation matrix, where similar variables can be grouped into the same cluster. In other words, the strongly correlated variables will be selected. In our example,

---

[1] https://ggplot2.tidyverse.org/, *ggplot2 is a system for declaratively creating graphics, based on The Grammar of Graphic.*

Table 1 Head of the dataset (© ifb SE)

Company	Object.Type	Object	Value	Address	Post code	City	Country	DUNSNr
Company 52	Airplane	Airbus A340-500	250,000,000	Tschamlerstr. 2	6020	Innsbruck	Austria	747,241,213
Company 52	Airplane	Boeing 747-100 Transport	650,000,000	Tschamlerstr. 2	6020	Innsbruck	Austria	747,241,213
Company 52	Tractor	John Deere 9570RX	600,000	Tschamlerstr. 2	6020	Innsbruck	Austria	747,241,213
Company 52	Truck	Mercedes Actros	500,000	Tschamlerstr. 2	6020	Innsbruck	Austria	747,241,213
Company 52	Airplane	Airbus A321-200 (Sharklets)	160,000,000	Tschamlerstr. 2	6020	Innsbruck	Austria	747,241,213
Company 52	Tractor	Case IH Stelger/Quadtrac 600	540,000	Tschamlerstr. 2	6020	Innsbruck	Austria	747,241,213
Company 52	Tractor	Fendt 1100 MT	400,000	Tschamlerstr. 2	6020	Innsbruck	Austria	747,241,213
Company 52	Airplane	Boeing 777-200 Passenger Model	550,000,000	Tschamlerstr. 2	6020	Innsbruck	Austria	747,241,213
Company 52	Airplane	Boeing 727-100 Passenger Model	150,000,000	Tschamlerstr. 2	6020	Innsbruck	Austria	747,241,213

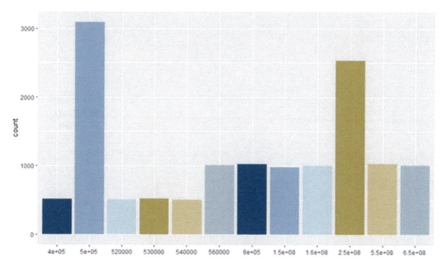

Fig. 4 Overview of label "Value" (© ifb SE)

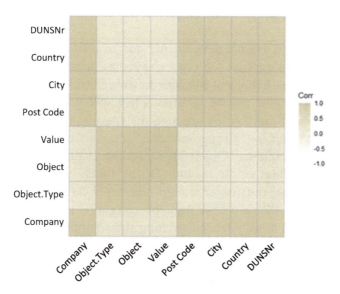

Fig. 5 Correlation matrix (© ifb SE)

we can directly read that the columns "Company," "Address," "Post code," "City," "Country" and "DUNSNr" are strongly correlated, since they are all geographic based. On the other hand, columns "Value," "Object" and "Object.Type" should be grouped together. This indicates that we should select "Object" and "Object.Type" for building the machine learning model.

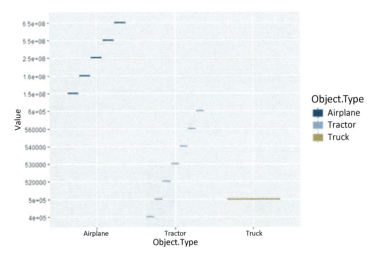

Fig. 6 Object.Type vs. Value (© ifb SE)

4.3.3 Features—Object and Object.Type

In the following, we provide some further statistical analysis for the columns "Object" and "Object.Type." As we already mentioned in other articles (Liermann and Li, Methods of Machine Learning 2021), these classic statistical intuitions should not be ignored. They will provide a deeper look at the dataset and are able to improve the training efficiency during the development of machine learning models.

Figure 6 plots column "Object.Type" against "Value." We are not able to separate the values of the column "Value" finely according to column "Object.Type," since the invoice announcements of category "Airplane" take values across 1.5e+08 to 6.5e+8 and the category "Tractor" covers values between 4e+5 and 6e+5. After considering the column "Object," the separation becomes sharper. As illustrated in Fig. 7, we are nearly able to identify the value of "Value" based on "Object.Type" and "Object." The result of the analysis is not surprising, since we used deterministic conditions to generate datasets, as introduced in Sect. 4.3.

4.3.4 Model Training—Random Forests

One of the traditional classification models—random forest—is chosen. Recalling the statistical analysis provided in the last section, it is unsurprising to see that a small forest with five trees is already able to achieve an excellent accuracy beyond 99.9%. Cross-validation results are shown in Fig. 8. In

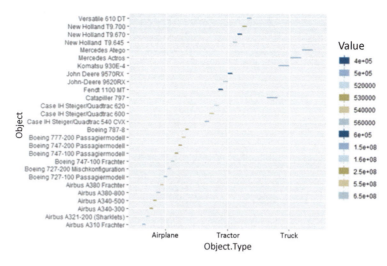

Fig. 7 (Object.Type, Object) vs. Value (© ifb SE)

Cross-Validation Metrics Summary:

	mean	sd	cv_1_valid	cv_2_valid	cv_3_valid	cv_4_valid	cv_5_valid	cv_6_valid
accuracy	0.99963856	5.075365E-4	1.0	0.99857855	0.99923897	0.99928266	1.0	1.0
err	3.6141448E-4	5.075365E-4	0.0	0.0014214641	7.61035E-4	7.173601E-4	0.0	0.0
err_count	0.5	0.70710677	0.0	2.0	1.0	1.0	0.0	0.0
logloss	0.040052153	0.0055257706	0.03954867	0.046860714	0.0452101	0.04388479	0.03501095	0.048248984
max_per_class_error	0.010186633	0.015246954	0.0	0.045454547	0.01754386	0.02	0.0	0.0
mean_per_class_accuracy	0.9991511	0.0012705795	1.0	0.9962121	0.998538	0.99833333	1.0	1.0
mean_per_class_error	8.488861E-4	0.0012705795	0.0	0.003787879	0.0014619883	0.0016666667	0.0	0.0
mse	0.006535436	0.0010166838	0.00628277	0.0073929336	0.008134246	0.0073786057	0.005536854	0.0076509146
r2	0.99950916	7.699056E-5	0.9995331	0.99945414	0.99939126	0.99945265	0.9995807	0.9994127
rmse	0.08062427	0.0062506427	0.079263926	0.085982166	0.09019005	0.08589881	0.074410036	0.0874695

Fig. 8 Random forest: cross-validation result (© ifb SE)

practice, we might face more complicated data structures and need to use more advanced models.

5 Practical Application: Machine Learning UiPATH

In this section, we present an example technical implementation of the previously circumscribed use case. As the RPA tool we use *UiPath Studio Pro 2020.6.0-beta.93 Community License* from the company *UiPath*. This offers the integration of the Python programming language as an external tool.

Fig. 9 UiPath.Python.Activities module in the UiPath Packages manager (© ifb SE)

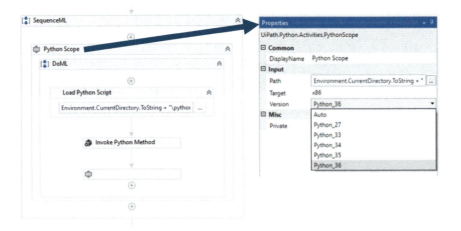

Fig. 10 Python scope and properties in UiPath (© ifb SE)

5.1 Python Integration in UiPath

For the technical integration of the externally installed Python programming language, UiPath provides an adapter package module called *UiPath.Python.Activities*, which is found in its Packages manager,[2] see Fig. 9.

Once installed, UiPath provides a so-called *App Invoker* for Python in its listed activities that include objects like *Invoke Python Method*, *Load Python*

---

[2] Note that we used the English language setting for UiPath.

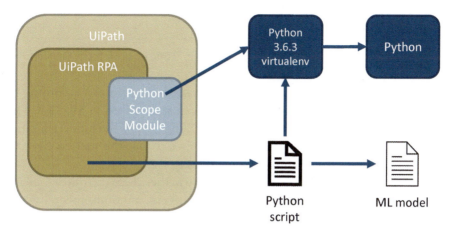

Fig. 11 Architecture of the integration of Python into UiPath (© ifb SE)

Script or *Python Scope*. Python is connected to UiPath via the *Python Scope* environment, see Fig. 10.

To make the connection work, three input attributes are key, namely Path, Target, and Version. The *Path* argument points to the folder containing the externally installed Python interpreter, not the interpreter itself. This can be the globally installed version or a virtual python environment created by virtualenv or the like. The tag *Version* corresponds to the Python version. As you can see in Fig. 10, several versions are supported. We used the latest supported one, version 3.6, as older versions tend to lose support by developers. Python 2.7 has even reached its end-of-life status (Python Software Foundation, Sunsetting Python 2, 2020). Last but not least, the *Target* differentiates between the 32bit and 64bit versions of Python. A Windows executable for Python 3.6.8 is available at (Python Software Foundation, Download 2020).[3]

After the Python scope is set up, an externally programmed Python script can be used via the *Load Python Script* module. This simply specifies the path to the script. Within this script, one defines functions or methods that can then be invoked and used via the *Invoke Python Method* module. Here you can forward parameters from UiPath to be used as input for the Python function. The return values of the function can then be read out by UiPath and processed further. In the scope of this use case, we created machine learning models beforehand, see Sect. 4.3. These models are invoked by the Python script. For a visualization of the interplay of the different components, see Fig. 11.

---

[3] We used the 32bit version of Python 3.6.8.

5.2 Example in UiPath

As a proof of concept and a technical example, we now sketch the implementation of phase two implemented in UiPath.

At this point, we assume that initial data has been recorded according to phase one. In our example case, it was generated as described in Sect. 4.3. The first step of phase two and ultimately a preparatory step is the model training, which was also covered in Sect. 4.3. The onset is that the user receives an email in MS Outlook like the one shown in Fig. 12.

The UiPath procedure starts by checking whether there are unread emails in the inbox regarding a certain topic, here "Invoice announcement." Upon finding one, its content gets read, processed and the relevant details assigned to UiPath variables. Most important for us are the variables "Value," stating the amount of the invoice, "Object type" and the "Object." At the end of the entire process, UiPath checks for the next unread email until none are left, see Fig. 13.

The detailed automation steps of the data processing are grouped in the "check mail message" box of Fig. 13. There, the logical steps begin by filling in the necessary UiPath variables, in our case the ones mentioned in the previous paragraph. Secondly, a function from a Python script gets invoked with the UiPath variables for the "Object Type" and "Object" as input for the function. The Python function refers to a previously calculated and provided ML

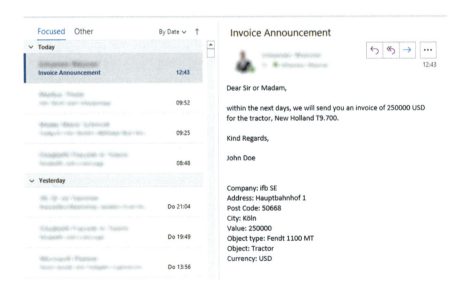

Fig. 12 Email regarding an invoice announcement (© ifb SE)

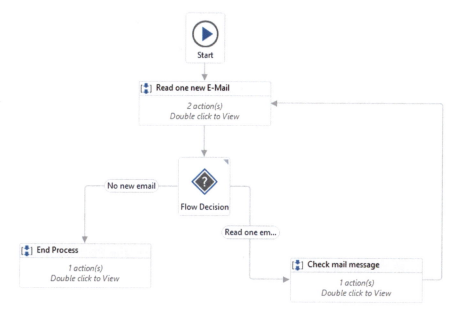

Fig. 13 Coarsest grained flow graph of the automation procedure in UiPath (© ifb SE)

model which yields a predicted value for the invoice that is returned by the Python script to UiPath. The user then gets prompted with two values: the originally announced invoice value from the email and the predicted value from the ML model. Since it is only semiautomatic in phase two, i.e., level B from Fig. 3, the user still needs to decide which one to choose or where he or she would like to use a third, new value as provisions.

6 Summary

The chapter shows a practical example of an important pattern in automating processes. The challenge is to have a step-by-step approach to achieve the benefits of true automation (modern RPA using automated decision-making). Full automation including automated decision-making cannot be implemented as a big bang, in one-step or one project task. The important aspect is to gain and integrate the knowledge of the manual process and its decision-making.

The three-step meta process (see Fig. 3) is mirrored in Bitcom's popular "five-step decision automation model" (see Fig. 2). Label generation can be a tricky task, especially if there is no electronic data history regarding the label. Supervised learning—by definition—only works with labels. The use of RPA capabilities to collect these important information labels is the crucial point in the approach. Only with an approach that collects the label data "en passant" (without any entries to an additional tool) and stores it electronically without slowing down the manual human process will it be accepted by the original process owner.

The potential of the approach is huge. The automation initiatives do not have to stop when more intelligence is required than simple rule-based approaches can easily cover. Defining a rule requires context knowledge and the definition of the rule is still manual and static (no learning without a human interaction), while machine-learning-based pattern recognition can define the rule autonomously and can adapt and learn from new situations. The only, but important, requirement is that the labels are available. Thus, RPA can automate simple, recurring, and stable tasks. In addition, RPA can collect the labels in the existing process and discover the decision-making patterns (using machine learning). Therefore, the way for a full automation is paved.

RPA is well established in most banks and insurance companies. Now is the right time to start collecting the labels (using RPA) so the cost-saving potential can be tapped just in time.

Literature

Bitcom. 2017. *Künstliche Intelligenz verstehen als Automation des Entscheidens Leitfaden*. Berlin: Bitcom Bundesverband Informationswirtschaft, Telekommunikation und neue Medien e.V.

Gartner. 2019. "Gartner Top 10 Strategic Technology Trends for 2020." *Gartner.* Accessed November 15, 2020. https://www.gartner.com/smarterwithgartner/gartner-top-10-strategic-technology-trends-for-2020/.

———. 2020. "Gartner Top Strategic Technology Trends for 2021." *Gartner.* Accessed November 15, 2020. https://www.gartner.com/smarterwithgartner/gartner-top-strategic-technology-trends-for-2021/.

H2O.ai. 2019. *h2o.ai Overview*, January 29. Accessed January 29, 2019. http://docs.h2o.ai/h2o/latest-stable/h2o-docs/index.html.

Liermann, Volker, and Norbert Schaudinnus. 2019. "Real Estate Risk—Appraisal Capture." In *The Impact of Digital Transformation and Fintech on the Finance Professional*, edited by Volker Liermann and Claus Stegmann. New York: Palgrave Macmillen.

Liermann, Volker, and Sangmeng Li. 2021. "Methods of Machine Learning." In *The Digital Journey of Banking and Insurance, Volume III—Data Storage, Processing, and Analysis*, edited by Volker Liermann and Claus Stegmann. New York: Palgrave Macmillan.

Liermann, Volker, Sangmeng Li, and Norbert Schaudinnus. 2019. "Deep Learning—An Introduction." In *The Impact of Digital Transformation and Fintech on the Finance Professional*, edited by Volker Liermann and Claus Stegmann. New York: Palgrave Macmillan.

Maddox, Teena. 2019. "Top 10 Technology Trends for 2020 Include Hyperautomation, Human Augmentation and Distributed Cloud." *TechRepublic*. Accessed November 15, 2020. https://www.techrepublic.com/article/hyperautomation-human-augmentation-and-distributed-cloud-among-top-10-technology-trends-for-2020/.

Python Software Foundation. 2020. "Download." Python. https://www.python.org/downloads/.

———. 2020. "Sunsetting Python 2." *Python*. Accessed November 15, 2020. https://www.python.org/doc/sunset-python-2/.

Schröder, Daniel, and Marian Tieben. 2021. "Sentiment Analysis for Reputational Risk Management." In *The Digital Journey of Banking and Insurance, Volume II—Digitalization and Machine Learning*, edited by Volker Liermann and Claus Stegmann. New York: Palgrave Macmillan.

Wikipedia. 2020. "Natural Language Processing." *Wikipedia*, November 15. https://en.wikipedia.org/wiki/Natural_language_processing.

RPA Use Case—"IFRS 9/SPPI"

Jens Gabriel

1 Introduction

1.1 Initial Situation

With the introduction of IFRS 9 (Financial Instruments),[1] new requirements were formulated in the context of the classification of financial assets, which, in addition to an examination of the underlying business model, also require an examination of contract components at the level of individual transactions. In particular, the examination of contract components (contractual clauses, ancillary agreements, options, covenants, etc.) in the case of wholesale loans (non-retail loans)—this is referred to as the examination of the so-called cash flow criterion—requires those responsible for this process to have financing and accounting expertise. In addition, wholesale loans (non-retail loans) involve a wide variety of heterogeneous and individual contract components. This is—as the term "wholesale loans" already suggests—due to the financing requirements of just such constellations. And as a rule, the contractual components are not geared to the balance sheet requirements, but

---

[1] See (IFRS.org 2020).

J. Gabriel (✉)
ifb SE, Grünwald, Germany
e-mail: Jens.Gabriel@ifb-group.com

rather to the needs of the respective sector and customers. However, IFRS 9 breaks with this paradigm. Particularly since the large number of companies preparing their balance sheets is unlikely to have any interest in increasing volatility in the income statement. However, this is precisely what happens if the financial instruments within the scope of IFRS 9 have contractual components that trigger fair value. Last but not least, this is a sub-process within the scope of financial instrument accounting that is highly manual because the relevant information (data) is not available in the IT systems and is therefore highly error-prone. In addition, the sub-process is characterized by the fact that it ties up a lot of time with the persons carrying out the work and—depending on the financing—requires a lot of queries from other departments and areas. However, since the sub-process is also to a high degree rule-based and is carried out regularly, the question inevitably arises as to how to automate this process so that people can be assigned to higher-value tasks that create real added value for the company.

1.2 Structure of the Article

The section starts with the business requirements in order to address the challenges and problems of these. In a further step, it is examined to what extent this is a process that can be automated with the help of RPA and what advantages can be gained from this. Finally, digitalization as a possible driver for greater efficiency in accounting and controlling is discussed in order to demonstrate the potential of RPA.

2 Business Requirements in the Context of IFRS 9 and SPPI

Financial Accounting, especially in financial services companies, credit institutions, and insurance companies, but also in some industrial companies, has been characterized by an enormous dynamic of regulatory and legal requirements over the past one and a half decades.

Especially after the global financial and capital market crisis in 2008, the standard setters for International Financial Reporting Standards (IFRS) radically changed the essential requirements for the accounting of financial instruments.

The accounting of financial instruments according to IFRS is one of the most complex areas of international accounting.

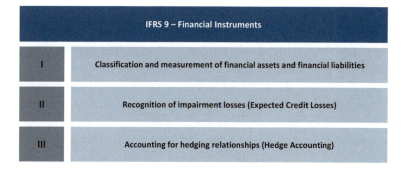

Fig. 1 Focus of IFRS 9 (© ifb SE)

IFRS 9 (Financial Instruments) is the IASB's[2] replacement of IAS 39[3] (Financial Instruments: Recognition and Measurement).

The Standard focuses on the following areas (Fig. 1).

Since January 1, 2018, financial instruments in IFRS financial statements must be accounted for in accordance with the requirements of IFRS 9 (previously IAS 39).[4]

In the following we limit ourselves to the requirements for the classification of financial assets.

According to IFRS 9, all financial assets are divided into three classification categories—those measured at amortized cost and those measured at fair value. When classifying financial assets at fair value, a distinction must be made according to whether changes in fair value between reporting dates are recognized in profit or loss (P&L) or directly in equity (OCI, Other Comprehensive Income).

The classification of financial assets is based on the characteristics of the cash flows of the financial asset (cash flow condition) and the business model within which the assets are held (business model condition).

In addition, options exist in the form of the fair value option (for debt instruments) and the fair value through OCI option (for equity instruments). These options must be performed at initial recognition of a financial asset and result in changes in fair value being recognized directly in profit or loss (P&L) or equity (OCI).

Subsequent reclassification is generally not or only in rare cases envisaged.

---

[2] IASB = International Accounting Standards Board.
[3] See (IFRS.org 2020).
[4] IFRS 9 was endorsed for use in the EU on November 22, 2016.

The following diagram shows the classification process for financial assets in accordance with IFRS 9.[5]

While derivative financial instruments are per se recognized at fair value and changes in fair value are recognized in profit or loss and equity instruments (e.g. shares) are also required to be recognized at fair value and changes in fair value either in profit or loss or directly in equity (OCI), the situation is significantly more complex for debt instruments (e.g. loans, securities, etc.).

Most preparers of financial statements have an interest in being able to control and predict P&L volatility. However, fair value-triggering agreements make this goal difficult. The contractual terms and conditions are generally determined by the front office, the back office and the legal department. For an audit-proof evaluation, a closer exchange between these departments and the accounting department is necessary. If new types of clause are to be included in the contracts, they must first be subjected to a joint assessment by the accounting principles department as part of a New Product Process (NPP). The final decision on the assessment is the responsibility of the accounting department. The extent to which fair value clauses may be used in contracts requires a decision by top management (Fig. 2).

In the following, the business requirements for the classification of financial assets (IFRS 9) are explained in detail in order to subsequently assess whether they are suitable for implementation in RPA.

Without taking into account a possible exercise of the fair value option, "an entity shall classify financial assets as subsequently measured at amortized cost, fair value through other comprehensive income or fair value through profit or loss on the basis of both:

(a) the entity's business model for managing the financial assets and
(b) the contractual cash flow characteristics of the financial asset."[6]

"A financial asset shall be measured at amortized cost if both of the following conditions are met:

(a) the financial asset is held within a business model whose objective is to hold financial assets in order to collect contractual cash flows and

---

[5] The classification process of financial liabilities according to IFRS 9 is not discussed in this section, as the process (a) is much more trivial and (b) is not suitable for implementation with RPA.
[6] IFRS 9.4.1.1.

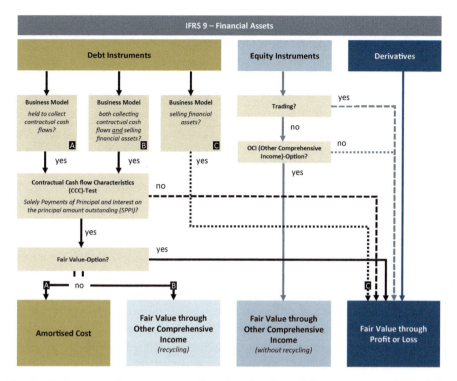

Fig. 2 Business requirements regarding classification of financial assets (IFRS 9) (© ifb SE)

(b) the contractual terms of the financial asset give rise on specified dates to cash flows that are solely payments of principal and interest on the principal amount outstanding."[7]

"A financial asset shall be measured at fair value through other comprehensive income if both of the following conditions are met:

(a) the financial asset is held within a business model whose objective is achieved by both collecting contractual cash flows and selling financial assets and
(b) the contractual terms of the financial asset give rise on specified dates to cash flows that are solely payments of principal and interest on the principal amount outstanding."[8]

---

[7] IFRS 9.4.1.2.
[8] IFRS 9.4.1.2A.

"Principal is the fair value of the financial asset at initial recognition. [...] Interest consists of consideration for the time value of money, for the credit risk associated with the principal amount outstanding during a particular period of time and for other basic lending risks and costs, as well as a profit margin [...].[9]"

"A financial asset shall be measured at fair value through profit or loss unless it is measured at amortized cost [...] or at fair value through other comprehensive income [...]. However, an entity may make an irrevocable election at initial recognition for particular investments in equity instruments that would otherwise be measured at fair value through profit or loss to present subsequent changes in fair value in other comprehensive income [...].[10]"

"IFRS 9 requires an entity to classify a financial asset on the basis of its contractual cash flow characteristics if the financial asset is held within a business model whose objective is to hold assets to collect contractual cash flows or within a business model whose objective is achieved by both collecting contractual cash flows and selling financial assets, unless the fair value option applies. To do so, the conditions of IFRS 9 require an entity to determine whether the asset's contractual cash flows are solely payments of principal and interest on the principal amount outstanding.[11]"

"Contractual cash flows that are solely payments of principal and interest on the principal amount outstanding are consistent with a basic lending arrangement. In a basic lending arrangement, consideration for the time value of money [...] and credit risk are typically the most significant elements of interest. However, in such an arrangement, interest can also include consideration for other basic lending risks (for example, liquidity risk) and costs (for example, administrative costs) associated with holding the financial asset for a particular period of time. In addition, interest can include a profit margin that is consistent with a basic lending arrangement. In extreme economic circumstances, interest can be negative if, for example, the holder of a financial asset either explicitly or implicitly pays for the deposit of its money for a particular period of time (and that fee exceeds the consideration that the holder receives for the time value of money, credit risk and other basic lending risks and costs). However, contractual terms that introduce exposure to risks or volatility in the contractual cash flows that is unrelated to a basic lending arrangement, such as exposure to changes in equity prices or commodity

---

[9] IFRS 9.4.1.3.
[10] IFRS 9.4.1.4.
[11] IFRS 9.B4.1.7.

prices, do not give rise to contractual cash flows that are solely payments of principal and interest on the principal amount outstanding. [...]"[12]

Examples of contractual terms or clauses that could trigger a classification at fair value through profit or loss[13]:

- Inverse variable interest rate
- Payment of interest only if the issuer remains solvent immediately afterward
- Deferral of interest without compound interest
- Payments in excess of interest and principal that are not attributable to the time value of money and the risk of default
- Interest rate with mismatched maturities (e.g. 3-month LIBOR and maturity schedule of six months)
- Leverage features
- Variable payments
- Contingent compensation
- Margin step-up clauses
- Right of conversion into equity instruments
- Option of currency exchange with conditions fixed in advance.

3 Challenges in Practice

The new requirements as well as the stronger principle orientation of IFRS 9 present discretionary scope and challenges for implementation. Why? There is scope for interpretation and assessment with regard to materiality when determining the business model and thus the classification of a financial asset. Furthermore, IT systems and processes need to be adapted in order to provide extended product information (in particular, information on the contractual terms included, which relate to the cash flow criterion) and to derive the classification criteria. Furthermore, there are increased documentation requirements in the context of classification. Last but not least, systematic reviews as well as business policy decisions are required to adjust current contractual terms and conditions in order to avoid higher volatility in earnings (P&L) and in the equity shown in the balance sheet and for regulatory purposes.

In practice, the handling of the SPPI criterion, in particular, presents a wealth of challenges (Fig. 3).

---

[12] IFRS 9.B4.1.7A.
[13] The valuation may vary from customer to customer.

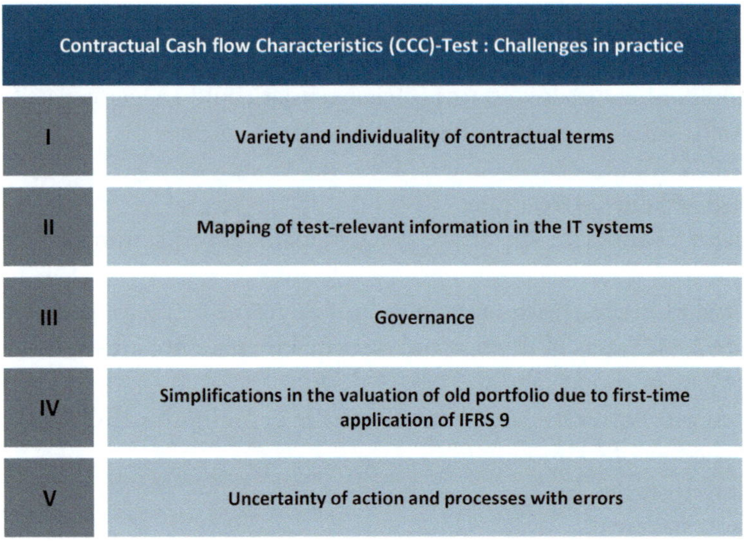

\multicolumn{2}{c}{**Contractual Cash flow Characteristics (CCC)-Test : Challenges in practice**}
I	Variety and individuality of contractual terms
II	Mapping of test-relevant information in the IT systems
III	Governance
IV	Simplifications in the valuation of old portfolio due to first-time application of IFRS 9
V	Uncertainty of action and processes with errors

Fig. 3 Challenges in practice (© ifb SE)

I. Variety and individuality of contractual terms

In the case of retail loans, there is usually a high degree of standardization in the contractual terms used. As a rule, these loans do not contain any contractual terms that trigger a classification at fair value through profit or loss. However, especially in the case of wholesale loans (non-retail loans), there are a large number of individual agreements and conditions that make it difficult to derive the SPPI criterion. Frequently, different formulations in and designations of clauses are used, which have identical contents with regard to the SPPI criterion. In other cases, identical designations of clauses are used, which have different effects in terms of content with regard to the SPPI criterion. Frequently, the contractual clauses used differ according to the industries financed (e.g. shipping, aircraft, commercial real estate, etc.) and the jurisdiction in this environment. The contract documents often comprise several hundred pages and are written in many different languages.

II. Mapping of test-relevant information in the IT systems

The test-relevant information for deriving the SPPI criterion is not or not completely available in the legal (= inventory management) systems. This circumstance leads to a high manual effort, which is connected with the risk that contracts and especially the SPPI criterion are evaluated incorrectly.

III. **Governance**

The contractual terms and conditions are generally determined by the front office, the back office, and the legal department. For an audit-proof evaluation, a closer exchange between these departments and the accounting department is necessary. If new types of clause are to be included in the contracts, they must first be subjected to a joint assessment by the accounting principles department as part of a New Product Process (NPP). The final decision on the assessment is the responsibility of the accounting department. The extent to which fair value clauses may be used in contracts requires a decision by top management.

IV. **Simplifications in the valuation of the old portfolio due to first-time application of IFRS 9**

Due to the first-time application of IFRS 9, simplifications were made in dealing with the old portfolio on a customer-specific basis in view of the challenges described above. This means that these contracts have been frequently and globally assessed as not triggering fair value. If these contracts are substantially modified and would subsequently have to be derecognized and re-recognized in the balance sheet, a different classification (fair value instead of amortized cost) may arise. This may lead to an undesired volatility in the income statement.

V. **Uncertainty of action and processes with errors**

Most preparers of financial statements have an interest in being able to control and predict P&L volatility. However, fair value-triggering agreements make this goal difficult. This is also due to processes that contain errors.

4 General Classification as well as Usability and Advantages of RPA for This Use Case

The classification of the RPA use case "IFRS 9/SPPI" can be seen in the following figure (Fig. 4).

In order to be able to make a statement as to whether a use case is suitable for implementation using RPA, one or more of the criteria listed below must be checked. This is virtually an RPA suitability test that should be performed for all potential use cases.

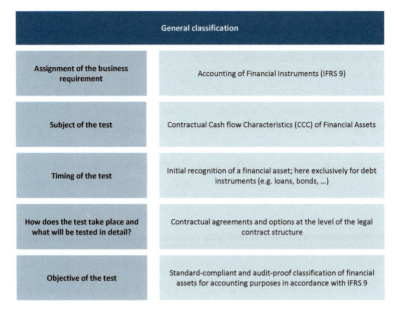

Fig. 4 General classification of use case "IFRS 9/SPPI" (© ifb SE)

The RPA use case "IFRS 9/SPPI" is intended to increase efficiency in financial accounting by applying a predefined set of rules at the time of initial recognition of a financial asset at the level of individual transactions (e.g. loan agreement) in order to check the existence of contractual components that trigger fair value.

The overriding aim is to ensure that the SPPI criterion is derived in a standard-compliant and audit-compliant manner, thus taking over a significant sub-process within the scope of the classification decision.

The robot is based on a set of rules—namely a collection of all known and documented contract components and their classification in terms of "fair value trigger = yes, no or maybe."

The robot will then scan the contracts using the rulebook and at the end of the process will generate a report showing potential sources of fair value-triggering contract elements with a reference to the page and the text passage concerned.

The person responsible for checking the SPPI criterion in accordance with governance must validate in an ICS[14] process (including the principle of dual control) whether the robot has arrived at the correct result in deriving the SPPI criterion. As part of an approval process, the information on the

---

[14] ICS = Internal Control System.

SPPI criterion required for the IFRS 9 classification is then passed on to the accepting, productive accounting systems.

If previously undocumented contractual elements are identified during the process, these are subsequently evaluated by the accounting principles and rules department in accordance with IFRS 9 requirements and stored in the rules for future processes.

This is a rule-based process, as the process is based on a set of rules. This set of rules provides clear and comprehensible structures. The sub-process of SPPI derivation as part of the process of classifying financial assets is a process that is highly dependent on the business model and the number of new transactions concluded by the reporting entity in terms of frequency and periodicity. Depending on whether the reporting entity has a large number of new business transactions, particularly in the area of special financing (non-retail/wholesale), the derivation of the SPPI criterion takes a long time. Furthermore, it is a very error-prone process, as it is usually a manual one.

The following figure shows the usefulness of the use case "IFRS 9/SPPI" for an RPA implementation (Fig. 5).

The following explains the requirements for the RPA process "IFRS 9/SPPI" and shows what an interaction between human and robot could look like.

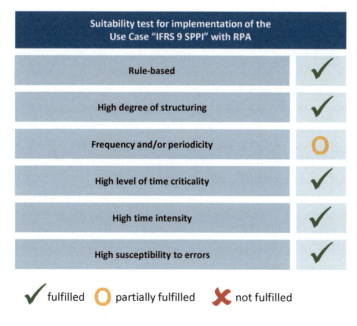

Fig. 5 Suitability test for implementation of use case "IFRS 9/SPPI" with RPA (© ifb SE)

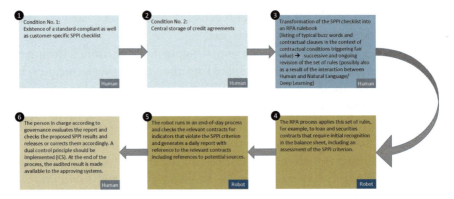

Fig. 6 Proposed process for use case "IFRS 9/SPPI" using RPA (© ifb SE)

An obligatory prerequisite is, on the one hand, the existence of a standard-compliant and customer-specific SPPI checklist and, on the other hand, access to the electronically stored contracts (loans, valuable paperwork, etc.). The contracts must be available in the respective valid version relevant for initial recognition and stored in pdf format (Fig. 6).

Based on the SPPI checklist, the accounting expert must then create an RPA rulebook that assigns to each fair value-triggering contractual term corresponding keywords or combinations of terms that the robots search for. Especially at the beginning of the implemented RPA process, the set of rules needs to be regularly adapted and extended.

The robot then has the task of applying the defined set of rules during the initial recognition of a loan or security. As a rule, this should be an end-of-day process. At the end of this process, the robot generates a report that assigns or does not assign a list of potentially fair value-triggering contractual terms to the corresponding contracts. The list then contains a reference to the corresponding page of the contract where a keyword was found. The report should also list the text passages before and after the keyword in order to have a more reliable basis for SPPI assessment.

Afterward, the human being comes into play again. He now has to assess the correctness and completeness of the fair value-triggering contractual conditions found by the robot and, as part of a dual control principle, he has to have the final SPPI evaluation released in order to provide the information to the accounting systems.

In addition to all the advantages of an RPA implementation described above, the implementation naturally also has weaknesses. The weakness is that the robot must not only have an understanding of individual words and sentences but must also be able to grasp and evaluate complete text contexts and facts. This requirement is due to the complexity of human language and ambiguity. How does the robot manage linguistically, for example, in the case of a double negation that leads to a completely different result?

This is exactly where Natural Language Processing (NLP) gains in importance. NLP has the goal to capture natural language and process it with the help of rules and algorithms. NLP draws on methods and findings from linguistics and then produces results with the help of artificial intelligence and machine learning methods. A brief introduction to NLP is given in Chapter 3 in (Liermann et al. 2019).

In order to use NLP successfully, large amounts of data are required in advance so that the procedures and methods from artificial intelligence and machine learning can recognize text meanings, sentence contexts and sentence relationships as well as recurring patterns holistically.

5 Digitalization as a Driver for Increased Efficiency in Accounting and Controlling

The use case shown is an example for the use of RPA in Accounting and Controlling.

Further use cases in this area can be found here, for example:

- KPI early warning system (in the context of Financial Reporting)
- Automation within the scope of consolidation
- Filling of Reporting Packages
- Corrections and validation processes
- Reconciliation issues.

The use of RPA should also increase efficiency in these areas. An increase and optimization of efficiency can be achieved through standardization, automation, and harmonization. In order to achieve this, various conditions must be met.

First and foremost, a digital corporate culture is required (Fig. 7).

If digitalization is to take a company to the next level, technology is only one of many prerequisites. In any case, it is necessary to create a digital corporate culture or adapt the existing one. All this with the aim of putting the leadership, behavior, and views of employees into a digital context. And on the way to a digital goal, it is of central importance that mistakes are allowed. Only in a trustworthy and error-accepting environment will things of value be created.

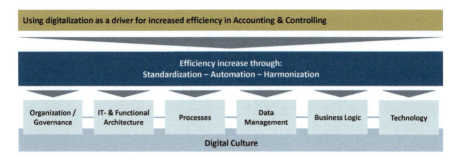

Fig. 7 Using digitalization as a driver for increased efficiency in Accounting and Controlling (© ifb SE)

An essential prerequisite for the introduction of RPA is to create a high level of acceptance of RPA.

Not all business processes can be automated. Furthermore, no faulty processes should be automated. For a fast and error-free result, all processes must therefore be checked for functionality and usefulness before automation.

Here it makes sense to launch a company-wide initiative to collect possible use cases in an agile project approach and then subject them to an implementation review (cost/benefit).

In order to assess the benefits of RPA for the company, the key performance indicators (KPIs) must be defined in advance and continuously monitored. Transparent reporting is necessary to create acceptance among employees.

Furthermore, clear responsibilities for an implementation of the digitalization strategy as well as new roles (e.g. Chief Digital Officer, Chief Visionary Officer, Chief Value Officer, Chief Data Officer, RPA Agents, SCRUM Master for implementation of agile project management, etc.) need to be created.

In addition, an Enterprise Architect could be positioned centrally in the overall organization in order to combine strategy and functional requirements (business logic) with architectural principles.

Another important point is that governance must clarify what control mechanisms and reports exist for monitoring the robots. Human beings must continue to be both the initiating role for the implementation of RPA processes and the "last line of defense" in the context of approvals, ensuring compliance with laws and regulations.

A further, not insignificant prerequisite for the successful implementation of RPA is the choice of the Operation Model. This model describes what the value chain of service delivery to the recipients looks like. The Operating Model answers the questions by whom and with which applications and processes the robots are introduced and operated. The all-important question is whether RPAs are operated centrally, decentrally, or in the form of a hybrid model (see Soybir and Schmidt [2021]).

Just like human employees, robots must handle sensitive data conscientiously and, just like other software, they must be protected against external attacks. There is a need for a coordinated and legally watertight framework that applies to the programming and operation of robots and in which the data security and integrity of the company and the interests of customers are fully protected at all times.

Last but not least, the selection of a suitable, sustainably usable, integrable application and thus the choice for an RPA software provider will be of great importance.

6 Summary

The general conditions described here illustrate why automation by means of an RPA is sensible and target-oriented. The susceptibility of the process to errors is minimized by the successive further development of the rules and regulations and the human being can be used for higher-value and value-added activities.

The improvement of the process is reflected in a higher quality of financial reporting. The audit and revision security is the duty, the possibility of a better planning of balance sheet and P&L the voluntary exercise, with which every CFO should find enough reasons to have this and other suitable processes checked for existing RPA potential.

The extent to which humans will want to use robots in the future also depends to some extent on the digital corporate culture and the confidence in themselves and the machines. Anyone who takes this path consistently and sincerely will also identify areas of activity that would not have existed without the involvement of the robot.

Literature

IFRS.org. 2020. https://www.ifrs.org/. Accessed December 15, 2020. https://www.ifrs.org/.

Liermann, Volker, Sangmeng Li, and Norbert Schaudinnus. 2019. "Deep Learning—an Introduction." In *The Impact of Digital Transformation and Fintech on the Finance Professional*, edited by Volker Liermann and Claus Stegmann. New York: Palgrave Macmillan.

Soybir, Sefa, and Christopher Schmidt. 2021. "Project Management and RPA." In *The Digital Journey of Banking and Insurance, Volume I—Disruption and DNA*, edited by Volker Liermann and Claus Stegmann. New York: Palgrave Macmillan.

Open Source

Open source has become a significant driver of innovation in the software industry and thus the financial services industry. The only chapter in this part looks at the development of open source in recent years. It searches for the different origins of open source and analyzes the tasks for which the open-source toolkit works best.

Open-Source Software

Volker Liermann

1 Introduction

In the early days of computing (1950–60), the software was a free addition to the hardware. The later rise and the market capitalization of software companies like Microsoft, Oracle, and SAP show the importance of software. Until the ascent of the big technology companies, the paradigm of proprietary and copyright-protected software was the recipe for success. These software companies soon noticed the threat of open source to their business models and tried to fight it.

At the beginning of the century, community-based concepts, such as Wikipedia and Linux, gained more and more supporters. Many of the big technology companies (BigTechs) were open to open-source concepts, certainly also because they could fight the established players.[1]

Around 2015, the open-source idea gained dynamism and the BigTechs provided quite a few groundbreaking technologies via an open-source-oriented license model. Two aspects have driven these developments: Firstly,

---

[1] The free Android paved the way for the end of Symbian-OS (Nokia) and Windows Phone (Microsoft).

V. Liermann (✉)
ifb SE, Grünwald, Germany
e-mail: Volker.Liermann@ifb-group.com

the tech companies' business model is advertising and not software, so they are not reliant on this extra income. Secondly, their business model is so successful that they can make huge investments if the subject is of strategic importance. In addition, their innovation model gives them space to try out new things with deep pockets.

In the course of this article, these aspects will be broken down for the financial sector and its software and infrastructure demands.

1.1 Structure of the Chapter

Section 2 gives a short overview of the open-source setting, touching on legal requirements and the main players. The open-source success factors are discussed in Sect. 3, including an assessment of which domains and use cases open source is best used in. The final Sect. 4 summarizes and gives an outlook.

2 Open Source—The Community Idea

The open-source concept cannot be separated from the idea of people networking and organizing themselves in communities and using these communities for sharing.

Although software (operating systems, databases, data processing frameworks, …) is an important part and often associated with open source, the collaboration idea is much broader. Applications can be found in (a) media and education, (b) science and medicine, and (c) manufacturing, production, and agriculture.

2.1 A Short History of Open Source (Software)

The idea of sharing instead of keeping rights to innovations does not originate from our current century. The first noteworthy implementation of this kind of sharing in the industrialized world was the US car industry, which openly shared patents without the exchange of money in an association that became the Motor Vehicle Manufacturers Association afterward.

In the early days (around 1950), software was a free addition to the hardware, and even in the early 1980s DEC shared software with source code through the DECUS[2] tapes. In the 1960/70s, common sharing between hackers and the hacker movement itself set the scene for a free exchange. In 1983, the GNU project was launched by Richard Stallman. Two years later, he outlined the importance of free software[3] in the GNU Manifesto (Stallman 1985).

2.2 Further Examples

A milestone in open source was the Linux kernel by Linus Torvalds in 1991, which was a freely modifiable released source code. After 1996, it was no longer entirely free software because it contained proprietary licensed components. Another key moment was the essay "The Cathedral and the Bazaar",[4] which motivated Netscape to release the source code of its Navigator in 1998. In October 2000, Sun Microsystems released the Lesser General Public License StarOffice office suite under the GNU.

Other important applications are (a) programming languages like Python (in 1991), R (in 1993), Ruby (in 1995), and Scala (in 2003), (b) distributed version control like Git (in 2005), (c) mobile operating systems like Android (in 2008) and Chromium OS (in 2009),[5] (d) databases like MySQL (in 1995) and its derivatives,[6] MongoDB (2009) and Hyperledger[7] (2015), (e) distributed storage and computing like in Apache Hadoop (in 2003) and Apache Spark (in 2009), (f) container virtualization like docker (in 2013) and Kubernetes (in 2014), and (g) data processing like Knime (in 2006) and Apache Kafka (in 2009).

2.3 Legal Variants

The term free software instead of open source is misleading, because open-source software follows legal boundaries that give a clear setting for the copyright and reuse of this work. Open source therefore became the most common term.

---

[2] DECUS was a worldwide system for wiring free software for users of DEC equipment.
[3] Open source vs. free and open-source software (FOSS).
[4] The Cathedral model: Each software release is developed between releases by an exclusive group of software developers and then made public. In the Bazaar model, the code is developed in view of the public (internet). The central thesis of the essay is: "given enough eyeballs, all bugs are shallow".
[5] Android and Chromium OS are based on Linux.
[6] MariaDB and Drizzle.
[7] Hyperledger is a framework for cross-industry blockchain technologies (see [Bettio et al. 2019] and more current information at [The Linux Foundation 2020]).

There are three standard licensing variants commonly used in the open-source setting: (a) copyleft license, e.g., GNU General Public License (GPL), (b) licenses with limited (or weak) copyleft, e.g., GNU Lesser General Public License (LGPL) or Mozilla Public License, and (c) license terms without copyleft, e.g., BSD license (Berkeley Software Distribution) or Apache Software License.

The major difference between the three variants shows if the source code of any derivative work needs to be made public: while all variants allow unrestricted redistribution of the software without charging license fees, the copyleft requires the source code to be delivered.[8]

2.4 Main Players

There are three groups of players in the open-source domain: (a) private persons,[9] universities, and other research institutes, (b) providers of commercial distribution and university-affiliated corporations, (c) BigTech and companies with a business model not focusing on selling software licenses.

In the early days, some push was generated by universities, other research institutes, and private persons. Examples include the GNU project, Linux, Berkeley Software Distribution (BSD), and Apache Software Foundation (ASF). Some of these initiatives come with their own open-source license legal frameworks, e.g., BSD Licensesand MIT License.

For most of the successful open-source initiatives, there are commercial distribution providers available.[10] for Linux, Cloudera[11] for Hadoop, Confluent for Kafka, Databricks of Spark are a selection of the commercial distribution providers relevant today. All of these corporations provide additional commercial services for the associated open-source framework. The services range from training to implementation support up to providing servers in a ready-to-use state.

The third group are the BigTechs. They developed and used the frameworks internally for their specific business needs and then contributed to an open-source community.[12] Examples include Kafka (developed by LinkedIn and contributed to Apache Software Foundation), Tensorflow (developed by

---

[8] Or an offer valid for 3 years; also download of the source code via website.
[9] E.g. Richard Stallman and Linus Torvalds.
[10] Red Hat was acquired by IBM in 2018.
[11] Before the merger with Cloudera, Hortenworks was a significant player.
[12] See (The Apache Software Foundation 2020).

Google[13] and released under the Apache license 2.0), PyTorch (developed by Facebook[14] under the BSD license), and Hive (developed by Facebook).

Universities and other research institutes are still significant drivers of important projects like Apache MXNet, which is supported by the Carnegie Mellon University, MIT, the University of Washington, and the Hong Kong University of Science and Technology.

3 The Success of Open Source (Software)

3.1 Why is Open Source so Successful?

Seeing the rise of open-source initiatives in recent decades, one interesting question is: Why are these initiatives so successful? The non-software-related community initiatives like Wikipedia are an interesting topic too, but we will focus on the software-related projects.

3.1.1 Reduction in Initial Costs

Since open-source software is often free (or only costs an amount for the distributor), the initial costs are significantly lower than standard software license costs. These low boundaries make it attractive for fintech startups and projects that are not clearly defined, such as Proof of Concept (PoC) or Proof of Value (PoV). Even in projects with a clear business case, the low initial license cost enables the stakeholders to shift the budget to individual functionalities.

The low initial cost creates space to develop business-specific functionalities that stand out from the competition.

The IT companies responsible in the financial sector used to argue that open source came with exploding costs, due to the lack of support and long-term maintenance. Both aspects can lead to unbalanced and unexpected high total costs of ownership (TCO). The argument originates from the experience of the IT companies responsible in the financial sector with software components of their own devising.

To some extent, the lack of support and long-term maintenance is provided by distributors with long-proven success like Red Hat for Linux.

---

[13] Google Brain team.
[14] Facebook's AI Research lab (FAIR).

3.1.2 Agility

In these days of groundbreaking changes and transformation, agility and the ability to adapt is an important component for the success of many companies (banks, insurers, fintech and technology companies). Many standard software vendors provide the customers with parameterization options and even the user exits and other more technical opportunities to adjust the given software to the clients' needs.

This structured opening of standard software can work to some extent if the vendor has a strong understanding of the current and upcoming business needs. In practice, experience is rather mixed: some parametrizations are limited, as are the user exits and the data provided for client-related data transformations.

In some implementation projects, half of the project budget is spent on these extensions, but the more important point is time lag for the implementation of new business features and business functions. If the structures are insufficient for the required extension, the clients must wait for a major software release and, given dependencies with other software modules, this could easily take more than one year.[15] Again, the big technology companies are setting the standards for flexibility and agility.

A full open-source environment—even when relying on strong contributors—offers the possibility to adjust code and meet the given deadlines. This creates the ability to respond quickly.

Agility comes with a price: the stability of the system. If the adaptation is conducted by a person who is not sufficiently skilled, the stability could be uncertain. But leveraged, this flexibility is exactly what is often demanded these days.

3.1.3 No Dependencies on a Single Entity

Another advantage often mentioned is the freedom to adjust and extend the code. Users of open-source software are never dependent on a particular vendor. If a user requires an enhancement or the correction of a program error, they are free to make this change or to commission someone to do so.

---

[15] Some standard software vendors moved to more agile releases by deploying new software in a two-week frequency.

Nonetheless, the big contributors can shift capacities between the different open-source construction sites and even away from open source. The reduction in the degree of support can have a significant impact on the life cycle of specific open-source projects or initiatives.[16]

This is a risk that must be taken by all software vendors, but if an institute has invested significantly in the use of such an open-source project, it can continue to use and extend the project with its own resources. This option is not available with proprietary software by a vendor that might have other intentions (e.g. to promote other products from its portfolio—planned obsolescence see [Bulow 1986]).

3.2 Where is Open Source Successful?

The key to analyzing the success of open source is the homogeneity of the business requirements. An additional question is whether the design individualization is a key differentiator to the competitors. In Fig. 1, three general areas of individualization are illustrated.

On the left-hand side, there is the slot of standard software with homogeneous requirements of large user groups. On the right-hand side, there is highly individualized software development in which the capability and flexibility of the software are key differentiators to the competitors. Standard software vendors can use the broad customer base (and the license revenue) to develop the best-of-breed software. They focus on use cases or the challenge many people or organizations face. Examples include Microsoft Office, SAP ERP, and Salesforce. Accounting or the databases (Oracle, Mircosoft, IBM) are other examples.[17] Individual software development was common in the 1980s and 1990s, due to a lag in sector-specific standard software (and not because it was a key differentiator). But banks and insurers today have a zoo of legacy systems (partly originating from individual development). The systems are costly and hard to maintain. In addition, modern technology stacks like Kafka[18] or even REST-APIs[19] are difficult to connect to these monolithic

---

[16] Example: In 2018, IBM decided to no longer support the Hyperledger composer (see [Liermann and Dahmen 2019]) and shifted, for good reasons, the developing capacities to the Hyperledger core. The Hyperledger composer was no longer used.

[17] Other examples include RPA (see [Soybir and Schmidt 2021]) and Process Mining (see [Rautenburger and Liebl 2021]) in which open-source software is almost irrelevant due to the excellent standard software provided by vendors (e.g. UiPath and BluePrism [RPA] and Celonis [Process Mining]).

[18] Kafka is a streaming technology platform (see [Steurer 2021]).

[19] Representational state transfer is a software paradigm that aims to improve performance and reliability by using a stateless protocol.

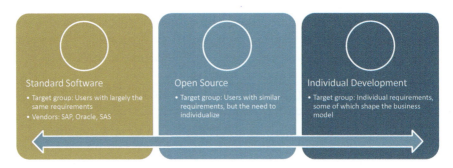

Fig. 1 Standard software—open source—individual development (© ifb SE)

systems. The transformation to modern technology standard software is still one of the biggest challenges for the financial sector.

Open source stands in between the two slots and targets users with similar requirements but the need to individualize. The individualization can be executed by each institute, but it can also be a "community project" with a group of contributors. To a huge extent, the business requirements will not differ between the institutes, but the ability to extend and even adjust existing components has a tremendous appeal. The extension and adjusting can be realized without any restrictions by a vendor; only the employees' capabilities and availability can limit the opportunities. Capabilities and availability can be managed, in contrast to plans by software vendors that are fixed and highly dependent on release.

The boundaries of the slots mentioned in Fig. 1 are fluid and will move over time. In some contexts, a standard software vendor might arise and offer a sufficiently customizable solution to cover all or at least most of the clients' needs. In other areas, the business requirements will change so dynamically that the existing and established standard software does not deliver the problem adoption in time.

Individual development can profit from a community-driven open-source approach. To a large extent, requirements are similar in many institutes and no secret is disclosed by sharing certain approaches or structures. The obvious advantage of individual development (in the open-source context) is that maintenance and change (and improvement) cost can be shared and more business value can be generated. This serves the clients and improves the customer experience as well as the variety of functions or channels. Therefore, open source is even an option for highly individualized development.

It is important to bear in mind that the legal environment of open source—depending on the license chosen—can force a sharing of the individual development code. One way to face the challenge of keeping business secrets or other differentiating components is to use parametrization for the structures defining the business model.

3.3 Peer Production vs. Vendor-Driven Standard Software

It might sound unusual and maybe a bit uncomfortable to share knowledge with institutes in the same sector or even with competitors. However, costs and time pressure are rising continuously. Only huge institutes have the profits to cover the innovation cost alone. Even for the strongest and biggest player in the financial industry, the competition—in terms of technological innovation and software—with GAFAM and BATX will be a challenge.

Standard software vendors can provide exceptional and user-oriented software if they have the sufficient client base and the ability to leverage business standards with individualization/customization. Only if the number of clients with similar requirements reaches a certain level are standard software vendors able and willing to invest. The clients must be willing to share their knowledge with the vendor. Furthermore, they need to adopt the processes and structures of the standard software vendor as part of their business models. In the area of standard accounting or regulation, most clients can work with these restrictions because they save money and resources for standard procedures.

Nonetheless, in fast-moving and changing domains, the passion for standard software is significantly lower than in the (more or less) clearly defined regulated domains. Standard software is always the ideal solution if the vendor can predict the institute's future requirements due to stability and technological superiority. The more business-driven (and not technology-driven) the key differentiators are, the larger the institute's need to find a vendor with a prophetic view of future business requirements.

In times of disruption, when most institutes struggle when asked about predicting the future developments in their sector, this vendor will be hard to find.

3.4 Community Editions

Most vendors[20] offer free community editions besides their standard packages (enterprise edition). This approach is often referred to as dual licensing or

---

[20] Microsoft, Oracle, R-Studio, IntelliJ, Neo4J, Cloudera to name just a few.

open core. The community edition often has reduced functionalities and does not scale like the enterprise editions. The community editions aim for low- or no-cost evaluations, testing, and small-scale development/implementation and proof of concepts. The community editions have good leverage in generating bigger client bases and thus help to improve the quality of early products (in terms of product life cycle).

Most vendors offer additional preconfigured systems in their clouds to test and get to know the functionalities. These systems lower the barrier for testing new concepts and prove the value of the framework or approach. As an extended support, the systems are offered in a software-as-a-service deal (SaaS). This gives the institute the opportunity to concentrate its IT resources on supporting the core business model.

The Commercial Open Source Software Index (COSSI) by COSS[21] gives an overview of the size and revenue of companies in this setting.

3.5   Open-Source Maturity Model

The Open Source Maturity Model (OMM) is a framework and methodology structuring the quality and reliability of FLOSS[22] and more specifically the FLOSS development process. The OMM is available under the Creative Commons license. The different levels[23] defined in the methodology help to evaluate the maturity of an open-source software project (see [Petrinja et al. 2009]).

4   Summary

Although the open-source idea has been established for quite some time, the open-source setting has gained momentum in recent years. The drivers of this development are without a doubt the companies that contributed their own development to the community (such as GAFAM & BATX and LinkedIn with Kafka), particularly BigTech and some other tech companies that have left the startup phase.

The open-source software components are already part of university education. The workforce familiar with open-source concepts is getting bigger and bigger (for some it is like a religion). Therefore, companies with a

---

[21] See (COSS Media 2020).
[22] Free/Libre Open-Source Software.
[23] Basic, intermediate and advanced level.

clear open-source strategy can make themselves stand out in the "War for Talent."[24]

In the financial sector, fintech companies especially have demonstrated the momentum and reliability that open-source software can contribute to their business models. The key elements are agility and low starting costs. The low initial cost enables an organization to experiment and explore the technology in their business context and experience how to leverage the technology in their business domain.

There will always be proprietary standard software, especially for common and standard tasks. Open source will take its place between standard software and full individual development. It is expected that open source will gain territory from both sides (standard software and individual development). The development is driven by social developments, such as cooperation and peer development (as a general trend not only affecting software development), and is a perfect fit with agile development[25] (and trends like design thinking and cultural change, see also [Merkt et al. 2021]).

Literature

Akhgarnush, Eljar, Fabian Bruse, and Ben Hofer. 2021. "New Project Structure." In *The Digital Journey of Banking and Insurance, Volume I—Disruption and DNA*, edited by Volker Liermann and Claus Stegmann. New York: Palgrave Macmillan.

Beister, Uwe, and Milica Zeljkovic. 2021. "Hybrid Project Management." In *The Digital Journey of Banking and Insurance, Volume I—Disruption and DNA*, edited by Volker Liermann and Claus Stegmann. New York: Palgrave Macmillan.

Bettio, Martina, Fabian Bruse, Achim Franke, Thorsten Jakoby, and Daniel Schärf. 2019. "Hyperledger Fabric as a Blockchain Framework in the Financial Industry." In *The Impact of Digital Transformation and Fintech on the Finance Professional*, edited by Volker Liermann and Claus Stegmann. New York: Palgrave Macmillan.

Bulow, Jeremy. 1986. "An Economic Theory of Planned Obsolescence." *The Quarterly Journal of Economics*, November 1: 729–749. https://doi.org/10.2307/1884176.

COSS Media. 2020. *COSS Media*. Accessed December 21, 2020. https://coss.media/.

Liermann, Volker, and Gereon Dahmen. 2019. "Hyperledger Composer—Syndicated Loans." In *The Impact of Digital Transformation and Fintech on the Finance Professional*, edited by Volker Liermann and Claus Stegmann. New York: Palgrave Macmillan.

---

[24] See (Michaels et al. 2001).
[25] See (Akhgarnush et al. 2021) and (Beister and Zeljkovic 2021).

Merkt, Rainer, Veronika Lang, and Anna Schmidt. 2021. "Digi-Cultural Mindset." In *The Digital Journey of Banking and Insurance, Volume I—Disruption and DNA*, edited by Volker Liermann and Claus Stegmann. New York: Palgrave Macmillan.

Michaels, Ed, Helen Handfield-Jones, and Beth Axelrod. 2001. *The War for Talent*. Bosten, MA: Harvard Business Press.

Petrinja, E., R. Nambakam, and A. Sillitti. 2009. *Introducing the OpenSource Maturity Model*. Vancouver, BC: ICSE Workshop on Emerging Trends in Free/Libre/Open Source Software Research and Development.

Rautenburger, Lars, and Alexander Liebl. 2021. "Process Mining." In *The Digital Journey of Banking and Insurance, Volume II—Digitalization and Machine Learning*, edited by Volker Liermann and Claus Stegmann. New York: Palgrave Macmillan.

Soybir, Sefa, and Christopher Schmidt. 2021. "Project Management and RPA." In *The Digital Journey of Banking and Insurance, Volume I—Disruption and DNA*, edited by Volker Liermann and Claus Stegmann. New York: Palgrave Macmillan.

Stallman, Richard. 1985. "The GNU Manifesto." *Dr. Dobb's Journal of Software Tools* 30.

Steurer, Ralph. 2021. "Kafka—Real Time Streaming for the Finance Industry." In *The Digital Journey of Banking and Insurance, Volume III—Data Storage, Processing, and Analysis*, edited by Volker Liermann and Claus Stegmann. New York: Palgrave Macmillan.

The Apache Software Foundation. 2020. "PLATINUM SPONSORS." *The Apache Software Foundation*. Accessed December 15, 2020. http://www.apache.org/foundation/thanks.html.

The Linux Foundation. 2020. *Hyperledger*. Accessed December 15, 2020. https://www.hyperledger.org/.

Summary

Volker Liermann and Claus Stegmann

1 Ethics Do Matter

When it comes to ESG (Environmental, Social and Corporate Governance), the environmental aspect (including climate change) is often viewed as the most significant. However, the social and corporate governance aspect should not be underestimated. Relying only on data can be and is discriminating because it is a model challenge to differentiate between correlation and impact. Being a "respectable" company has become ever more important for (retail and corporate) clients as well as for employees. This illustrates again the two perspectives of work—the internal and the external sphere.

So-called understandable AI can help to understand even the "black-box" models like ensemble models (random forest or gradient boosting) or even deep learning. These models have a far better predictive power than the classical models (decision trees and linear regression), so their use makes good sense. However, it is much harder to identify discriminating factors. These can be easily revealed by the classical models.

V. Liermann (✉)
ifb SE, Grünwald, Germany
e-mail: Volker.Liermann@ifb-group.com

C. Stegmann
ifb Americas, Inc., Charlotte, NC, USA
e-mail: Claus.Stegmann@ifb-group.com

Data protection and working with data protection regulations are important. Useful client and employee data therefore cannot be used for optimization, for—sometimes—good reasons. Here, regulation and the analysis of personal data have further evolved in areas with extremely restrictive personal data protection, like in Europe. In other areas (with less restrictive data protection), the understanding of interdependencies and how to use them will speed up and can form a knowledge gap that will be hard to close in the future.

2 Process Optimization and Automation

Process optimization (including process automation) is not a finished action but a continuous improvement process (like playing golf—you will get better but never reach zero). Most of the optimization processes still rely on incremental innovation, which of course helps to improve.

Only a clear and data-driven analysis (like process mining) can reveal the structural problems that can lead to a significant improvement and a more disruptive transformation. The confrontation with unchangeable facts produced by process mining can start the process of rethinking established patterns to a new and different compilation.

In addition, process mining and automation (RPA and ADM[1]) can help to keep up a high quality and high frequency in the processes. Both thinking new and keeping up high standards must be addressed to stay competitive in internal processing.

ADM needs data (ideally mass data), otherwise, the model will not be able to make reliable decisions. RPA can provide support by collecting the decision-driving data, and can therefore bring automation to the next level (hyperautomation).

3 Digital Transformation is an Irreversible Process

Digital transformation is an irreversible process, so financial service providers entered this one-way street a long time ago. Still, several institutes and their management do not want to believe this. Statements like "We have a strong and loyal customer base" are whistling in the dark. Others state "Our business

---

[1] Automated decision making.

is so special, there is no alternative to us," and it is true that some customized solutions meet the customer requirements. Open banking will enable existing and new market participants to compose the most suitable solution for niche market segments and at scale.

The only parameter an institute can select is the speed at which they travel on the digitalization path. Some institutions still puzzle over the important steps to take. A wise selection in the periodization is required, so that the one-way road does not turn into a dead end eventually.

The challenge is that, despite all industry and IT standardization, digital transformation is individual and institute-specific. It is necessary to understand the key technological elements and how to leverage them in the context of the institute's markets, customer demands (outside digitalization), and the culture and processes of the institute (inside digitalization).

With the help of use cases, one can model which technology to use. Additionally, one can test ways to improve the customers' "well-being" or to save unnecessary costs. Dealing with the use cases in the setting of institutes' challenges (inside and outside) will reveal the relevant patterns to leverage the technology.

A general understanding of the new technologies and the opportunities offered by the infrastructure are important. The third volume of the book series "The Digital Journey of Banking and Insurance, Volume III – Data Storage, Processing and Analysis" will provide insights into these subjects.

Index

A

ABACUS360 6, 10
Actor models 135
Adjusted sentiment scores 93
Advantages and challenges
　Business 245
　process mining 247
　robotic process automation 248
AFINN 89
Agent-based model 135, 137, 151
　agent classes 140
Agile development 323
Agility 318
AI-based fraud detection system 47
AML. *See* Anti-money laundry
Android 315
Apache
　Kafka 315
　MXNet 317
　Software Foundation 316
　software license 316
Apache Hadoop 315
Apache Kafka 315
Apache MXNet 317
Apache Software Foundation 316

Apache software license 316
Architecture
　R 47
Area under the curve 39
Argon2 185
ASF. *See* Apache Software Foundation
Asset-based models 120
Asset liability management 136
Asset returns 122
Asymmetric agent behavior 148
Asymmetric key encryption 202
Attended process automation 243
Augmented dictionary 92
　approach 94
Augmented dictionary approach 92, 94
Autoencoder 41
Autonomous decision-making 279
AWS 120
Azure 120

B

Bag-of-words approach 89

Balance sheet dynamics 136
Balance sheet dynamics simulator 116, 136, 138, 139, 145
  average number of actual loan agreements 143
  averaged incongruity of target and actual rating structures 143
  exposure of banks 142
  initial distribution 147
  initial states 146
  limiting conditions 143
  loan agreements 142
  Matching Efficiency 142
  model parameters 143
  ratio matched loan amounts 143
  reasonable model extensions 151
  Simulation Runs 148
  Technical Scenario 144
BATX 5, 322
Bayesian inference 87
Bcrypt 185
Berkeley Software Distribution 316
BERT 95
Bifunctor 225
Big data 36
Bigrams 89
BigTech 313, 322
Binary classification 84
Bing 89
Bloch body 212
Bloch sphere 211
Born rule 207
BPMN 2.0 240
BPMS. *See* Business Process Management Suite
BPM workflow systems 264
Braid group 217
Brute Force Attack 183, 184
BSD. *See* Berkeley Software Distribution
  licenses 316
Business model 295, 297–301, 305
Business process engine 240, 245, 254
Business processes 260
Business process management suite 240

C

C 146
Calibration 44
Carnegie Mellon University 317
Categorical Quantum Theory 203
Categorical theory 187
Category 222
  definition 222
  natural transformation 224
  theory 221
Change the Bank 2
Change the Insurance 2
Chief Data Officer 308
Chief Digital Officer 308
Chief Value Officer 308
Chief Visionary Officer 308
Chromium OS 315
Claim samples
  insurance 36
Classification
  binary 84
Classification algorithm 8
  configure 10
  optimize 11
  train 10
Classification engine 45
Classification model 11
Classification process 84
Clifford
  gates 208
  group 208
Cloudera 146, 316
Cluster algorithms 11
Clustering
  center 12
  hard 15
  soft 15
CNOT map 210
Collateral values 120

Combinatorial optimization 151
Combined parameter shifts 159
Commercial Open Source Software Index 322
Community editions 321
Competitive pressures 233
Complexity of processes 5
Complexity science 135
Complex systems 135
Component classification 250
Component combination 253
Confluent 316
Connections 99
Copyleft 316
   limited (or weak) 316
COSS. *See* Commercial Open Source Software
COSSI. *See* Commercial Open Source Software Index
Cost effects 18
Costly state verification 34
Cost of fraudulent claim 33
CreditMetrics 115, 120
   asset returns 122
   factor-loadings 122
   introduction 121
Credit portfolio models 115, 120
   asset-based models 120
   collatral values 120
   CreditMetrics 120
   CreditPortfolioView 120
   CreditRisk+ 120
   distributed calculation 133
   intensity-based models 120
   KMV 120
Credit portfolio risk models 120
CreditPortfolioView 120
CreditRisk+ 120
Credit risk 119
Credit risk management 136
CRM 249
Cross validation 42, 65
Cryptographical complexity 185
   SHA-1 185
   SHA-2 185
Cyber risk ix
Cyber security 228
Cypher 103

D

D3.js 178
Daniel Kahneman
   System 1 158
   System 2 158
DARPA 191. *See also* Defense Advanced Research Projects Agency
Dashboard
   Impairment Projection 166
   Portfolio Manager 160
Databricks 316
Data protection regulations 326
Data repartition 131
Decision making 158
Decoherence 217
DECUS tapes 315
Deep networks 40
Defense Advanced Research Projects Agency 202
Determine representatives 10
Deutsch algorithm 214
Dictionary 89
Dictionary-based approach 89
Digital corporate culture 307, 309
Digital footprints 260
Digitalization strategy 308
Digital transformation 326
Dirac ket symbol 206
Dirichlet 88
Distributed calculation 130, 133, 146
Distributed computation 135
Docker 315
Document-term matrix 85
D-Wave 190
D-Wave Systems 205
Dynamic Dashboarding 156

definition 156
Dynamic dashboards
  tools 171

E

Einstein-Podolsky-Rosen paradox 203
Embedded process engines 240
Ensemble Model 41
EPR paradox. *See* Einstein-Podolsky-Rosen paradox
EPR protocol 203
ESG 101, 119, 325
  risk 101
  social norm risk 101
  transition risk 101
ESG Risk
  example 101
European central bank 78
Evaluable process model 264
Event log 262, 264
Events 102
Example dataset
  German credit 13
Expected topic matrix 87

F

Facebook 317
Factor-loadings 122
Fast hashing algorithm 185
Financial loss 35, 100
Financial navigator 116, 136, 158
Financial Reporting 296, 307
Financial risk 119
Five-step decision automation model 278
Flask 178
Flexibility 318
Fraud classification engine 45
Fraud detection 33, 35, 44, 48
  manual 33
  process 45
  systems 35
Fraud detection systems 35
  aI-based 47
Fraud probabilities 46
  estimated 46
Frauds
  hard 34
  soft 34
Fraudulent claim
  cost 33
Functional analysis 202
Functor 224
  definition 224

G

GAFAM 5, 322
Gate-Based Quantum Computing 187, 206
  algorithms 209
Gates
  reversible 206
Gaussian-LDA 88
GDP growth factor 141
Geisterhafte Fernwirkung 203
General-purpose dictionary 89
General-purpose lexicon 89
Generative statistical model 87
Git 315
GNU 315
  General Public License 316
  license 316
  Manifesto 315
GNU project 315
Goldman Sachs viii
Google 205, 317
Google Cloud 120
Gottesman-Knill Theorem 209
Governance risk 101
GPL. *See* GNU General Public License
GPU 185
Graph aggregation 106

Graph databases 103
    query 103
    storage 103
Graphical calculi 221
Graphs 100
Graph theory 100, 135
Grover's Search Algorithm 216

H

H2O 27
Hadamard gate 210
Hadoop 134, 137, 146, 315, 316
Hadoop cluster 115, 146
Hard frauds 34
Hashcat 181
Hash cracking
    patterns 183
Hash cracking patterns 183
    Brute Force Attack 183
    Mask Attacks 184
Hashed passwords 181
    hacking 181
Hash functions
    security 182
Hashing algorithm 183
Heavyweight IT 250
HHL Algorithm 217
High-Performance Applications 115
Hilbert spaces 221
    unitary operators 221
Historical simulation 158
Hong Kong University 317
HR risk 2, 51, 52
    change and run risk 53
    communication risk 53
    conduct risk 53
    machine learning 62
    management 51
    predictive models 63
    resignation risk 54
        indicators 56
    resignation score 61
    risk of dissatisfaction in the office 53
    score values 60
    surveys 58
Human resources risk 52
Hummingbird 205
Hybrid encryption algorithm 202
Hyperautomation 231, 273, 277
    data collection 280
Hyperledger 315
Hyperparameter 85

I

IAS 39 297
IBM 189, 319
IFRS 9 295, 297–309
Imbalanced data 36
Impacted nodes 106
Impact graph 55, 100, 102
    aggregation 106
    analysis functions 104
    example 101
    Predecessor and Successor Analysis 105
Impact graphs 3, 57
    creation Ex-Ante 55
    creation Ex-Post 55
Impairment
    Projection 165
    Projection Dashboard 166
Indicators 57
Information asymmetry 34
Information visualization 156
    interactive 156
Inside digitalization 327
Inside view x
Insurance claim samples 36
Integrated stress test 169
Intelligent process automation 243
Intensity-based models 120
Interest rate in the banking book 137
Internet of Things ix

Intraday liquidity stress test 169
Inverse stress test 160
Investigative groups 35
    dedicated 35

K

Kafka 315, 316
Kaggle 36, 77
Key Performance Indicator 178
Key risk indicator 110, 158, 178
KMV 120
Knime 315
Know your customer 241
KPI 307, 308. *See also* Key
    performance indicator
KRI. *See* Key risk indicators
Kubernetes 315

L

Latent dirichlet allocation 84, 85
    Example 86
Law enforcement 35
LCSD. *See* Longest common
    substring distance
LDA. *See* Latent dirichlet allocation
LDA2Vec 88
Lemmatization 77
Levenshtein distance 2, 26, 31, 78
Lightweight IT 244, 251
Limited copyleft 316
Linear projections 155
Linguistic models 77
LinkedIn 316
Linux 313, 316
Longest common substring distance
    2, 26, 31
LSD. *See* Levenshtein distance

M

Machine learning 7, 33, 48, 62, 84,
    94

classification algorithms 8
classification engine 45
classifier 94
    HR Risk 62
Machine learning classifier 94
Machine learning models 94
Macroeconomy 140
Managing complexities 99
Mask Attacks 184
Mass transaction business 8
Matching Efficiency 142
MATLAB 178
Measure resignation risk 57
Microservices 47
Microsoft 197, 313
    Power BI 171
Microsoft Office 319
MicroStrategy 163, 174
Mircosoft 319
MIT
    licenses 316
Model
    calibration 43
    hyperparameters 85
    parameters 85
Model risk 35
Model selection 37
Modern computational
    infrastructures 135
MongoDB 315
Monte Carlo simulations 120
Multivariate gaussian distribution 88
MXNet 317
MySQL 315

N

Named entity recognition 3, 77
NASA 205
National Institute of Standards and
    Technology 228
Natural language processing 2, 77,
    227, 282, 307
    framework 77

vocabulary 80
Natural transformation 224
Negative effects 102
Neo4j 103
NER. *See* Named entity recognition
New regulatory requirements 6
Nexus server 144
NFR. *See* Non-financial risk management
NFR management 54
NIST. *See* National Institute of Standards and Technology
NLP 307. *See also* Natural language processing
No-cloning theorem 203
Node.js 178
No-deleting theorem 203
Non-financial risk 2, 71
   category 52, 102
Non-financial risk management 100
   ESG
      risk 101
   events 102
   financial Loss 100
   HR risk 110
      example 110
   impact graph 100, 102
   negative effects 102
   reporting 113
   risk categories 100
   risk events 100, 102
   taxonomy 100
   treat level 100
   vunerability 102
Nostro accounts 22
   matching 22
   matching - Brute force 22
   matching - Brute force search 25
   matching - example 23
   matching - match results 29
   matching - string similarity 25
NPP 298, 303
n-qubit state space 208
Nvidia 183

Nvidia GTX 1080 processor 183

O

OCI 297, 298
OMM. *See* Open Source Maturity Model
Open source 64, 311, 314
   Commercial Open Source Software Index 322
   concept 314
   history 314
   microservices 48
   solutions 47
   success 317
Open Source Maturity Model 322
Open source solutions 47
Operational risk 101
Opinion mining 74
Optimization potential 237
Optimize classification algorithm 11
Oracle 313, 319
Organizational structure 252
Outside digitalization 327
Outside view x

P

P&L 297, 298, 301, 303, 309
Parallel computing 123, 181
   hybrid approach to splitting 127
   natural splitting 124
Parameter shifts
   combined 159
Part-of-speech
   tagging 79
Password 181
   candidates 183
Password candidate 183
   keyspace 184
Password cracking 182, 185
   speed lists 185
Password hashing competition 185
Password recovery 181

Pauli group 209
Pauli spin matrices 208
Peer production 321
Pegasus chip 205
Pentagon axiom 226
Performance application 116
Planning process 136
PoC. See Prove of Concept
Polarized word 89
Portfolio Manager Dashboard 160
POS. See Part-of-speech
Post-quantum cryptography 192
  Code-Based 192
  Hash-Based 194
  Isogeny-Based 197
  Lattice-Based 194
  multivariate 196
PoV. See Proof of Value
pseudo random generators 181
Precision 39, 43
Predictive models 63
Probabilistic measure of relevance 78, 88
Process automation viii, 234
  attended 243
  intelligent 243
  unattended 243
Process automation solutions 243
Process design 45
Process engine 234, 240, 246
  embedded 241
Process mining 234, 242, 247, 255, 259–261, 326
  digital footprints 260
  project environment 263
  projects 270
  technology 259
Process mining projects 270
  organizational aspects 270
  responsibilities 271
  roles 271
Process opimization 231, 235, 239, 326
  magic triangle 239

Product and permutation category 226
Proof of Concept 317
Proof of Value 317
PROP. See Product and permutation category
Protocol
  EPR 203
  QKD 203
Public dataset 36
Python 77, 95, 172, 176, 315
  Dash 176
  Plotly 176
  Power BI 173
PyTorch 317

Q

QC. See Quantum computing
QKD
  networks 204
  protocol. See Quantum key distribution
QKD networks 204
QKD protocol 203
Quantum
  annealing 205
  circuit 209, 214
  communication 201, 202
  computers 187, 189
  computing 201, 205
  gate-based 187, 206
  topological 187, 221, 228
  cryptography 190
  dualization 203
  entanglement 202
  hypothesis 204
  imaging 204
  information 202
  metrology 202, 204
  optics 202
  probabilistic machine 207
  sensing 204
  sensors 201

simulation 201, 204
superposition 202
technologies 190
tunneling 202
Quantum algorithms 209
Quantum bit 206
Quantum category 225
  definition 225
Quantum computing x, 187, 201, 205
Quantum Experiments at Space Scale 202
Quantum gate 207
Quantum key distribution 191, 202
Quantum key distribution networks 191
  DARPA 191
  QUESS 191
  SECQC 191
  SwissQuantum 191
  Tokyo QKD Network 191
Quantum mechanics 222
Quantum processors
  Bristlecone 190
  Sycamore 190
Quantum programming 187
Quantum Simulator
  Hummingbird 205
  Sycamore 205
  universal 205
Qubit 206, 226
QUESS 191. *See also* Quantum Experiments at Space Scale

R
R 47, 77, 93, 172, 315
  Shiny 176
Random forests 41, 286
Random sampling 44
R architecture 47
React 178
Recall 39, 43
Reconstruction error 41, 42

Red Hat 316
Reduced test portfolio 10
Regression tests 6
Relevance probability 85
Representatives
  determine 10
  test portfolio 7
Reputation 73
  forecasts 76
  influencing factors 73
Reputational risk 2, 35, 73
  management 75, 95
  mitigation 77
Resignation risk 54, 64
  example model 64
  indicators 56
  measure 57
  resignation rate 57
  satisfaction index 57
  sickness rate 57
Reversible gates 206
RI. *See* Risk indicators
Risk driver 106
Risk events 100, 102
  loss potential 109
  probabilities 108
Risk indicators 110
Risk management 52, 135
  multiple-year view 133
Risk of governance 101
Risk of resignation 71
Risk to governance 101
Robotic process automation 234, 243, 248, 277
RoG. *See* Risk of governance
RPA 295, 296, 297–299, 301, 303–309
  autonomous decision-making 279
  classic 277
  Hyperautomation 277
  modern 277. *See also* Robotics Process Automation
R package
  sentimentr 93

shiny 47
R Shiny 47, 163, 166, 176
RtG. *See* Risk to governance
Ruby 315
Run the Bank 2
Run the Insurance 2

S

SAC. *See* SAP analitics cloud
Salesforce 319
SAP 313
SAP analytics cloud 173
SAP ERP 319
SAP SAC 173
Scala 315
Scoring resignation indicators 58
Scoring system 52
SCRUM Master 308
SECOQC. *See* Secure Communication based on Quantum Cryptography
SECQC 191
Secure Communication based on Quantum Cryptography 202
Security of hash functions 182
Sense2Vec 79
   model 79
Sensitivity 159
Sentiment analysis 74, 88
   general approach 74
Sentiment classifications 94
sentimentr 93
Sentiment score 76, 89
   adjusted 93
   benchmark 76
   calculation 90
   unigram 90
Sequence of agent actions and messages 141
Seven bridges of Königsberg problem 100
Shor's Factoring Algorithm 216

Similarity 80
   score 81
Simudyne 116, 136, 145
   Software development kit 145
Skip-gram window 78
Socialization of costs 34
Social norm risk 101
Soft frauds 34
spaCy 77
Spark 115, 316
Sparklyr 130
   configuration 130
   data repartition 131
Spooky action at a distance 203
SPPI 295, 297, 299, 301–307, 309
State verification
   costly 34
Status of vulnerability 112
Stop word 78
Stress test
   integrated 169
   Intraday liquidity 169
   inverse 160
String diagrams 221
Superposition 207
Supervised learning 39, 63
Supervised model 39
Surveys 58
SwissQuantum 191, 202
Sycamore 205

T

Teleportation 203
Tensor category 203, 221, 225
Tensorflow 316
Tensor product 225
Testing 6
   adaptive method 17
   cost effects 18
   existing functionalities 6
   new functionalities 6
   similar transactions 6
Test portfolio

representative 7
Text mining 78
   tool 78
The Cathedral and the Bazaar 315
Threat level 100
Threat situation 110
   estimation 110
Three buckets approach 46
Token 79
Tokenization 77
Token level 79
Tokyo QKD Network 191
Topic distribution 85
Topic modeling 84
Topological environment 139
Topological quantum computing 187
Topological quantum computing with anyons 221, 228
Topological superconductor 228
Topology 139
Total costs of ownership 317
Traditional oprisk approach 107
   example 108
Traffic light approach 46
Transition risk 101
Triangle axiom 226
Two-qubit system 207

U

UAT. *See* User acceptance test
UI. *See* User interface
UiPath 280
   MACHINE Learning 287
   Python 288
Unattended process automation 243

Understandable AI 325
Unigrams 89
Unigram sentiment score calculation 90
Unitary group 209
Unitary operators 221
Universal Quantum Turing Machines 206
Unsupervised learning 40, 62
Unsupervised model 40
User acceptance test 16
User interface 47

V

Valuable optimizations 260
Value at Risk 158
   historical simulation 158
Value chain 235
Value-driver-oriented planning 136
Vector representation 85, 87
   expected document-word 87
   expected topic word 87
Vision and value vii
Vocabulary 80, 87
Volkswagen 205
VUCA 157
Vulnerability 102, 112
   status 112

W

Wikipedia 313
Word embedding 79, 85
   models 78, 79
Word-level dictionary approach 91
Word vectors 80

Printed by Printforce, the Netherlands